FROM FEAR
TO AWE:

*A New Understanding of the Book of Job
Leads the Sufferer to Wholeness and Bliss*

JACOB ZIGHELBOIM, M.D.

Toren *Publishers*

For information address:
Toren Publishers
436 N. Bedford Dr.
Beverly Hills, CA 90210
Phone (310) 858-5730
Fax (310) 858-5733

ISBN: 0-9655676-0-5
Library of Congress Catalog Number: 96-90893

TABLE OF CONTENTS

PROLOGUE

NINE STAGES TOWARD WHOLENESS:
FROM FEAR AND DENIAL TO AWE

June 10, 1983, started out as an ordinary good day. I remember stepping out of bed at around 7:30 in the morning feeling elated. The day was bright, and I approached it with confidence and anticipation. I was, after all, a man at the top of my world—a tenured scientist/physician in a leading university, well married with healthy children, secure, young, and without apparent problems.

In the span of a few moments, however, my little world would collapse. I would look in the mirror and discover something bulging from the right side of my neck. "Jacob," an inner voice announced in disbelief, "You have cancer!"

Of the multitude of experiences I have had in my life, none has devastated me more than my own diagnosis that morning. It felt like I had had a head-on collision with an immovable object, which seemed to destroy or endanger much of what had seemed meaningful to me until then. In that precise moment, my innocence, most particularly was pierced: I ceased to live in the world of religious and cultural precepts handed down to me by my parents and teachers.

The experience of having cancer shocked me first by its unexpectedness, and then by its exposure of how little control I had over my life. In time, I have come to describe such experiences as "collisions with the world of God." I speak neither of occurrences that only religious people have nor of extraordinary life events that touch our human spiritual core. I refer instead to ordinary life experiences that we perceive as catastrophic because they run counter to our beliefs about the world's workings. We all have adopted implicit cosmologies that describe the world and how to be safe and secure in it. These personal cosmologies reflect, however, a world according to humans—one we can trust and rely on as long as the events confronting us are expected and logical. But when life presents us with threatening events that our cosmologies neither anticipate nor ameliorate, our psyches are brutally shaken, wounded, even crushed.

Ironically for me, of the many collisions with the world of God I had experienced before that morning in June, the one I had examined most intimately was the diagnosis of cancer in my patients. But this clinical background was no psychological protection for me. Like most of the men and women stricken each year with this disease, I also had enjoyed good health and expected to live for many decades, until the day the diagnosis was made. Then, the sudden realization that my life might be abruptly shortened was truly shattering. I reacted with the same shock and disbelief my less knowledgeable patients did when they heard my diagnosis. For all intents and purposes, my easy hopes in life, and my secure expectations, had been smashed.

But even while my psyche was being barraged by a multitude of frightening questions, and the events surrounding my diagnosis were unfolding rather quickly, I had a moment of inner clarity. I realized that I would choose to engage my challenge head-on. I also understood intuitively that standard medical treatment was not going to be sufficient to allay my fears and restore my sense of security. I was given an eighty to ninety percent chance of cure, but what that meant to me was that ten to twenty percent of people with my diagnosis die.

Thus, I came to dread the day when I might hear my doctors walk into the office, where I anxiously awaited the results of my latest tests, and say compassionately but all too clearly, "We are sorry, Jacob. The treatment we gave you did not work as well as we had hoped. The disease has returned and is now incurable." But even if that were to be the ultimate outcome of my illness, I had to be certain that I had taken charge of my life, and that I had done everything in my power to enhance my chances of survival. I wanted, in short, to feel that I had acted responsibly, had grasped my situation fully and had marshaled all my resources. I wanted to know that if the disease recurred, after my successful short-term treatment, I could rest assured knowing I had done the best I could, and that despite my efforts, this was how my life needed to unfold. Surprisingly, accepting the possibility of a recurrence of my cancer was all right with me. What I could not accept was the feeling that the recurrence was caused by my fear, my ignorance, my naiveté or my mental negligence. I had no choice but to thrust myself into a journey of exploration and learning, a journey that would eventually lead me to search out the secrets underlying my illness, the foundations of health and disease, and the means available to restore my emotional balance and my physical well-being. This journey took me into mysterious, and at times frightening, places, but it taught me how to find and use the awesome resources each of us contains for healing and for the attainment of human wholeness.

My journey began in the fall of 1983 and is still going on. I know now that this is a journey with a beginning but no real ending. It is a journey that deepens in stages, and the farther I go, the more resourceful I feel when I am challenged.

In the course of this journey, I have met numerous guides and teachers. Some were alive and present, while others had lived in the past and had left their wonderful teachings embedded in the lines of their profound poems, stories and other writings, pictures, sculptures, films, and all the other means of symbolic expression humans have used to reveal their truth.

Of the many teachers from the past I found on my path, there was one in particular, *The Book of Job*, whose content and rhythms resonated most intensely with my soul. I had, of course read this book before, first at the age of twenty-one and twice again before I diagnosed my illness in the mirror that fateful morning. Despite my attraction to its contents and to the questions it raised about humanity, God, and divine justice, I had never really understood Job until I read it for a fourth time during the winter of 1992.

On my fourth reading, I could not believe the amazing consistency between this man's hitherto mysterious and baffling story and the details of my own long healing journey. As I read, I was awed by the similarity of content between Job's experiences and mine, and by how much I could identify with his predicament, feelings, and thoughts. Later, in my doctor's work with cancer patients, I discovered similar relations between Job's progress and that of many other suffering people.

Hidden between the lines of this mysterious poem was not only a detailed account of how Job healed his body and his mind, but also a precise roadmap into the psychospiritual journey humans must undertake and endure to heal their souls. Here is a book that, if we know how to read it, gives us precise instruction as to how to find inner harmony and peace after our life has been torn asunder by events we cannot predict, comprehend, or accept.

From this perspective, this book provides critical guidance into a process that, when successfully negotiated, thrusts us into spiritual freedom and bliss but, when aborted or bypassed, subjects us to a life suffused with fear, uncertainty, and progressive psychospiritual impoverishment.

Before Job's remarkable journey was recorded (about 2,500 years ago), human beings knew that attaining wholeness was possible, and that we could connect with a "Higher Wisdom" that would guide our inner quest. Indeed, we knew about the lives of men (Abraham, Isaac, and Jacob, among others) who overcame their greatest fears and who managed to live in harmony in this ruthless and uncertain world. What we did not know was how these humans had done so. To the ordinary mind, they seemed to be the "chosen few," the human beings God selected to imbue with freedom and blissful serenity. Their stories gave insight into the reality of wholeness, but they did not address the intricate process required to attain it. In Job, however, I came to see delivered for the first time the Tao of healing: the sacred pathway that connects us with our strength, our resourcefulness, and most importantly our spiritual essence.

I urge everyone, therefore, to perceive Job's story as his or her own—a story highlighting humanity's struggles and its search for truth. Job's story is often looked upon either as one of undeserved punishment and proof of evil's dominion in this world, or as a parable illustrating God's inequity or His powerlessness. But either one of these readings overlooks the very essence of this tale's meaning. Job is one with each of us: his despair is clearly ours and, like him, we also have felt oppressed and betrayed by our friends, our superiors, and even by our God.

Job's journey, which may often seem amorphous, reveals upon close scrutiny nine stages. The successful completion of all these stages leads to psychospiritual bliss. Each stage has distinguishing features and characteristics that are sketched briefly below, and examined more fully in the detailed decoding of *The Book of Job* that occupies most of this volume. Over the past twelve years, I have seen a number of people who are struggling with cancer and other life-threatening conditions make their way through some of these stages, and from the context of understanding derived from my own journey, I have guided many of them in theirs.

Job's healing journey is described here in a sequential fashion, as a linear and orderly progression of critical life events. This is for clarification and organizational purposes. In reality, the healing journey I allude to is more complex and disorderly—it is a process in which occurrences can follow and overlap each other and even appear synchronous in time.

NINE STAGES TOWARD WHOLENESS:
From Fear and Denial to Awe

Stage I. Shock and Denial. As the story begins, Job, a person who is prosperous and wealthy, receives a crippling blow both to his body and soul. This man, who until then had everything he desires, sees his wealth, children, servants, and all else that matters to him taken away. This injury shatters his innocence and precipitates the collapse of his infantile world view. His initial reaction is one of shock, numbness, and complete denial.

Stage II. The "No-Man's Land" of Uncertainty and Reasonlessness. Until these injurious events took place, Job thought he knew how to function securely in the world, and he had had precise guidelines dictating what to do to be rewarded and what not to do to avoid punishment. But from this moment on, uncertainty grips him, and life ceases to be something he can take for granted. He has been thrust into a realm of existence I term no-man's land. He must cross this uncharted terrain if he is to survive, yet it is a place that frightens him, often to the point of paralysis.

When we first find ourselves in no-man's land, our initial reaction is to cast about desperately for something or someone to help us find our bearings. Each time a patient or a family member walks into my office, I know immediately whether that person has entered this inhospitable realm. Frequently, these people feign bravery and make bold statements, like "I am going to lick this thing," but inwardly they are desperate, seeking support and direction. No-man's land is a place we can know only if we have been there; otherwise, we never understand its stark ruthlessness. Only those who have inhabited its dismal expanses can fully comprehend the terror and alienation it evokes.

In reaction to this difficult stage of the journey, we tend to resort to all those rational and willful skills that we customarily use in moments of crisis (affirmations, positive thinking, imagery, hypnosis, and so on). This is a period of great mental agitation and instability, and it is one that persists until we are able to reassure ourselves that we have a strategy that will indeed help us survive.

Stage III. The Beginnings of Feeling as Shock Subsides. At first, Job makes himself appear composed even though he is inwardly agitated. Now he cannot hold his feelings back and bemoans his fate and ill fortune. As the sufferer's initial shock subsides, the numbness that overtakes him lifts and emotion floods his psyche, causing him to experience what can be called an explosion of feeling.

For psychospiritual healing to take place, becoming intellectually aware of our wounds is not enough; it is essential that we experience them in our hearts as well. Until our deepest sorrows are touched, that which has befallen us remains only a vague idea, a pale abstraction. Only when our thoughts are moored to feelings can they become realities of the flesh.

In my own life, before feeling pierced my awareness at this stage of the journey, I had been a different person, especially a different kind of doctor. I could speak easily about intriguing cases of cancer I had seen, or about difficult oncologic problems I had treated. This detached approach toward illness served me well and was sanctioned both by my colleagues and by our highest institutions of learning. But after I was diagnosed with non-Hodgkin's lymphoma, I experienced for the first time what it truly means to have cancer. I experienced the uncertainty and fear this diagnosis engenders, as well as the pain and confusion, the feelings of abandonment and betrayal, the social and economic implications of the illness, and the spiritual angst with which it is accompanied. Suddenly, the disease of which I had once spoken so glibly was vividly attached to a whole person with rich hopes and expectations—to a man who was someone's spouse and father, son and son-in-law, brother, friend, and colleague. My perceptions about illness moved swiftly from the arena of mental constructs to that of human experience and psychophysical truth. From then on, everything mattered, and what traditional medicine had to offer no longer sufficed. This reconnecting to feeling is undoubtedly one of the key steps in the resolution of our dramas, and it is one that we cannot bypass.

Stage IV. We are Victims of Injustice. Job's feelings deepen now, energizing his resentment at what has befallen him. He feels further victimized by those around him who don't understand his plight, criticize his handling of it, take advantage of it, even accuse him of being responsible for his own calamities. In time, these feelings also give way, and the sufferer realizes he must move on, but where?

Stage V. Understanding the Need to Transform. In his own search, Job comes gradually to a stage in which he realizes that if he is to proceed, he must undergo irreversible transformation. He understands this necessity with difficulty. Those around the sufferer are also too entrenched in their rigid roles to understand this need. They cannot see that to survive, the person must, in essence, die to his old and more limited self. As a consequence, the *compassion, and psychospiritual nurturance* required for this stage to unfold fully are often not easy to find either within our families or in our doctor's offices.

Psychospiritual counselors that I sought out in the months following the initiation of my journey told me that I "needed to die"—but, like Job, I first experienced these words as devoid of meaning. They were empty phrases meant to impress or frighten me, but not to be taken to heart. "What do they mean, die?" I asked myself repeatedly. "I know of only one type of death, and I am not interested in that at all! Anything else said about death is pseudospiritual verbiage."

I learned, however, as Job did, that whenever one meets a life-threatening challenge, a fundamental inner transformation is both necessary and vital. This notion is so overwhelming that we require *unconditional love, abiding friendship, and teachers* who can indeed usher us through the mystery of such a "death and rebirth." These teachers are people who can foster this awesome process because they themselves have died and emerged transformed and resourceful. This is precisely what gives them the credibility and the tools to support our transformation and to assist us in our inner quest.

Stage VI. The Emergence of the Inner Warrior. In this stage of the story, Job the innocent fool, the victim of life's darkness, is dying, and Iyov the "warrior," the resourceful human being who genuinely loves life, is soon to be born. I use Iyov, the Hebrew word for Job, to denote the man in his awakened or transformed state.

All the wisdom we seek externally resides within us, embodied in the energy of our own inner warriors. Our dilemma lies in discovering how best to tap these resources and bring them to the fore so that we can become whole.

During this stage of the journey, we rely on our teachers and guides to serve as catalysts for the induction of the warrior energy within us, this sensitive psychic presence that can conquer no-man's land and mend our wounds and broken hearts. We seek these people out as part of our effort to be illuminated by their energy, their unique skills, and their heightening presence.

In The Book of Job, the sufferer needed *Elihu* (the wise teacher) to help him become receptive to Higher Wisdom, which is the enlightened supervisor of his inner world. Without Elihu, Job was unable to reach genuine understanding and wholeness. My guides came in the form of people like Dr. Brugh Joy and Dr. Hal Stone, who inducted me into deeper levels of consciousness[1]. Meeting people with such reputable medical and psychological backgrounds who had the resources to explore new frontiers of knowledge prompted my awareness to stretch its boundaries and burst into a new appreciation of living. Unexpectedly, and to my amazement and delight, the warrior energy began to operate in me one day, and that was the day I started to tap spontaneously into the meaning of my dreams and those of others. It was the day my dreams came alive to become vibrant reflections of inner truth—realities I can now access with relative ease.

Stage VII. Finally Letting Go of Intellectualistic Constructs and Methods. Despite our deepening connection to the warrior energy and to an emerging inner wisdom, we cannot easily stop trying to overcome the challenges of the crisis using routine cognitive skills and willful maneuvers. After a while, Job realizes that such an approach is not helping him address his concerns and will not lead him to the psychic resolution and the physical wellness he seeks. Finally, after trying everything his rational mind can conjure, he *surrenders to life and awaits inner guidance.*

To let go of our intellectual controls and of our established ideas of how the world works is difficult under any circumstances. These are the foundations upon which we have built our lives, the coordinates with which we have charted our existence. How much more difficult, at the time of our greatest need, to relinquish those controls and *surrender to unknown teachers or unfamiliar principles.*

Amazingly, though, *as soon as we surrender to life's rhythms and we allow the deep feelings mandated by our situation to express themselves, we assent to healing.* Suddenly we begin to hear, to see, and to know more. Those who have experienced these moments know well the joy and awe with which they are associated. They know, too, the serenity, the feelings of well-being, and the transcending healthfulness such moments bring forth. In times like these, everything seems to fall into its proper place, and a new and awesome order makes itself perceptible. Often, unexpectedly, a powerful dream comes forth—one that is full of profound meaning, yet distressing. It is a dream we shall never forget, a dream that embodies so much substance that it fairly overwhelms us, as did the original disaster that crystallized our crisis. Now, however, we are better able to comprehend the message and to follow the directives and guidelines it implies.

Stage VIII. To the Deeper Levels of the Unconscious. As Job reconnects with Higher Wisdom, he begins to learn the secrets of his nature.

What follows is the most awesome experience we can ever know. I am referring to our entry into God's palace and our subsequent induction into a psychic state in which awareness of reality expands exponentially, and learning about our essence proceeds unhindered. In this state, we discover the very laws that unify our nature, and we begin to appreciate life as life is, as it has been for millennia. As we enter this sanctum, we begin to evolve as mature human beings, who have the newfound ability to view the world with a fresh, non-prejudiced eye and who at the same time can experience its rhythms and flow with far less fear and vulnerability. In this state of consciousness, the world is no longer one that is driven by the twin arbiters of reward and punishment, or by punitive deities wreaking havoc on their devoted servants. In this state of being, there is only life flowing freely, manifesting its profound diversity and expressing its full and breathtaking splendor.

When we enter this state of consciousness, we also become cognizant of how resourceful and capable we are. Through our dreams and meditations, we discover that we are not alone but rather are buoyed by an inner wisdom, an inner reality that is more objectively aware than we could ever be.

When we have connected with this wisdom and strength, fear begins to ebb and harmony manifests itself in our soul. Suddenly we feel more secure and relaxed. And the more we come to understand the world, the more congruent and meaningful our lives become. In this state of consciousness, fewer unexpected surprises await us. Yet in this state everything is not predictable and monotonous; on the contrary, life is full of magical occurrences and continues to unfold its intriguing mystery. Now, however, our responses to life are colored by awe, curiosity, appreciation, and genuine understanding. Do not get me wrong: Suffering—being aware of our fears, pains, sadness—endures. It is just that one is now far better equipped to place it in its proper perspective.

People who have entered this state of being are less fearful of living and hence of dying. They are replete with love and compassion for themselves as well as for others and, while they are highly knowledgeable, they maintain genuine humility. These people take life in stride, responding constructively to its every manifestation, and thus they are seldom in conflict. We are eager to associate with these people, and we seek to be imbued with their joyfulness and tranquillity.

Stage IX. Wisdom Experienced, Wholeness Attained. Job has experienced Higher Wisdom (God) and emerges radiant and whole. A new order has been established, and he has become a free and serene man who can truly appreciate the awesomeness of life. This is why, at the end of the story, we can finally say with assurance, "There was once a man in the land of Uz called Job: a sound and honest man who was in *awe* of God and shunned evil" (Job 1:1).[2]

Such wholeness cannot be attained until we embrace our shadow—that is to say, until we integrate those dimensions of our psyche we have long rejected or simply never known. Only then will harmony and freedom suffuse our consciousness and establish themselves in our personal relations. At this stage, outer and inner wholeness become identical, as they actually have been all along.

When we are in conflict with someone else, it is critical to understand that simultaneously there is a complementary part of ourselves with which we are equally at odds—an aspect of psyche that feels alienated from us, hanging desolate in search of nurturance and connection. Thus, I tell my patients: "The moment you can embrace all of yourself, you will become whole and feel it immediately within you. You will experience, then and there, the serenity that comes of being complete and harmonious. From that moment on, fear and disintegration will give way to a sense of security and to freedom of being."

From the point of view of healing work, God, the force we initially perceive as responsible either for fostering our fall from grace or for facilitating our redemption from misery, is innate to us and ever present. We rise and fall as part of a total reality, a system of psychospiritual coordinates that produces these effects in and of itself. This is how our universe has evolved, and this is how it functions—a universe in which all we need to do to remain vibrant and balanced is align ourselves with its wisdom, and in doing so, draw radiance and nurturance from its unfailing light.

An evolution of personality and understanding to such great heights, proceeding through what I have designated as no fewer than nine stages (many of them needing to be cycled through more than once), is seldom if ever a quick and direct process. The immense utility of *The Book of Job* is that it maps the journey for us in great detail, with a narrative rich in implication that allows us a profound emotional understanding of where we need to go and where we are at any given moment in our exploration. From it, we can gather clarity about our turmoil, the courage to persist, and the faith that we can triumph in the face of the most distressing events. Job and the divine book that bears his name can be our companions in a redemptive journey through pain and suffering of every kind. But for them to serve this function, we need to understand them in detail and from a new perspective. We must proceed to a new and close reading of this book, taking care, in a regular way, to illustrate its relevance to actual moments in the life we live today. To this end, I shall use examples from my own life and the lives of my patients.

PART I

THE COMING OF DISASTER AND JOB'S IMMEDIATE REACTIONS OF DENIAL AND SHOCK

One

Job Is Ripe For A Precipitous Fall

The Book of Job begins, like most of the times of our lives, in apparent peace, calm and security. We are in a world of family, work, saving for the future, regular recreations, and religious observances. In the manner of traditional writings from ages characterized by heroic poetry, the example of all such everyday qualities is not just normal but supernormal: family, work, prosperity, feasting, religious observances, even Job's character are all exemplary.

There was once a man in the land of Uz called Job: a sound and honest man who feared God and shunned evil. Seven sons and three daughters were born to him. And he owned seven thousand sheep, three thousand camels, five hundred yoke of oxen and five hundred she-donkeys, and many servants besides. This man was indeed a man of mark among all the people of the East. It was the custom of his sons to hold banquets in each other's houses, one after the other, and to send and invite their three sisters to eat and drink with them. Once each series of banquets was over, Job would send for them to come and be purified, and at dawn on the following day he would offer a holocaust for each of them. "Perhaps," Job would say, "my sons have sinned and in their hearts affronted God." So that was what he used to do after each series. (Job 1:1-5).

The Mystery of Perceptual Blindness

The description of Job's character and behavior offered in these introductory verses parallels, in its inner essentials, the lives of most people before they suddenly fall ill or otherwise experience disaster— it reveals an unconsciousness about much of the reality around and within them. To people like these, life is unfolding predictably and all seems to be well and under control.

Of all the events that followed my diagnosis of cancer, none astonished me more than discovering how unconscious I had been about hitherto hidden complexities of my psychic and biological life. The experience of being diagnosed with a life-threatening illness jolted me out of this stuporous state. It helped me realize how much of what I had held till then as truthful and real was either illusory or, at best, a small part of a much larger totality as yet unknown to me. As this awakening took place, the image that kept recurring in my mind was that of a blindfolded man whose blindfold was suddenly removed, thus allowing him to see a world he had not known before. Some of what he saw then amazed him and was awe-inspiring, and some simply overwhelmed him.

I can attest unequivocally that the psychic awakening I am alluding to made me more alert to, and present in, everything with which I was involved. I remember discovering realities in the events of my daily life and in the books I read, as well as in the many things I saw around me that had been concealed from me before the diagnosis.

This process began immediately after that June morning when I first saw an enlarged lymph node bulging from the right side of the area under my jaw. After I thought about it, I was perplexed about my lateness in this discovery. The enlarged lymph node had escaped my detection in an area of my face I daily regarded. As a physician, I knew that the tumor I was only now seeing did not develop overnight. How did my mind manage to exclude this knowledge from my conscious awareness while "seeing" it each morning for weeks if not months? Furthermore, what allowed me to see it the day I did? Clearly, something in me had censored this information until the date that it became impossible for me to continue excluding this information from my conscious mind.

Much later I had a similar, although less dramatic, experience regarding the material contained in *The Book of Job*, and particularly in its first verses. I shall never know whether the author was aware of the profundities he had encoded into its narrative, or whether he had included them on purpose. All I know is that, despite having read this book numerous times, one night in January, 1992, I had a moment of sudden clarity about its meanings, and from then on I began to see in the verses of this mysterious poem revelations of truth that evoked in me a feeling of awe and deep appreciation. From that moment, I stopped perceiving Job's need to offer exculpatory sacrifices for his children (lest "they have sinned") as a manifestation of his righteousness, moral rectitude, or piousness. Suddenly, I began to perceive them as obsessive expressions of recurrent tension and anxiety in a man afraid of God's wrath. From this perspective, the conclusion that Job was a man in trouble and on the verge of a physical and psychospiritual breakdown was easy to come to.

I read the text many times and had innumerable experiences before I began to discern Job's fear and deep-seated existential angst. Until then, I had perceived Job in the same light as most readers do: as a man who was the embodiment of health and success, a model citizen worthy of praise and emulation.

This discrepancy in perspective about a biblical text or about ourselves is not uncommon. I frequently encounter these discrepancies in my practice of integrative medicine/oncology. There I meet people with life threatening illnesses who, like me prior to my own experience with cancer, have little or no awareness of the destructive physical, psychospiritual, and psychosocial forces that have long combined to foster disease and disequilibrium in their lives. It thus does not surprise me to hear them exclaim, "Until the day I discovered my illness, I was in perfect health," or to insist, "I have never before been to a hospital or suffered from a significant physical ailment."

But when illness and disequilibrium underlie our physical and psychospiritual life, how can we talk about being healthy? We all agree that a tumor growing somewhere in the body is the most obvious manifestation of cancer and warrants the most urgent attention, but it is by no means the only cancer that might be manifesting in the life of the afflicted individual. Cancer, when seen as a pattern of material organization, reflects all those conditions in which an interference with normal maturation and differentiation—the process whereby new functions become expressed—has taken place. From this perspective, cancer can express itself not only in our cells but also in our psyches and spirits, in the social groupings we belong to and in our material environments. This is precisely why, to heal, we need a medical science that addresses all the cancers affecting our bodies and our minds. Otherwise, our therapies will be palliative at best, and we will continue to suffer illness in many real senses of the term.

For us to appreciate these insights fully, we must have a frame of mind that can be acquired only through *direct experience*, which means that these insights are difficult to communicate to those who have not experienced them. As long as the persons to whom we want to convey this information remain unaware of the disequilibrium that has governed their lives or of the injuries that have shaped their decisions, the information we attempt to impart will hold no personal meaning. Once having experienced these things firsthand, however, these people will understand that physical illness represents merely the tip of an iceberg—the overt manifestation of a deeper disequilibrium that is in need of engagement and resolution. They will also realize that the wounds we harbor within us foster distress in our inner world, regardless of how tranquil we may appear to ourselves or to others. Evidently, in addition to what we can all overtly detect, each of us holds within us patterns of thought, feeling, and behavior that can help a physical or mental illness take root. When realizations such as these move into our consciousness and take on personal meaning, we are prompted to search for help in engaging our hidden challenges and healing our lives.

The surgical and radiation treatments I received in the summer of 1983 cured the physical manifestations of my cancer, but I was far from feeling healed. The physical disease had shocked me, and I was slowly becoming aware that, in many ways, I had been and still was a frightened, naive man, stuck at an early stage of psychological development. My feelings of detachment and lack of commitment to living, before and after the illness, reflected this inner formlessness. I will never know for sure whether any of these psychological conditions contributed to the development of my cancer, but I do know that they fostered a state of unconscious inner disarray that was not healthy.

Interestingly enough, none of my physicians knew about these inner conditions or had the presence of mind to inquire about them. I, who was insufficiently clear about my feelings then, was not of much help either. My colleagues, seeing disease only as the product of external forces affecting a person, perhaps genetically vulnerable to cancer, approached my situation with similar simplicity. The result, for me, was a feeling of confusion and aloneness. I could not help but conclude that my colleagues were adept at treating the physical manifestations of my cancer, but they had no idea of how to help me heal any non-physical cancers I was increasingly aware I harbored. I had no other choice than to go out in search of new resources, and in search of people who knew how to address the underlying ailments I was slowly discovering.

Job 1:1-5, seen exclusively from an objectivistic and rationalistic point of view, parallels my own case. The verses describe a superficial human way of living—success, family conventions, ritualistic obedience—and we may easily overlook the great distress and fear that Job carries within him implied by his nearly compulsive burning of sacrifices lest his sons "perhaps" had sinned. Furthermore, this shallow perspective allows us to perpetuate the delusion that Job was indeed an epitome of success, that his life followed a predictable course, and that as long as he continued to adhere to God's commandments, all would remain well.

People who hold this perspective live in a world predicated on unfounded assumptions that allay their fears and help them endure some of life's torments, but these assumptions certainly do not favor discovery and healing. Such a restricted and fragile world view can be sustained for only a limited time, and when life's perceived ruthlessness breaks through, the brittle mental constructs shatter, and hopelessness and despair supervene.

By contrast, those who can view Job's story from a more awakened perspective see deeper realities in these initial verses. They are able to read Job's feeling patterns and perceive him correctly, as an objectifying man, in an objectified world, full of reasoned stratagems for conduct and prayer but without real insight into himself and his world. For them, Job is nothing more than a man so blinded by his mentality that he is foolishly and hopelessly walking into an abyss.

To read *Job* (and Job) this way is to feel genuine caring and compassion. The man is a walking time bomb. What else can one say of a man objectively blessed with everything desirable, the pride of his God and his community, who nonetheless experiences fear and inner tension every time his sons celebrate together? Why does he imagine them sinning, and why does the fear of Hashem's wrath overwhelm him? Because nothing in the text suggests that his children's behavior was anything but flawless, Job's fears must have a more subjective origin.

All psychology teaches us that unrealistic anxieties such as these are usually the product of repressed, unconscious material pressing forward for acknowledgement. In Job's case, what is repressed is nothing less than an awareness of all the rest of the great realities both within and without, which his restricted view of the world has, up to this point, not allowed. His repressed reality, the source of his anxiety, includes most notably the inner Self, that world of instincts and feelings, sensuality and passion, archetypes and the collective unconscious, intuitive knowledge, higher wisdom, and much more. All are parts of the larger existence that is God's, an existence radically different from that which Job has experienced thus far.

From reading *The Book of Job* in this new way, we learn that any time we meet a human being for whom everything is working out and whose life lacks blemish, we are witnessing, perforce, an individual who is temporarily disconnected from most of his existence—including the dark parts. No one who seems all good can remain that way indefinitely. Sooner or later, life will burst the bubble, and when that happens, we are so surprised, so overwhelmed, so deeply wounded that our very existence is put to the test.

We may take as a gloss on the first verses of Job, and as an eloquent statement of the urgency of the unacknowledged reality that readies itself to spring upon the superficially successful man, these famous verses from another part of the Old Testament:

> ...Pharaoh had a dream; he was standing by the Nile, and there, coming up from the Nile, were seven cows, sleek and fat, and they began to feed among the rushes. And seven other cows, ugly and lean, came from the Nile after them; and these went over and stood beside the other cows on the bank of the Nile. The ugly and lean cows ate the seven sleek and fat cows. Then Pharaoh awoke (Gen. 41:1-4).

Two

Job's Initial Response Is Denial and Total Numbness

Satan, the challenging angel, questions God's assessment of Job's character. "Job is not God-fearing for nothing," he proclaims defiantly, and pressing his point forward with conviction, he suggests that if God were to lay a finger on Job's possessions Job would curse Him to His face. God, despite his omniscience, swallows Satan's bait, and allows him to strike at Job in any way he wants except to his person.

> One day the sons of God came to attend on Hashem,[3] and among them was Satan. So Hashem said to Satan, "Where have you been?" "Around the earth," he answered, "roaming about." So Hashem asked him, "Did you notice my servant Job? There is no one like him on the earth: a sound and honest man who fears God and shuns evil." "Yes," Satan said, "but Job is not God-fearing for nothing, is he? Have you not put a wall around him and his house and all

his domain? You have blessed all he undertakes, and his flocks throng the countryside. But stretch out your hand and lay a finger on his possessions: I warrant you, he will curse you to your face." "Very well," Hashem said to Satan, "all he has is in your power. But keep your hands off his person." So Satan left the presence of Hashem.

On the day when Job's sons and daughters were at their meal and drinking wine at their eldest brother's house, a messenger came to Job. "Your oxen," he said, "were at the plow, with the donkeys grazing at their side, when the Sabaeans swept down on them and carried them off. Your servants they put to the sword: I alone escaped to tell you." He had not finished speaking when another messenger arrived. "The fire of God," he said, "has fallen from the heavens and burned up all your sheep, and your shepherds too: I alone escaped to tell you." He had not finished speaking when another messenger arrived. "The Chaldaeans," he said, "three bands of them, have raided your camels and made off with them. Your servants they put to the sword: I alone escaped to tell you." He had not finished speaking when another messenger arrived. "Your sons and daughters," he said, "were at their meal and drinking wine at their eldest brother's house, when suddenly from the wilderness a gale sprang up, and it battered all four corners of the house which fell in on the young people. They are dead: I alone escaped to tell you" (1:6-19).

With ironic swiftness, the shadow half of life denied by Job's introduction in the first five verses reveals itself, as calamities pierce Job's innocence. These reach a climax in those very disasters to his children which, with vague anxiety, Job had tried to avert by conscious means (ritual sacrifice) based on a rationalistic understanding of how the world works. Before the disasters strike, however, the text offers us a myth to explain why they have befallen such a worthy man as Job—God is persuaded by the iniquitous and skeptical angel, Satan to test the very best of us (1:6-12). What is made obvious (at one level) in this passage is our bewilderment with such occurrences and our need to explain how and why bad things happen to good people.

God's Wager With Satan: A Travesty of God's Truth

Whenever we are stricken by tragedy, illness, or any other unexpected and unseemly event, we always pose the same questions: "Why me? What have I done to deserve this fate? Why have I been singled out for punishment?"

How many times have similar questions been articulated by patients who come to work with me? "Jacob," they ask, "why have we been afflicted with cancer? Did we bring this on ourselves? Was it a result of our dietary habits, our inner conflicts, or our stressful lifestyles?" These questions are accompanied by unyielding fear and dismay. "We need to know," they clamor. "We thirst for answers. Please help us!"

Invariably, I try to reassure these men and women that their cancers were not invoked by acts of volition, nor dispensed as punishment for sins they feel they have committed or for the lifestyles they have embraced. Instead, I emphasize, their medical problems were the product of complex interactions between physiochemical and bio-psychosocial forces operating both synchronously and sequentially to produce change—a foundation of our physical beingness. Because these interacting forces of nature operate largely beneath the threshold of our conscious awareness, how can we claim personal responsibility?

It would be even more ridiculous for people beset by tragedy to feel such responsibility if they have led an impeccable life, and are therefore beyond our, and God's reproach. Thus, the author of the text of Job offers an even more bizarre and clearly wrong-headed mythical explanation. If taken literally, it forces us to accept the premise that the God we have so dutifully worshipped for the last few thousand years questioned the loyalty of His most faithful follower, and fell prey to tricks and manipulations by one of His own creatures. Such assertions, however, make no biological, psychological, or metaphysical sense. Nature, we know, acts in opposition to what these verses imply, in a purposeful and meaningful way, and it is invested in promoting wellness and survival. Nature's pursuits are indeed relentless, but never are they arbitrary, capricious, or, least of all, tricky.

The key verses quoted at the beginning of this chapter, which form the backdrop of the whole book of Job, should not be taken in such a naive and childish manner. Rather, they should be seen as expressing an implied critique of our difficulty in accepting God's truth: that we are in fact vulnerable to injury regardless of our conduct and that, despite all our efforts to the contrary, tragedy can still befall us. Such basic truths are so stark, however, that they often leave man no recourse but to create a cosmology that places in a merely rationalistic context what is otherwise incomprehensible and unacceptable to us.

This human cosmology first holds that our universe is ruled by a God that is a caring and merciful King (the epitome of loving kindness) and who is at the same time a fair, albeit strict, overseer of man's every action and thought (the epitome of absolute justice). This omnipotent God, states the myth, oversees and scrutinizes all aspects of our lives from His vantage point in heaven, rewarding us appropriately when we are good and punishing us appositely when we are not. How then can we explain the suffering that good people are so often made to endure?

Evidently, the reality that good people suffer unjustly forced us to amend our cosmology and introduce a flaw into the character of our ruler. This all-loving, caring, and just ruler was conceived, therefore, as harboring some insecurity and animus in His heart. Thus, when challenged to show trust in His followers, He buckled under pressure and put His innocent servants to the test. This unfortunate flaw, the cosmological myth goes on to state, would never have surfaced had it not been for the presence of Satan in our midst. Satan, who, according to these beliefs, is introduced into the world by our sins, is a trickster, a troublemaker—an energy who is able to provoke God and wreak havoc in the lives of people like Job, whose behavior is indeed beyond reproach. By this reasoning, Job's misfortunes are the price commendable people pay for the sins of their brethren, those primitive and unenlightened beings who do not live according to the precepts set forth by Hashem.

As we can see, this myth fashioned by humans succeeds in offering a palatable explanation for why Job's life was overtaken by tragedy. While circumstance forced humans to acknowledge that God was indeed vulnerable to the cunning of Satan, they were able to shield God from responsibility for the many calamities poor Job ultimately received. These calamities, as well as all other injustices we may find in our universe, are interpreted instead as a direct consequences of our sinfulness and as a product of our imperfections and frailties.

But the very implausibility of this sort of myth making—including that reflected in the text of *The Book of Job*—undercuts any impression we may have that it is the fruit of divine revelation or an accurate reflection of the way God's world works. What this cosmology represents instead is the handicraft of frightened and overwhelmed people who cannot tolerate naked truth or, more specifically, the complexity of God's awesome creation.

Job's Response to His First Encounter With God's World is Denial of His Feelings

Job rose and tore his gown and shaved his head. Then falling to the ground he worshiped and said:

"Naked I came from my mother's womb,
   naked I shall return.
Hashem gave, Hashem has taken back.
   Blessed be the name of Hashem!"

In all of this misfortune Job committed no sin nor offered any insult to God (1:20-22).

Job's response to calamity is measured, deliberate and controlled. He does not allow feeling to dominate him. Instead, he performs rituals of mourning, and utters professions of resignation and submission in highly stylized repetitive phrases ("naked...naked...Hashem...Hashem"), which are themselves verbal equivalents of his prefabricated ritual gestures. These traditional measures are at once canalizations and, paradoxically, denials of feeling.

Denial is, without doubt, one of the most often misunderstood of our psychological defenses against pain and harm. I frequently hear people say things like, "We must break through his or her denial; denial is bad." I have often wondered: "Why is it bad? Why is it so important, especially when disaster strikes, to be instantly and steadfastly aware of our unfortunate circumstances?"

Once I worked with a 40-year-old woman whose advanced cancer was unresponsive to conventional therapies. After many attempts with complex chemotherapy regimens to achieve a lasting remission, she decided to stop all treatments and handle her illness with her own personal resources. Despite the advanced stage of disease, she managed to remain fully functional, enthusiastic, and invested in living. There was, however, a limit she imposed on all her efforts: She wanted to remain in total denial of her impending death. She had made it clear, over and over, to all those who came in touch with her, that this was her wish, her request, and the way she was going to handle her condition. From my point of view, she managed her disease remarkably well, and she was a true symbol of courage and determination. At a certain point, however, a smart and "very well trained" health care professional came along (in this case it was a Hospice social worker) who, in his wisdom and with no knowledge whatever of the person's psychology and soul, declared in unequivocal terms to the afflicted person's family: "For us to provide service to your loved one, she must be told she is dying. Her denial is definitely not good for her. It must be breached to help *her die peacefully*." I wondered where such false wisdom comes from? How we frequently, with the best intentions, cause harm to those we are trying to help, and particularly when we enter their delicate psychophysical and spiritual situations with abstract agendas that, by and large, disregard people's continual effort to avoid despair and hopelessness.

To speak more personally, when I discovered my own cancer, I was a 37-year-old married man and the father of three young children, a physician/scientist working at one of the most acclaimed universities in the country. Imagine the shock I experienced when I suddenly realized that my future was uncertain. What could I be expected to do other than deny the whole thing and pretend, at least temporarily, that nothing of import had happened? What other course of action will usually prove as productive in moments such as these? I can thus empathize greatly with Job, who, when first informed of the calamities that had been visited upon him, became numb and grew distant and alien. The significance of what had just happened was so overwhelming that his best recourse was to detach himself from it and deny it had occurred at all. Job, as do most of us afflicted by adversity, retreated into the fortress of everyday reasonableness and ritual behaviors to a place where he felt safe and invulnerable.

Job's initial emotional detachment helped him uphold his composure and his faith in the idea of the God he understood. This detachment also prevented his sense of the world's order from collapsing forthwith and, though his belief systems were being seriously challenged, he could keep them intact, allowing him to cleave to the notion of God's and his own righteousness as a key to his eventual salvation.

Those who have suffered sudden disaster will identify wholeheartedly with Job's initial response. When I was diagnosed with non-Hodgkin's lymphoma, the whole experience automatically seemed to me like a cosmic joke God was playing: A young Medical Oncologist/Immunologist develops a cancer of the immune system! I even laughed at it all, with a certain humorous detachment. In retrospect, I can see that I was even then aware of the fear and sadness that gripped my interior. But at the time, I was instantly able to feel nothing at all. In the long run, as time passed and things settled down, detachment and denial gave way to feelings that spurred my growth and allowed me to heal my wounds, but when disaster first struck, detachment and denial were indeed effective and practical reactions.

Three

Job's Healing Journey Has Begun

The story progresses rapidly now, new torments being visited upon Job. However adaptive Job's denial of truth may be in the short term, a second preparation for his further trials implies that this denial will not succeed in the long run.

> Once again the Sons of God came to attend to Hashem, and among them was Satan. So Hashem said to Satan, "Where have you been?" "Around the earth," he answered, "roaming about." So Hashem asked him, "Did you notice my servant Job? There is no one like him on the earth: a sound and honest man who fears God and shuns evil. His life continues blameless as ever; in vain you provoked me to ruin him." "Skin for skin!" Satan replied. "A man will give away all he has to save his life. But stretch out your hand and lay a finger on his bone and flesh; I warrant you, he will curse you to your face." "Very well," Hashem said to Satan, "he is in your power. But spare his life." (2:1-7).

Cosmic and psychic forces work to pierce Job's detachment and to ensure that his encounter with God's world is acknowledged. To accomplish this healing breakthrough, these verses suggest a person's very body must be injured.

It distresses me to think that we can successfully bypass the transformational power of hurtful events that affect critical domains of human existence, such as our financial well-being, our social status, and even the welfare of our children. But this is the case, in most instances. Only when our lives are truly on the line, and when we face the possibility of extinction, do the conditions for substantive change move to the fore and foster genuine transformation. This reality is a sad and honest testimony to our resistance to transcending patterns of psychospiritual action that have long inflicted damage on our health, and also on how difficult this undertaking is, even when we are intellectually committed to fulfill it.

According to *The Book of Job's* narrative, Job never witnessed the terrible occurrences that initially befell him; he only heard about them. In other words, he knew about them cognitively but did not experience them emotionally. This is why the penetration of this psychic material into his conscious awareness was incomplete, and why it did not foster significant change. For Job to begin to transform himself, he had to receive a direct blow.

> So Satan left the presence of Hashem. He struck Job down with malignant ulcers from the sole of his foot to the top of his head. Job took a piece of pot to scrape himself, and went and sat in the ashpit (2:7-8).

Job has now received an initiatory injury, a direct hit to the body—something that threatens his existence. Job's wealth, his servants, and even his children, however precious to him, were all in a certain sense replaceable. His very health and life, however, were not. Once his flesh was touched, he became truly aware he was mortal. Now he is wounded in his very substance, and his illusion of invulnerability is irreversibly shattered. Job's life will never again be the same. He has been thrust into a ruthless, uncertain and forbidding world. Job has entered no-man's land and feels lost and confused.

Why Did Job Fall Ill?

The story of Job's predicament has raised many questions over the years, but the question I am asked most frequently is, "Why did Job fall ill? How do you explain this phenomenon without invoking the image of a conscienceless God wreaking havoc on the life of His most faithful servant? If, as suggested before, the sequence between Satan and God was but a myth, a picture of our feeble attempt to mitigate nature's truth, what is the true explanation of Job's illness?"

At one level are the complex and mostly unknown interactions of physical and non-physical causes—all parts of God's world. But at another level of meaning, we can see Job's illness as an example of an underlying psychosomatic condition caused primarily by his inability to permit, express, and release deep-seated emotions, specifically his rage and profound resentment. The sages in commentaries tell us that it took approximately a full year for Job's calamities to unfold. Imagine then, what might have happened to his body if for a full year it was being affected by calamity, after calamity while all he managed to say was:

"Naked I came from my mother's womb,
   naked I shall return.
Hashem gave, Hashem has taken back.
   Blessed be the name of Hashem" (1:21).

Such a feeble and essentially maladaptive reaction probably caused a serious perturbation in the physiology of Job's body. Job's denial of feeling immediately upon hearing of his ill fortune was initially useful and, in fact, necessary. But as time went on, this same detachment from feeling encouraged the development of disease. In the absence of feeling, neither Job nor anyone else had a clue as to what needed to be done to encourage healing. Detachment from feeling heightens our body's vulnerability to illness and significantly lowers our capacity to respond to serious challenges and threats, trapping us in our own disease process. Our negative conditioning against our own feelings (in particular the unpleasant ones) has fostered the creation of a psychosocial world where rationalistic-mentalistic constructs rule and where feelings play a minimal role. This type of world, however, is inherently unhealthy. It cannot sustain itself indefinitely, and it tends to cause serious disequilibrium and disease in us. People who live in such a world have no clear sense of their own existence and identity; therefore, they have no clue as to what goes on inside their own bodies. After being ignored for a long time in this way, the body, in a last-ditch effort to restore its wellness, forces the emergence of disease in the person's life. This is a natural attempt to break through the restrictive conditioning and allow for the restitution of equilibrium and health. But don't try to convince the sufferer of this truth.

Job 1:6-19 and Job 2:1-8 suggest that the many wounds inflicted on Job occurred over a relatively short period of time. It is quite likely that Job was just recovering from one injury before the next one hit him. In this case, he may not have had sufficient time to recover from his wounds and initiate the process of psychological repair. Regardless of what precisely caused his physical illness, however, it is fair to say that Job's inability to express his feelings could not have been advantageous to him. Energy trapped within the body tends to seek manifestation and release, and when *strong feelings are repressed*, they inevitably seek alternative channels for expression. From this perspective, Job's skin ulcers could have been the product of his inability to give vent to his despair in a natural and constructive fashion, thus validating the notion that psychospiritual imbalances (repressions) may have been important factors in his disease, as I believe they were in my case.

Certainly, shortly following my diagnosis, I became totally invested in finding out why I had become ill. As a physician/scientist committed to the investigation of the causes of neoplastic diseases (disorders caused by the uncontrolled growth of cells that accumulate and produce tumors) and of the mechanisms available to the body to defend against them, it was imperative I find adequate answers to my inquiry. I knew this information would be unavailable within the framework of traditional medicine, and that I needed to look somewhere else. But where?

From a purely biomedical perspective, the recommended approach to my sort of predicament was merely to submit to the most effective treatment available at the time, and go on with my life as if nothing had occurred. I, however, could not do that. I needed to understand my reality better. The idea of a cancer developing inside my body frightened me and fueled my quest. I could not accept the idea that cancer could develop in a totally normal and healthy individual. And yet was I not healthy by all medical standards? Moreover, I could not understand how I differed from the millions of other men and women in my age group, who ate the same foods and drank the same water as I did, and yet did not develop cancer. All this confused me and spurred my efforts to review all aspects of my life in search for clues and understanding. I wanted to know whether I was involved in patterns of psychic activity or in behaviors that promoted disease. I wanted to discover if I was living in an unhealthy environment and, if so, what to do to correct this. More generally, I needed to know what health was all about, and how to harness it and augment it to the maximum. I could not rest until I had addressed and dealt with all these concerns.

The process of exploration I initiated then has continued unabated. I discovered many realities as I went along that made the development of my disease more comprehensible. One of the most critical realizations I made during this time was that I had lived most of my adult life under the influence of an infantile psychic pattern that made me appear as an attractive and charismatic boy-man, who felt bored and often disgusted with ordinary living. I wasn't truly committed to my own earthly existence, and exhibited instead a lack of vitality and staying power. The pattern I am referring to is that of the divine child/ fool, which, to my chagrin, is prevalent among many males these days. People who live under the influence of this pattern tend to be highly idealistic, sensitive, ethereal, adventurous, imaginative and seductive individuals. To them, simple day-to-day tasks are unattractive and offend their sensitivity and divine nature. I came into full awareness of my involvement with this pattern in 1986 after reading a book by

Marie-Louise Von Franz, *Puer Aeternus*. The text mesmerized me, particularly when it quoted Jung as saying that men who carry this pattern tend to die young[4]. I cannot explain how angry I felt then. I experienced a crushing disappointment and felt I had betrayed my own capacity for existence by falling into this configuration of self. At first, I couldn't believe that this innocent little child had almost taken me to the grave. Later, I became committed to overthrowing the power of this tyrannical ruler. I wanted him out of my life immediately. I understood the suicidal component in this pattern of life, and its danger to my health and well-being. To my relief, a part of me fully committed to living (perhaps my inner warrior) awoke when I most needed it, seized the moment, and became invested in ending the dominance of this infantile psychic form.

I am certain that the influence this childish pattern exerted over my interior created the equivalent to a "psychic" cancer in me and supported or permitted physical cancer to take hold. How this occurred I don't know. But I know in my heart of hearts that this was so. Though I will not, unfortunately, be able to convince many of my colleagues of the validity of my assertion, what I did with the intuitive knowledge I gained did not require the validation of others. Understanding this information gave meaning to my illness and made me feel I could manage the illness better. First, it gave me clear knowledge of the fundamental personality pattern that was detrimental to me. Second, it pointed, in a general way, in the direction of what I needed to avoid, and to transcend, psychologically. Today, the knowledge of similar limiting psychospiritual forces operating in me helps me engage them preventively and hence, avoid their toxic effects and propensity to cause disequilibrium later. While I am still vulnerable to the cancer-promoting forces that exist outside my being, I feel that I live now in an internal milieu that is stronger, more supportive, and more committed to health and healing, and hence more capable of avoiding and handling disease.

The Truth About What Happened to Job

It will benefit us to ask why the text goes to so much trouble to explain why Job's life was overcome with calamities. Why was it necessary to present Job's illness as the product of a second full-dress meeting and unholy agreement between God and Satan, aimed at testing Job's devotion to God? The very unreasonableness of the myth serves, above all, to emphasize the desperate need we have to find adequate answers for why horrific things happen to good people. This terrible truth makes us feel vulnerable, desperate and hopeless because it suggests that we will never be able to control the two things that trouble us most: illness, in particular when it is life-threatening; and death. This is precisely why *The Book of Job* is so challenging. It presents us with a man whose life lacks blemish, and so forces us to address the question of why his life is so brutally shattered. To deal with this quandary, the story forces us to give up our innocence and acknowledge that good behavior even if it means following all of God's ten commandments and the 613 others prescribed as Mitzvot in Leviticus will not spare us from serious illness, material loss, and death. Once we can truly accept this fact, the whole story of Job falls into perspective and becomes comprehensible. We are then able to see Job for what he was: a denier of realities, an innocent and unsuspecting child/fool, a man who believed "it can't happen to me," and who believed that prayers and good behavior could turn back even nature's laws. Indeed, Job was scarcely aware of the mundane facts of what was going on around him, let alone the mythical meetings of God and Satan in heaven. Evidently, for instance, Job was so naive that he believed everyone's intentions were as good as his own, and therefore he grossly misinterpreted the way the world works. Job's child/fool way of living blinded him to the envy and resentment his wealth, privilege, and seeming moral flawlessness naturally inspired among many of his fellow men, especially those less fortunate. He became a highly vulnerable target for his envious neighbors (the Chaldaeans and the Sabaeans), but he had no idea this was so. A buildup of tension then took place, which would not be relieved without bloodshed to his servants, his symbolic extensions.

Even the death of Job's children could have been anticipated, by anyone not identified with the child/fool within him, and prevented. They perish in a whirlwind that topples their homes. Surely if Job had been less lost in wishful thinking, he might have remained aware that he and his children lived in a dangerous and unstable area. He might then have chosen to live elsewhere. Job is indeed a wounded soul deserving of infinite support and compassion and his encounter with God's world has clearly overwhelmed and destroyed him. But he was forewarned of his fate, if he had been willing to acknowledge the facts.

Similarly, those of us who have chosen to live in places more or less regularly visited by earthquakes, tornadoes, hurricanes, floods, ice storms, avalanches, or other natural disasters should be well aware of the risks and dangers inherent in our decisions. In the back of our minds, we all know that in the event of a major earthquake, we and our loved ones might be seriously injured or even killed. Wouldn't it be ludicrous if, in the event of such an unfortunate and most painful occurrence, we were to invoke the actions of a Satan manipulating God's will and resolve? But, as has been said, "man cannot bear too much reality" and so we resist knowing the truth about ourselves and our world, just as Job did.

None of what befell Job requires for its comprehension either invoking divine intervention or some weird and debasing wager between an omniscient, all-powerful God and His trickster son. All we need to place these events in context is to remember that when we are naive and disconnected from truth, we are highly vulnerable to experience a ruthless and earth-shattering awakening. "Welcome to the world of God," I say. "I hope you enjoy it."

Four

The Voice Of Wisdom Helps Job Overcome His Emotional Numbness

It is not uncommon for people who face calamities of one sort or another to receive advice and recommendations from family and friends. While some of these well-intentioned recommendations can at times be quite unusual, none surpasses in weirdness the one Job received from his beloved wife. In her first and only appearance in the book, she addresses Job, her shell-shocked husband, and says:

> "...Do you now still mean to persist in your blamelessness? Curse God, and die" (2:9).

Most of us who read this verse for the first time react to it with bewildered disbelief. "What an insensitive woman Job's wife was," we say. "How did she dare address her husband, a broken man mourning the death of his children? Weren't these her children as well, and wasn't she facing the possible loss of her beloved husband? Why, of the innumerable things she might have said, did Job's wife elect to communicate such a brutal message?"

To comprehend Job's wife's surprising intervention, it is necessary to shift our perspective. The situation is desperate, and something drastic needs to be done in order for Job to save his life. I have given Job's wife a fictitious name, Naomi. Naomi is for her own part bereft, having lost all her children, and now her husband of 35 years has been taken gravely ill. She has no time to equivocate; either something dramatic must happen or Job will be lost to her forever. Realizing that no one else understands the situation as clearly, and that no expert help is to be found, it is up to her alone to jolt her husband from his deadly stupor and into a process of recovery. So, despite her own deep affliction and abiding despair, armed with the courage of knowing that her message comes from the highest source, Naomi applies a form of psychological shock therapy: "Do you now still mean to persist in your blamelessness? Curse God, and die." Here, the voice of wisdom comes forward through Naomi to help Job overcome his emotional numbness. If Job can curse God, Naomi senses, the denial that oppresses her husband, which is based on a good-boy compliance with conventional notions, will begin to lift, enabling him to move toward recovery. Naomi also understands that, for Job to overcome his tragedy, he needs to "die"—not in a physical sense, but rather by undergoing a profound and irreversible psychospiritual transformation. To her, Job's submissive goodness and rigid blamelessness are part of his disease—part of what he urgently needs to free himself from. Job, however, clings tenaciously to his old beliefs and patterns of behavior, thinking that they are instead precisely what will secure his salvation.

When we are blinded by prior conditioning, nothing short of a miracle will open our eyes. I am reminded of the bewilderment and even resentment that often greet me when at a certain time in their illness, I first tell my patients, "If you want to live, you must die!"

"No," they answer. "You have it all wrong. We want to live, not die; death is not what we are interested in."

"Precisely," I say; "that is why you must die, and rather soon." In a gentle way—much gentler than Naomi's—I am trying to open a door for them to something new. I don't push it unless I see that the patient has budged the door open at least a crack. Often, I have to make my hard point and then back off, until the patient's inner psychological evolution opens the door some more.

Many of us are naturally slow to understand why and how dying may serve as a foundation for living. The idea seems a contrivance, an irrelevant trick. And this is indeed the case as long as death is perceived as a phenomenon that pertains only to the physical realm of our existence and, therefore, is always undesirable or evil. By contrast, when death is understood as irreversible change, as a transformation that may occur at any of the levels of organization in which we participate (physical, psychological, social, sexual, spiritual, etc.), the subject takes on another hue.

From this emerging perspective, it would be inconceivable for anyone afflicted with a life-threatening illness to defend him or herself automatically against dying. "What is it," I may ask, "that you seek to preserve? The psychic patterns that may well have fostered illness or allowed the latter to develop? Your impaired psychobiologic structures? Is there a course of action more sensible than dying when one is faced with a life-threatening condition?" In fact, dying so that new and healthier patterns of mental organization can emerge is precisely what the doctor ordered.

Conditioning, however, can be unremittingly rigid and exceedingly hard to extinguish. It is remarkable how many of us conduct our lives on the basis of patterns and rules of behavior into which we were inducted thirty, forty, or even sixty years ago, often during the initial stages of our childhood. Certainly, these beliefs are now at least partly outdated and may well have outlived their usefulness altogether. Why, then, should we not rethink some of the assumptions that have been shaping our every thought and action?

"Be your own Einstein," I encourage my patients. "When he encountered a physical phenomenon that he could not explain, he did the most sensible thing: He accepted the phenomenon as valid and began to search for new laws to integrate it into the context of physical reality. This move resulted in the discovery of a new set of principles that heightened our understanding of the physical world."

Similarly, people with cancer and other life-threatening conditions need to change their understanding of reality to integrate and adapt to the new information they have received. As long as they continue to perceive the cancer experience from their old and obsolete perspectives, they will continue to feel victimized, frustrated, and weak.

After recovering his composure from the impact of his wife's brutal pronouncement, Job replies:

> "That is how foolish women talk...If we take happiness from God's hand, must we not take sorrow too?" And in all this misfortune Job uttered no sinful word (2:10).

Job's reaction to his wife's words is both predictable and understandable. Job the victim is still in shock. So much has happened so fast that he can not allow himself to break down or he will not be able to assimilate it. It is a little too early for Job to "die." People who feel as devastated as Job did at this point tend to become even more tightly attached to what is familiar, and therefore comfortable, to them, even though it is frequently exactly what they need to move away from.

Job thus calls his wife's counsel foolish and then proceeds to make one of the most emotional obtuse statements a man can utter: "...If we take happiness from God's hand, must we not take sorrow too?" (2:10). His clearly is the response of a mind that is operating in disjunction from his body. There is no feeling in what he says; to the contrary, Job acts completely detached, as if he could not care less about what has happened to him. His wife is beside herself. "Where is your anger, your rage?" she protests. Job, however, remains calm and collected. He is incapable of feeling anger; this is not part of his emotional repertoire. Instead he looks at his wife with bewilderment and confusion. "Why is she so worked up?" he thinks to himself.

All Job offers are perfectly reasonable answers. And these in themselves are not invalid. But his reaction is only a fragment of a fully appropriate response to what is actually happening to him. His voice here is not, then, that of true understanding and wisdom. Rather than reflecting moral superiority or higher understanding, Job's reaction illustrates instead his extraordinary detachment from his feelings.

As a physician, I have seen this detachment from feeling many times before, and not just with patients. In this regard, I have been particularly struck by what goes on in those weekly meetings attended by specialists in the diagnosis and treatment of neoplastic diseases called "tumor boards."

If you were to walk into one of these meetings, you would find yourself in a high-tech auditorium, where a projector flashes pathology slides prepared from surgically removed tissue, and television monitors show CAT scan pictures of body organs. A speaker would be pointing out the presence of tumor lesions in particular body sites and giving diagnostic conclusions and therapeutic suggestions on the basis of the information about the case he or she has just presented. Following this, the case would be opened up for discussion and final recommendations. After a few other doctors had offered their opinions, a consensus decision would be made and later conveyed to the afflicted person and his or her family. The meeting would then be adjourned and everyone would stand up and engage in social chitchat.

I can assure you that no one entering the room a few moments after the start of the meeting would be able to determine whether the case in question involved a human being or a non-human primate. This lack of a fundamental distinction is emblematic of a type of medical practice that is centered on the study of disease rather than on people with disease—a study in which the structural and functional features of an *illness* are what counts rather than the person in whom the illness has become manifest. Feelings do not matter. In this type of medicine, it matters little whether an illness happens to occur in a human being or not. The parameters and considerations are quite similar and the treatment approach virtually the same.

Many people, particularly physicians, may react to these assertions with outrage. My statements, however, are valid, and they warrant acknowledgment so that the problem may be properly addressed. Moreover, what I am conveying is neither said in a judgmental spirit nor intended as a technical criticism of the practitioners of this craft. I am certainly not implying that physicians either don't feel for or don't care about their patients, because that is not the case. What I am saying, however, is that engagement with the patients' feelings, acknowledgment of patients' existential concerns, and the activation of patients' psychospiritual resources for healing and recovery are not significant parts of traditional medicine's paradigmatic understanding of health and disease, or of conventional physicians' training and skills.

Some of my colleagues try to transmute this gross deficiency into a positive attribute: "If you become emotionally involved with your patients," they argue, "it will certainly cloud your clinical judgment and have detrimental and at times disastrous effects." Obviously no one would advise health practitioners to do something that would cause them to lose their minds or their good judgment. Why then this wrong-headed resistance to such obvious needs in the improvement of health care? The answer is to be found in the great difficulty people, including physicians, have in handling their own feelings. They are frequently overwhelmed by them, and by and large they seek refuge from their own pain and despair by detaching themselves emotionally. Unfortunately, most physicians try to conceal this characteristic and present their behavior in a positive light. But if this is what so-called professionals do with their own feelings, what can we expect them to do with those of their patients? Encourage and appreciate them? Unfortunately not. Encouragement and appreciation are simply not possible, and, when physicians attempt them, they seem hollow and contrived to all concerned.

I don't want to leave the impression that each and every physician can or should be expected to engage these powerful and most complex areas of being, or that abstraction on a doctor's part is in and of itself bad or detrimental to our health or our health care. Neither am I asking people who approach illness from a rational standpoint to alter their perceptions of reality or their way of engaging the world. What I am suggesting, instead, is that we remember that healing an illness involves more than just attending to its symptoms and its physical manifestations. Many of today's medical practitioners may not yet know how to help others heal and repair the sickness of their soul. This deficiency does not constitute medical malpractice, but it does invest us with the responsibility of encouraging fellow practitioners who do know these secrets, in every authentic effort to promote an integrated wellness in those whose illnesses we treat. To do any less is unrealistic, irrational, and, we could even venture to say, unscientific.

Five

The Voice(s) Of Reason Protect Job From His Feelings

> The news of all the disasters that had fallen on Job came to the ears of three of his friends. Each of them set out from home—Eliphaz of Teman, Bildad of Shuah and Zophar of Naamath—and by common consent they decided to go and offer him sympathy and consolation. Looking at him from a distance, they could not recognize him; they wept aloud and tore their garments and threw dust over their heads.
>
> They sat there on the ground beside him for seven days and seven nights. To Job they spoke never a word, so sad a sight he made (2:11-12).

As the news of Job's devastating tragedy spreads through the land, his three best friends hear about his misfortunes and come to console him. Like Job, the three men are all men of learning, scholars who had taught together and had respected each other's individuality and breadth of knowledge. They, too, had counseled the masses on many issues of personal and communal concern. Their capacity to remain calm under even the most trying of circumstances was naturally held in high regard. After their initial expressions of grief, they followed religious tradition and sat with Job silently for seven days, mourning the deaths of his beloved children.

At first glance, the actions of Job's three friends seem entirely commendable. After all, Job was facing the most trying moments of his life, so we would expect his best friends to act in this fashion; anything less would be incomprehensible. On the surface, what Job's colleagues did was indeed appropriate, but most of what we do is not what it seems, and altruism is all too often a cover for something else less appealing and glamorous. Job's friends' response to his misfortunes, while reflecting in part their devotion to their colleague, reflect in equal measure the internal dynamics of their personal needs. After all, didn't they have something precious to protect and defend, something so valuable to them that it made it imperative they be by his side at all times?

Let's be realistic: Job was an injured man fighting for his life and survival, and the explosion of feeling that such a powerful struggle may evoke in people is often deeply feared by those closest to them. Job's friends understood that if feelings were to flood Job's psyche, they could cloud his mind and make him act erratically and unpredictably. They saw, too, that their life's work of so many years, their accomplishments, and the very foundations that supported their culture were all in danger of crumbling if a man like Job, their respected spiritual leader, was allowed to denounce the beliefs and ideologies on which those foundations were based. It was therefore essential that the friends monitor Job's every step and action and that they remind him by their steadying collective presence, of how he ought to think and behave in the world after unexpected tragedy. Above all, it was imperative that Job's malefic emotions remained in the recesses of his unconscious, where they belonged.

Just as Job's friends came to sit with him after hearing about his misfortunes, so my colleagues came to me after finding out about my illness. I don't believe their intentions were to prevent deep-seated emotions from rising to the surface, but I too had the sense that my colleagues were unconsciously committed to keeping things quiet, calm, and normal. Let business go on as usual above all, lest we dwell on the shock and pain of the natural disaster happening to one of us. Our commitment, to Science and its incarnation in the University must remain transcendent. Unbeknownst to me, we were behaving like members of a sect worshipping a god that demanded obedience, loyalty, and devotion. It didn't matter to this god whether I lived or died, or whether I was healthy or ill, as long as I continued to abide by my institutional obligations and responsibilities. The fundamental message I received from my colleagues was: "You must continue your work and your scientific pursuits, perhaps even with more zeal now. We hope that your illness does not distract you from the path we all have chosen and cause you to stray away from your purpose and our aims."

Naturally, I, as the person with the cancer, was not as professionally focused as these co-workers were. One experience in particular brought to the fore the wide gulf that had arisen between me and my old ways of looking at my situation. Just after completing my radiation treatments at Stanford, I returned to my office and laboratory at UCLA, and while I was sorting my mail one of my colleagues and friends walked in to welcome me back. After a few cursory questions about my experience at Stanford, he plunged into a discussion of several projects for research and new possibilities for funding that he had been exploring during my absence. These were wonderful opportunities for venturing into exciting areas of work, and he wanted me to consider doing them with him. Two months earlier all this good news would have tickled my fancy, but that morning I could not have cared less about everything he was telling me with so much enthusiasm.

I was clearly in a different world from his world, and I felt totally detached from and unmotivated by his grand projects. From his perspective, however, all seemed to point to business as usual. There I was in the same office, wearing the same lab coat, and looking pretty much the same (except for the second-degree burns on both sides of my neck from the radiation, and the modest loss of blond hair at the back of my scalp), and ready to resume the scientific race. To him, what had happened to me had become only a small inconvenience, a temporary detour, which had been successfully managed and taken care off. For me, however, my experience felt like a plunge into a strange, uncharted world, where I still faced a ten to twenty percent chance of dying within five years. That statistic was too high for comfort; moreover, it was unacceptable to me. I was not going to merge blithely back into a lifestyle that had yielded (even though not necessarily causally) this illness. Moreover, my interest and concerns had shifted: I needed and wanted to explore my new, existential world. This would be my next research project: to investigate my own life as profoundly as I could for clues to an understanding of my new reality. It is ironic, though, that while I was becoming an ever more dedicated scientist, embarking upon the newly unknown by exploring the mystery and the secrets of my own selfhood, my university colleagues and the larger institution they represented (society's center for study of the mysteries of nature) did not consider the investigation of certain of these realities sufficiently scientific or interesting. No one among my many well-known colleagues in cancer research took the time to reflect that perhaps my personal experience provided a unique opportunity to learn important new things about what cancer is and what happens to people when they get it. My personal experience with the illness offered us all a unique occasion to learn directly about the biology, psychology and spiritual dimensions of this condition. Yet somehow these matters were of limited interest to that scientific community. Information being gathered directly, experientially, was obviously less relevant than whatever scientists can study by manipulating mice on laboratory benches or cultures in test tubes and petri dishes.

Attunement to The Wisdom of The Body

Like Job, I also received recommendations and advice from family and friends following the onset of my illness. Most of the information involved traditional and, mostly, non-traditional methods of treatment, which promised what I most wanted to hear: that a 100% cure was possible. But how do we know which of these many approaches to choose? How can we effectively discern which of the many voices we are hearing are the voices of wisdom and which are the voices of foolishness and ignorance? How do we know which approaches will be productive?

For some, the best way to handle this flow of information is to try everything that seems reasonable and not obviously harmful. People who choose this alternative are concerned with leaving no stone unturned, and hence they take an all-encompassing approach. This strategy, however, can be exhausting, costly, and often counterproductive. Its driving force is usually fear and ignorance, and therefore it seldom leads to a wholesome outcome. There is, however, an alternative pathway that in my opinion is more valuable. This pathway connects us to our heart and teaches us to follow the dictates of our intuitive selves. When my two specialist physicians were deciding on the best treatment available for my condition, they could only agree to disagree. Both these oncologists were highly respected, world-renowned figures in the diagnosis and treatment of lymphomas, yet, despite their extensive experience and profound knowledge of the disease, the best they could do was disagree with each other about what was right for me. To my surprise, they placed the ball in my court and asked me to decide on one of their recommendations. As had been the case with my physicians, however, nothing in the medical literature could help me decide between these choices. To my pleasant surprise, a subtle but precise feeling began to stir in me then, and that feeling guided my decision. I am glad that I was able to respect this inner feeling, although, to be perfectly honest, I had no other choice. Since this particular event took place, I have learned to identify this inner state better and to use it more readily. I think of it as part of the wisdom of the body, that side of us that allows us to discern between possibilities that from an objective view point are equally reasonable. Being in touch with this inner wisdom has also made the rest of my life much easier, providing me with a guiding light for the continued exploration of other wonders of living.

The importance of being attuned to the wisdom of our body is illustrated when we experience a life-threatening illness. Then, our investments and beliefs, the soundness of our commitments, the wisdom of our choices, our lifestyle, and our cosmology are all challenged by the uncertainty the disease causes and by our compelling desire to survive. This provides another way of describing the need to "die" because of illness and the benefits illness thus brings. Nothing now can remain sacred, or off limits to our critical scrutiny. We feel we must, under the circumstances, ask ourselves: Is the fulfillment of the obligations we have assumed (whatever they are) enhancing our chances to overcome our predicament? Is the maintenance of our public persona, and the responsibilities thereof, something we should keep up or not?

As everything in our lives comes up for revision, requiring new engagement and resolution, our career, our vocation, and our life's work are rightly questioned. Recently, a young woman struggling with a metastatic cancer for which there is no effective treatment, came to me for help. Outwardly, this woman looked good and healthy. Inwardly, however, we both knew she was riddled with a disease that was advancing and slowly compromising her health. A highly visible public figure, who had made a full commitment to community work, she had been used to spending a great deal of her time attending to matters of collective need; her daily activities were dominated by her many social and political responsibilities and obligations. As she began to review her life, these commitments came immediately under the magnifying glass of an attention enhanced by the threat to her life:

"I have to go to this dinner tomorrow," she said emphatically. "I promised: it is very important I be there. A person in my position, with my obligations, cannot say no."

"But why?" I asked. "Does the community for whom you work and whom you serve really care about your health and well-being? Do they know your predicament, and if they do, would they genuinely care?"

These questions stunned her. "I have dedicated my life to this cause," she insisted. "This has been a most important part of my life."

"Yes," I said, "but is this cause invested in you?" "Listen," I persisted. "Your time on this earth may be quite limited. You have been given the privilege to prioritize your time. Your life is precious, so please use your time wisely."

"But they need me. I have made commitments," she replied.

"The only commitment that matters now is the one you are making to yourself," I told her. "If under the circumstances, knowing what you know, you still feel compelled to do your political service, then please do it by all means. But just do what is most meaningful to you, what is congruent with your inner feelings. Your body contains a wisdom that reveals itself to you quite often. Listen to your body messages. Learn to follow your bliss. If you do, you will not be conflicted or unduly burdened. I would rather see you live a while longer and have people say: 'have you noticed what a self-centered, self-absorbed person she has become,' than for you to continue being perceived as totally devoted to work and dead!"

Six

Job's Psyche Is Flooded With Unbounded Emotion

In the end it was Job who broke the silence and cursed the day of his birth. This is what he said:

May the day perish when I was born,
  and the night that told of a boy conceived.
May that day be darkness,
  may God on high have no thought for it,
  may no light shine on it...
May that night be dismal,
  no shout of joy come near it.
Why did I not die newborn,
  not perish as I left the womb?
Why were there two knees to receive me,
  two breasts for me to suck?
Had there not been, I should now be lying in peace,
  wrapped in a restful slumber,

with the kings and high viziers of earth
  who build themselves vast vaults...
Or put away like a stillborn child that never came to be,
  like unborn babes that never see the light.
Why give light to a man of grief?
  Why give life to those bitter of heart,
who long for a death that never comes,
  and hunt for it more than for a buried treasure?
Why make this gift of light to a man that does not see his way,
  whom God balks on every side?
My only food is sighs,
  and my groans pour out like water (3:1-4, 7, 11-14, 16, 20-24).

These beautifully moving verses give voice to the depths of Job's despair and suffering. The images blaze with the previously smothered feelings of the pious sufferer. Psychologically speaking, Job's victimized inner child, the one who became mute so early in life, has awakened, and cries out his immense grief.

As Job curses his very birth, we sense that a profound transformation has begun to take place inside him. Before, he took things calmly and resolutely, but now, he is breaking down and feels victimized and forsaken by his God. "My only food is sighs," he protests to the Almighty when everything he has tried fails to still his anguish. Whatever semblance of composure he had left is gone. As Job the victim begins speaking, his words pierce our hearts like arrows. His voice wails profound disappointment, anguish, and helplessness, as he sees no escape from his agony other than through death. Job has recognized, with his feelings, his collision with God's world.

Anyone who has experienced an unexpected eruption of feeling knows the profundity of such an event. The intensity of emotion can be so high that its effect on the body often feels more overwhelming than the calamities themselves. Yet it is these same emotions that provide the most reliable indicator that a person is indeed beginning to heal. For this reason, whenever situations such as these arise, I say to my patients: "Believe me when I tell you that the worse you feel now, the better you will feel tomorrow. This may seem paradoxical to you, but more often than not, the beginning of healing is excruciating, and there is no way to bypass the pain without compromising the restorative process. Your pain and anguish now have purpose, and they are part of your body's effort to overcome your challenges and to repair your wounds. Your suffering is useful; take comfort in that fact.

"Incidentally," I add, "it was an innate fear of the intensity of your feelings and the further devastation they can provoke that prompted you to disconnect from them in the first place. But now you can take it, a proof that you are already stronger, more resourceful, and, in ways you do not yet understand, more knowing. With this new progress, you are on your way to higher healing and greater wellness. Enjoy the journey now and be healthy!"

On the other hand, I must stress that we must listen to our own inner process of unfolding, and not some crude, routinely held axiom that emotional expressiveness is always good. The tendency of others to urge emotionality on patients can be a particularly frequent problem in our highly psychologized age where, too often, to quote Pope, "a little (psychological) learning is a dangerous thing," and "fools rush in where angels fear to tread." Among the many difficult problems confronted by people who face life-threatening illness, a critical problem is how—and whether—to communicate with family, friends, acquaintances, and co-workers about their feelings and intimate moments concerning their illness.

Typical for instance, was my experience with a 42-year-old, accomplished, and highly conscientious bright woman who had just completed a course of intense chemotherapy prescribed to treat a recurrence of her disease that had perturbed us all. The side effects of the chemotherapy had been severe, and she was just beginning to feel better. While in the throes of this recovery, she was deeply concerned with how to respond to certain people with whom she had not been particularly close and who had been inquiring about her illness.

"I don't want to spill out my guts to everyone who calls," she said. "I don't want people out there talking about me as a terrible case of colon cancer, for whom they feel pity and sorrow." Unfortunately, she said her concerns had been heightened by a magazine article that suggested that long-term survivors from cancer were those patients who did not mind speaking about their experience to whoever was interested in listening. This may have been her interpretation of the material, but in any case this information raised doubts about the possible detrimental effects of her reticence to spill out her heart. I had to reassure her that there was no foundation to the idea of absolutely necessary self-disclosure. I reassured her that it was perfectly okay to withhold information from anyone, especially from those with whom she didn't feel comfortable or safe. I further emphasized that the most important thing was that she stay connected to her feelings and follow the dictates of her heart. "Your heart," I said, "will seldom mislead you. There is no one way of handling the decision of how much feeling to disclose, which feelings and to whom," I continued. "If and when you feel comfortable in disclosing feelings and other intimate information to others, by all means do so. But don't think for a moment it is automatically necessary for your recovery. Don't let yourself be unduly influenced by what others tell you is right for you. When you are in no-man's land, what others say or do may not apply to you at all. Remember, you do need guidance to overcome this stark and scary territory, but the guidance you need most is aimed at helping you learn to trust and support your own inner wisdom about your developing psychological process. Go forth in your quest for recovery, and remember to listen to your inner feelings for direction."

* * * * * * * * * * * * * * * *

Unmitigated fear as well as despair flooded Job's psyche, and in his agony he lamented:

Whatever I fear comes true,
    whatever I dread befalls me.
For me, there is no calm, no peace;
    my torments banish rest (3:25-26).

At last, the anxieties betrayed by Job's compulsive post-banquet sacrificial offerings for his sons are out in the open. He confesses to a mountain of worries, a host of fearful fantasies, all of which have come true. But why was such a good and prosperous man so fearful? From a psychological standpoint, this habitual dread was the ongoing price Job had paid for his success at being so controlled and limited about what his unconscious mind allowed into consciousness. He felt always a stirring within a whole inner world of realizations, and rather than deal with them, he pretended the monster was not there. The more disconnected he remained, the more fearful he became as the monster seemed to take on ever larger proportions. Finally, when all these efforts failed, and when the sacrifices he had made to avoid and suppress life's ruthlessness seemed as if they were for naught, Job felt doubly destroyed.

When psychic repressions persist in time, it is not uncommon for them to emerge and cause serious disequilibrium, and even physical disease, in the individual's body. In Job's case, the disease fostered by his repression initially manifested itself in the form of chronic panic states, during which Job's fears of being punished by the forces of evil were exponentially magnified. But psychic concealment can last only so long, and in the end, everything that seeks to be acknowledged ironically emerges into our consciousness and demands scrutiny and resolution. As Job said, "Whatever I fear comes true, whatever I dread befalls me."

A Return to Full Living

In this verse, Job's eruption of feeling and his acknowledgment of his many concerns constitute a pivotal moment in his healing journey. In a way, these experiences mark his return to full living, and with it the beginning of the death of his old self. Being able to feel again, and hence to experience what has befallen him, will help him gather the strength and resourcefulness to overcome his despair and heal his battered soul. Feelings instigate revolt and protestations, though. If we are not aware of our feelings, we shall never know the oppression, repression, and abuse that suffuse our lives. As long as we remain detached from feelings, we shall continue abiding by the conventional wisdom that asks us to accommodate our reasonableness and accept a world in which change, repair, and transformation are not integral or possible. But when feeling erupts, it causes us to question the validity of the information we have received, and that we continue to receive daily. This connection to feeling demands answers and brings up for review a good deal of what we have learned from our parents, teachers, and general authorities. It even questions what we have been taught about God Himself or Herself. When feeling pierces our delusion, it is difficult to forget what we know now and re-enter our detachment and obliviousness. We have experienced an irreversible loss, which we hope will sustain our reconnection with revealed truth.

None of this, however, is easily welcomed or accepted by the up-holders of the status quo. When we experience an explosion of feeling, we receive severe rejection, and disapproval, and we will be engaged in a long and bloody battle with those who oppose us. Not only will we have to fight our own fears and psychological limitations, but also those of our family, friends, and society at large. We will have to battle against the ignorance and misunderstanding that run quietly rampant in our world, and against the defensiveness that comes from our inherent resistance to change. If we allow ourselves to emote freely, to vent our anger, disgust, and disappointment with God, we are in the eyes of our contemporaries heretics, and for this we will receive the highest degree of condemnation and be threatened with the most serious punishments. Feelings, and the insights about the world which they help configure, are profoundly disturbing to those asleep in the false securities of the status quo.

PART II

THE INNER BATTLE FOR CONTROL OVER JOB'S PSYCHE

Seven

The Struggle Between Logos And Eros Takes Shape

I will call the neglected power asserting itself within Job's psyche from Chapter 3 of *The Book of Job* on, "Eros," and the rationalistic power that guided his friends' psyche and formerly his own, "Logos." The developing conflict between Job's Eros and his friends' Logos described in the text (4:1 to 27:24) gives external or symbolic manifestation to a struggle that has raged within the psyche of humanity since the beginning of time. Logos, the seat of rationality and mental prowess, battles with Eros, the seat of desire, creativity, and feeling. This inner battle will never yield a winner, and even though Logos (the symbolic representation for the functions associated with the left cerebral hemisphere) has seemingly ruled supreme for thousands of years, his victory has been Pyrrhic at best.

Unresolved inner battles, as we might expect, inevitably project themselves outward, and they give rise to the cruel conflicts that have engulfed our nations, communities, and families throughout the centuries. These are the timeless battles being waged between men and women, scientists and artists, church and state, proponents of democracy and dictatorship, intellectuals and existentialists, and so forth. Each idea, individual, or group polarizes itself rigidly around the energies of Logos or Eros, and it is invested in seeing the supremacy of its chosen ruler come to pass. It is no surprise, then, that these conflicts permeate almost every one of our activities, institutions, and relationships demanding our continual attention and concern.

When seen from this vantage point, *The Book of Job* gives a powerful and inspiring account of the rise of Eros (the feminine dimension of the human psyche) from the throes of submission and repression 2,500 years ago. Eros' demands for equality and representation have continued unabated till today, and these demands will continue until we finally find a constructive way to integrate our psychic worlds (the worlds of the heavenly Father and the earthly Mother) into one singular and wholesome totality—one in which Logos and Eros are dancers rather than combatants of life, who bring inner peace and harmony to us all.

Unfortunately, we are far from accomplishing this psychospiritual ideal of the integration of self, and we were even further away from it when Job's Eros made her unwelcomed appearance many centuries ago. So don't expect too much tolerance or acceptance from Job's friends. These are men deeply invested in maintaining the conventional order and in bringing Job back to his old, "good" self.

Logos, in the Form of Eliphaz, Reprimands Job for Becoming Emotional and Losing His Composure

At this stage, Job's intense despair begins to create friction with his three best friends. Each of them is severely distressed by his emotion and by the despairing angry words he utters. Each then feels bound to defend his God, who stands implicitly accused as Job's victimizer. What Job's friends are doing, however, is using their intellectual capacities to defend against their own agony.

Eliphaz of Teman spoke next. He said:

If one should address a word to you, will you endure it?
    Yet who can keep silent? (4:1-2).

Though Eliphaz sympathizes with Job's plight, he also feels duty bound to defend what to him must be both just and proper. Knowing instinctively that what he is about to say will not be well received, he cannot hold himself back:

Many another, once, you schooled,
   giving strength to feeble hands;
your words set right whoever wavered,
   and strengthened every failing knee.
And now your turn has come, and you lose patience too;
   now it touches you, and you are overwhelmed (4:3-5).

Eliphaz' words might be modernized as follows: "You who have been such a commendable guide and teacher to others, how is it that when your turn to suffer came, you faltered? Come on, Job, stop playing the victim; get hold of yourself and behave as you are supposed to!"

Eliphaz is deeply troubled: Here is his teacher, the wise old man, the counselor of counselors, falling apart. "How could Job fail me so?" Eliphaz implicitly asks himself. "Was Job a charlatan? Didn't he believe or have faith in his own counsel? Was everything Job had taught me and the others no more than empty words?"

Evidently, when one pillar of the conventional community falls, the others tremble and are afraid. But Job was no charlatan, rather an innocent fool. Lacking the direct experience to support his leadership, Job was in essence a man of mere intellectualism—a human being who combined rationality and erudition with a vast naiveté.

Job surely knew some of what to say to people in distress, but these communications would have been ineffectual. Lacking the depth of feeling required to help him discern what these people really needed, he was unable to guide them into true healing. Hence, when his turn came, and he found himself personally challenged, he indeed faltered: He was overtaken and temporarily drowned by that very feeling he had tried so diligently to suppress for so many years. Nevertheless, under the troubled surface of his being, a neglected power was strengthening itself and beginning to pose a serious threat to the supremacy long held by a limited rationalism in Job's psyche.

Connecting To Feeling Energizes The Healing Journey

One of my first realizations following the diagnosis of cancer was that I could not return to the ways in which I had been used to working at the University. Gradually, I came to see that I could not continue to practice a medicine that was abstracted from my feelings; nor could I do scientific research that did not integrate my inner life. The changes I was increasingly experiencing in my own existence—connection to feeling, attunement to intuition and the wonderful world of dreams, a reverent respect for all life forms, and so forth—had altered my perceptions of who I was and how I wanted to express myself in the world. Later, I would see that I was being inducted into the path of the healer: the person invested in repairing his inner and outer worlds and in helping others repair their own. This is a path illumined by direct experience. Regardless of how erudite we may be, we will not be able to conduct others along it very far without personally acquired wisdom. From this perspective, healers can help others repair only what they themselves have repaired in their own lives. For example, a person who has never been married cannot be an effective healer of marriages; a person who has never made love cannot induct others into the pleasures and mystery of love-making; and a person who has never experienced a life-threatening situation does not know about no-man's land and how to survive in it. This is why the admonitions of Eliphaz were ineffectual, and why he could not induct Job into higher understanding. How could he if whatever he dispensed was school-book truths? Those who attempt to guide others into the uncharted lands of healing must themselves understand what they teach and counsel. This requires continual and honest examination (by themselves and others) of their skills, limits, and experience, or lack of it. Healers then, are people who frankly communicate who they are—not only is this ethical, it is the only way to be effective. Patients will see through hollow pretensions to wisdom, and the greatest truths when sounded by those who don't understand them, will fall on deaf ears. Honesty is the *sine qua non* for healing work, and without it the entire effort will fall apart.

Such honesty, and the providing of nurturance and compassion, are only some of the elements in healing practice that create both a gratifying and a challenging path. The healer in a culture dominated by reason alone will often suffer quick, harsh judgement from those whose lives are suffused by fear and ignorance. The path of the healer inevitably is seen as threatening by many practitioners of conventional medicine, raising, as it does, questions about the nature of life and self that few people confront willingly. It is naive, therefore, to believe that healing work will be well received by traditional institutions or by their followers. The rejection to which healers may be subjected is as much a part of the healer's path as the accolades and the genuine appreciations of grateful patients, families, and colleagues. It is naive and dangerous not to anticipate negative reactions, just as it is dangerous to be unprepared to handle them, or to believe that, because the intent of the work is wholesome, others will always perceive it that way. Unfortunately, many people who are blinded to the darkness of the healer's path have not handled a significant part of their shadow material, or the psychological traits and characteristics that are denied and rejected by the conscious mind. These people will feel bitter disappointment when other health care professionals automatically and ignorantly belittle them or their work.

Logos Attacks Job's Eros by Making Him Bear Responsibility for His Suffering

Does not your piety give you confidence,
   your blameless life not give you hope?
Can you recall a guiltless man that perished,
   or have you ever seen good men brought to nothing?
I speak of what I know: those who plow iniquity
   and sow the seeds of grief reap a harvest of the same kind.
A breath from God will bring them to destruction,
   a blast of his anger will wipe them out (4:6-9).

Eliphaz begins by offering hope, but he then appeals to Job's rationality and sense of fairness in preparation for the horrific accusation he is about to level. "You are guilty as charged, and there will be no discussion," Eliphaz asserts. "I speak of what I know. Have you ever seen good men brought to nothing? Those who plow iniquity reap a harvest of the same kind." In effect, Eliphaz tells Job: "Stop playing the innocent, because you are not. You must have plowed iniquity, because that is what you have reaped. If you are being punished, accept it, because it is well deserved!"

Job is shocked by Eliphaz's words (6:1-4) and his condition grows more desperate by the minute. Not only has he had to withstand seemingly unendurable losses, but he is now being accused of having brought this unbearable pain upon himself.

Eliphaz's placement of responsibility for his own misfortunes on the shoulders of such a man as Job is both unjust and ill-advised. Most individuals have little or no notion of why and how they are taken ill or visited by tragedy. To blame them for their fates constitutes sheer cruelty, a sad testimony to our need to project our own fears and limitations onto hapless sufferers.

The importance of how we interpret the sudden onset of calamities such as a serious illness was illustrated for me last week when I met Lina, a 36-year-old woman who had recently been diagnosed with breast cancer. My first impression of her was of a somewhat idealistic and innocent person who was trying to deal naively with a life-threatening condition. "I brought this on myself," she affirmed decisively. "I know that my stresses and lifestyle hampered my immune system, and this is why the disease developed. Can you help me get my immune system back in order? Can you help me get rid of my disease?"

Affirmations such as these are not at all uncommon and, in fact, are repeated daily in the offices of physicians, therapists, and healers who work regularly with cancer patients. Sometimes it is the patient who introduces this notion, as was the case with Lina, while at other times it is an unfortunate commentary put forth by the "healers" with whom these people may associate.

After some reflection, I think I have come to understand why some people are given to supporting this unfounded belief. Above all, it permits them to hold on to the idea that if they caused their illnesses, they can rid themselves of them as well. What we can bring on we can also eliminate, the saying goes, and while bearing the burden of having caused such a serious illness is indeed distressing, it does carry with it the consolation of allowing us to feel we are still in command of our lives. This is why I am not adamant about dispelling such notions when they seem to originate with the afflicted people themselves. But if the notions are introduced and supported by a patient's counselor or physician, then they are as unconscionable as the blame Eliphaz attempted to inflict on Job.

I don't mean to imply that our behaviors and attitudes—smoking, indiscriminately exposing ourselves to the sun, or eating a diet high in saturated fats, for example—are wholly irrelevant to the development of certain types of cancer, because they surely do play a critical role. But to reprimand people who are already ill for a behavior that may or may not have contributed to the development of the illness is both cruel and unwarranted. Moreover, to blame them dogmatically, as Job was blamed—to maintain that their cancer must have been engendered by their destructive lifestyles, their poor eating habits, or inadequate attention to their spiritual needs—is ludicrous and detrimental. I hasten to add that there may well be bio-psychosocial forces that foster and promote disease. But if these are unconscious, why should we be made to bear responsibility for them?

Logos Tries to Trick Eros Into Retreating by Suggesting that His Directives and Commands Come from None Other Than the "Higher Authority" Itself.

Now, I have had a secret revelation,
   a whisper has come to my ears.
At the hour when dreams master the mind,
   and slumber lies heavy on man,
a shiver of horror ran through me,
   and my bones quaked with fear.

Someone stood there—I could not see his face,
  but the form remained before me.
Silence—and then I heard a Voice (4:12-14,16).

Eliphaz received the information he is about to deliver to Job during that mental state that is interposed between sleep and awakening. The language he uses to describe the experience suggests, however, that this information is coming from a transpersonal source, a higher being—perhaps God Himself. By using this approach, Eliphaz tries to lend credibility to the statements he is about to make. If he spoke in his own name, why would anyone listen? If he speaks in the name of the Lord or that of a higher being, however, then his insights are likely to be taken to heart. What we are about to hear, therefore, is not Eliphaz's personal counsel but rather information emanating from a "Higher Authority" channeling itself through him.

"Was ever any man found blameless in the presence of God,
  or faultless in the presence of his Maker?
In his own servants, God puts no trust,
  and even with his angels he has fault to find.
What then of those who live in houses of clay,
  who are founded on dust?
They are crushed as easily as a moth,
  one day is enough to grind them to powder.
  They vanish for ever, and no one remembers them.
Their tent peg is snatched from them,
  and they die for lack of wisdom" (4:17-21).

The message Eliphaz's "Higher Authority" delivers is clear and un-ambiguous: Everyone is at fault in the presence of the Lord. For Him there is no such thing as a blameless, faultless person. No one, regard-less of external appearances, is beyond His reproach.

What Eliphaz has just stated, while valid, does not reflect any deep personal insight. Eliphaz, like most of us, has vented similar sentiments about man's innate guilt since childhood and easily repeats such cliches. This is why his counsel cannot alter Job's behavior, and why he must continue to insist on his shallow point of view.

During childhood it is normal, even desirable, to look up to authority figures for guidance, and to abide strictly by their directives and counsel. This is a time of life when we need help to solve our problems. As we grow older, however, we are expected to move from blind obedience to authority, and toward respect and admiration for skill, resourcefulness, and experiential wisdom. We are to stop abiding dogmatically, and begin to use discrimination and discernment in our actions and thoughts. This applies to all levels of our involvement, including our health and well-being. Before the calamities struck, Job heeded his teachers' counsels and never rebelled against authority or transgressed any rule. But now that his eyes have been opened, how can he continue to respect such authorities or believe in their teachings?

For me, and for many cancer patients, the psychological transition forced on us by life-threatening illness was highly traumatic and frightening. At first, most of us would rather continue trusting our physician's efforts to attain resolution than look somewhere else for additional resources and skills. But when, as so often happens, what our physicians can offer us is far removed from what we desire, we have no other choice than to roam the world (our world) for new answers and solutions.

Logos Uses All His Cunning in an Effort to Regain His Lost Standing. This Time, He Tries to Weaken Eros' Position by Intimidating the Child in Job.

Resentment kills the senseless,
    and anger brings death to the fool.
I myself have seen how such a one took root,
    until a swift curse fell on his House.
His sons at a single blow lose their prop and stay,
    ruined at the gate with no one to defend them;
their harvest goes to feed the hungry,
    God snatches it from their mouths,
    and thirsty men hanker after their goods.
If I were as you are, I should appeal to God,
    and lay my case before him.

His works are great, past all reckoning,
  marvels, beyond all counting.
Happy indeed the man whom God corrects!
  Then do not refuse this lesson from Shaddai.
For he who wounds is he who soothes the sore,
  and the hand that hurts is the hand that heals (5:2-5, 8-9, 17-18).

Eliphaz's insistent message to Job is simple. "Emotions are bad. They will kill you and bring bitterness and desolation to the lives of your family and friends. Give them up and accept that you have sinned. I cannot tell you what you have done, but I can assure you it must have been severe to justify God's having torn your soul apart! You are being asked to accept these injuries with dignity and to uphold God's name and your faith in Him. If you do so—if you learn your lesson in earnest—then Hashem will forgive you and love you even more than before. He will protect you, heal your wounds, and imbue you with inner peace. You will then feel secure, stable, and joyful."

In time of famine, he will save you from death,
  and in wartime from the stroke of the sword.
You shall laugh at drought and frost,
  and have no fear of the beasts of the earth.
All this, we have observed: it is true.
  Heed it, and do so to your profit (5:20, 22, 27).

Eliphaz is making Job an offer he will have a hard time refusing. "Acknowledge that you have sinned and that God is just and merciful, and receive from Hashem the most wonderful gifts. All you have to do, Job, is cover up your emotions that tell you you are being wrongly abused, and in return your Abuser will give you everything you ever wanted and more."

Eliphaz's language is seductive, and Job, like anyone, will have difficulty keeping his inner child in check here. The inner child believes Eliphaz's promises and wants to follow his suggestions. "Okay, so what if I have to cover up for a little bit of abuse?" the child in Job mutters to itself. "To be honest, I am not even sure that what I experienced was abusive at all! It may all have been an unfortunate misunderstanding, a product of my youth and naiveté, that allowed those people who are invested in belittling God make me claim something that is untrue and terribly distorted."

Many patients, shortly after they are stricken, go through a stage where they too try to take this regressive path—complying, or pretending to comply, with some malevolent higher power, trying to seem obedient, bargaining with God by being a good little child and so forth. But, as so often happens, this tack cannot long be followed. Eventually, our more mature aspects emerge and bring balance to the inner world. Then, we see that to allow the child to take over our psyche once again will have disastrous effects. So Job understands he must remain acutely aware of the truth he has just uncovered: Life can indeed be ruthless and amoral. Job senses that Eliphaz's approach cannot work; indeed, it has not worked for Eliphaz himself. Had Eliphaz's soul matured and unfolded, he would have been more compassionate and would have felt less compelled to respond to Job's words and inflict additional pain on his friend. Moreover, he would have become attuned to Job's feelings, and he would be able to lend him support. Healed souls, as every sacred text testifies and as we see throughout history, are capable of infinite compassion and love.

Job's Immense Suffering Protects Him from the Seductiveness of Logos' Reasoning.

In reply to Eliphaz's facile explanations and counsels, Job bursts forth with all his pain and says:

If only my misery could be weighed,
　　and all my ills put on the scales!
But they outweigh the sands of the seas:
　　what wonder then if my words are wild?
The arrows of Shaddai stick fast in me,
　　my spirit absorbs their poison,
　　God's terrors stand against me in array (6:2-4).

With every moment that passes, Job becomes less stuporous and increasingly in touch with his feelings. He looks around at his circumstance and recognizes the immense loss he has sustained. He looks at his friends and sees their incomprehension, and even their blame. When a calamity like that Job experienced befalls us, we try at first to remain calm and collected. Only later, when it is safe to do so, do we allow the feelings evoked during these moments to emerge and permit ourselves to acknowledge their intensity. Often we go through many cycles of denial and feeling. Sometimes days may elapse before these feelings come to the fore, but it could just as easily be months, years, or decades—and in some cases it is only immediately before death that they are finally made manifest.

* * * * * * * * * * * * * * *

"Jacob?" a feeble voice questioned me as I walked into the dim room.

"Yes, Jon, I am here," I answered.

"I am so afraid, Jacob. I feel so lonely," the voice exclaimed almost in a whisper.

"Do you want me to get closer?"

"Please do. I need to tell you something that has been bothering me for quite some time. I want you to know that all my life I have been a coward. I have shied away from honesty."

"Why do you say this, Jon?" I asked him calmly.

"I say it because in all my 40 years of marriage, I never mustered the courage to acknowledge to my wife how much I loved her, how much I needed her, how important she was to me."

"It is not too late, Jon; it is certainly not too late."

"Are you sure? Don't you think she resents me for having been so detached and ungiving?"

"I don't know, Jon. What she feels I can not tell you, but what I can say is that we are all wounded souls seeking comfort and repair. Regardless of how old these wounds might be, it is still our responsibility and privilege to attempt to heal them. This is our God-given gift—our capacity to redeem our pain and overcome our torment."

"Thank you, Jacob. I hope I muster the strength to reveal my truth."

"I do, too, Jon."

"Goodbye."

* * * * * * * * * * * * * * * *

It is not uncommon for people like Job, who are stricken into journeying to the farthest recesses of their souls, to complain of loneliness and isolation there. Life has plunged us into Eros, but our family, lovers, friends and physicians almost automatically take the part of Logos. Reflecting the most superficial of perspectives, they tell us, "you look so good, you will get well promptly," or "do not worry—everything will be okay." And this contradiction arises precisely at a time when we have the greatest need for an empathic understanding from others. To be told that "all will be well" when we are in the middle of an inner wilderness, beleaguered, and at the mercy of potent yet unseen forces, is of little solace. Moreover, it makes us feel as if all our struggles to have our journey acknowledged are exercises in futility. "Our lives will never be healed," we think to ourself. "How could it be so if, despite all our efforts, we continue to go unnoticed and a part of us remains unrecognized?" It is critical to understand, though, that this desperation reflects primarily an inner state of alienation and repression. And it is precisely the lack of our own internal recognition, when we feel emotionally or physically distressed, that causes us to feel so bad when others follow suit.

When long-repressed material finds expression in our objective world, however, the results can be devastating. All that we were once intent on banishing from our psyche rears its head, and we can no longer elude it. Dejection and helplessness descend on us when there is no way to deny them any longer. But, paradoxically, it is this very dejection that prevents our listening to the old conventional wisdom. Job feels so stricken, he wishes for death:

May it please God to crush me,
to give his hand free play and do away with me! (6:9).

From a psychological developmental perspective, Job is still largely trapped in his infantile stage, which is to say he sees himself as helpless, lacking volition with which to confront life as he now knows it. He wants God to kill him and free him from his despair. But he is already moving beyond this child stage. In his disasters, Job has experientially discovered he is a vulnerable and mortal human being. Before, he knew about death, but only intellectually. After all, no one in his immediate family had yet died. His parents were still living, and while his grandparents were not, he was too young at the time of their deaths to have experienced their passing as a true loss. Job had formerly spoken about death and dying but had not fully understood his own words; death, in point of fact, had never posed a direct threat to the world he knew. Now, however, he begins to understand its full import and thus ceases to feel secure or knowing. Death could be imminent; he feels it in his bones. He is aware for the first time that his future is uncertain and that, for all he knows, these might be his last moments. An acute sense of dejection mixed with urgency overtakes him, and paradoxically these powerful emotions give him the firmness to reject Eliphaz's facile viewpoint:

My brothers have been fickle as a torrent,
    as the course of a seasonal stream.
So, at this time, do you behave to me:
    one sight of me, and then you flee in fright.
Have I said to you, "Give me this or that,
    bribe someone for me at your own cost,
snatch me from the clutches of an enemy,
    or ransom me from a tyrant's hand?"
Put me right, and I will say no more;
    show me where I have been at fault.
Relent, and grant me justice;
    relent, my case is not yet tried (6:15, 21-24, 29).

This refusal prepares the inner ground for Job's uniting with essential but repressed and disowned parts of himself. Those parts, Jung would say, can be described in a comprehensive single term: the shadow. Job was encountering his shadow, which in his case included the aspect of him that challenges authority, defies convention and conformity, and is relentless in its pursuit of accountability. He had denied and re-pressed this facet of himself for so long that it forced itself into his consciousness to become light. From the point of view of the superfi-cially conscious lives that most of us generally live, we are in the light, and what is not known or acknowledged in ourselves is dark, and usually felt to be threatening, alien, and evil. Job had, among other aspects, rejected the non-conformist, questioning, challenging side of himself. Indeed, he had felt it to be Satanic. So, lo and behold, to whom do you think he fell prey? Satan, of course. The more Job sought to escape this "evil"—that part of him that wanted to explore and un-derstand more of life's mysteries, that felt uncomfortable abdicating its freedom to choose and to question—the more it stuck to him like glue.

From an integrative psychological perspective, what was happening, as painful as it seemed to him, was part of the repair process needed to cure his disease, rather than a manifestation of the disease itself. To that part of him that felt like a victim, to Job's wounded child and to his conventional adult, what was happening seemed purely and simply a curse.

Job, Despite His Connection to Feelings, is Still Unable to Understand the Truth that Eros Brings Him in Dreams

As the gateways to unbound emotion open even further, Job's de-spair becomes greater. His is the language of a man in intense emo-tional and physical pain:

Is not man's life on earth nothing more than pressed service,
 his time no better than hired drudgery?
Like the slave, sighing for the shade,
 or the workman with no thought but his wages,
months of delusion I have assigned to me,
 nothing for my own but nights of grief.

Lying in bed I wonder, "When will it be day?"
  Risen I think, "How slowly evening comes!"
  Restlessly I fret till twilight falls.
Vermin cover my flesh, and loathsome scabs;
  my skin is cracked and oozes pus...
  and my eyes will never again see joy.
If I say, "My bed will comfort me,
  my couch will soothe my pain,"
you frighten me with dreams
  and terrify me with visions.
Strangling I would welcome rather,
  and death itself, than these my sufferings.
What is man that you should make so much of him,
  subjecting him to your scrutiny,
that morning after morning you should examine him
  and at every instant test him? (7:1-5, 7, 13-15, 17-18).

All that has ever meant anything to Job has been lost, and his life seems empty and devoid of purpose. When it is day he clamors for night, and in the darkness of night he wishes for the clarity of day. He is a man in the throes of such agony that nothing solaces him. Job yearns for powerful narcotics to still his anguish, but none is forthcoming. The numbness he experienced at the outset has lifted, but what he sees ahead of him is unmitigated pain. Job can see no way out of his torment.

Yet in the midst of his suffering, Job hurls a most intriguing question at Hashem: "what is man that you should at every instant test him?"

Eros' rebellion against the order of things previously understood and accepted by a superficial Logos intensifies further. Eros clamors for acceptance and respect, yet when she shows Job her true colors and designs, Job reacts to her presence with confusion and dejection. Job still has no understanding, for instance, of the truths that Eros, working through dreams, can bring him. To the sufferers, the unpleasant feelings our dreams evoke seem like further torments, which are confusing to a person who had seen God's ways as simply and straightforwardly beneficent. Thus, Job confronts Hashem, asking: "Why is it that, whenever I begin to feel a tiny bit better and a ray of hope for rest pierces my darkness, you (God) shatter my illusions with horrible dreams and terrifying visions? Why are you doing this to me? Can't you let me have a breather? Don't you see that I am a defeated man on the brink of disintegration? Don't you have compassion for your loyal and devoted servant?"

There is a liveliness in this despair that leads to protest, and in it, we already taste one redemptive effect of affliction. But Job's despair prevails. Job's inner blindness is still such that all appears lost and hopeless to him. Indeed, as long as his old psychospiritual patterns continue to dominate him, nothing in his desperate situation will change. Caught in the mire of his old ways, Job is still rapidly sinking. The fight must continue if he is to save himself. Psychologically speaking, Job's consciousness was still disconnected from his inner world and from the messages that were being conveyed in his dreams and visions or fantasies. He could not appreciate his inner Higher Wisdom, which has been trying all along to help him overcome his challenge. Rather than seeing Higher Wisdom's interventions as beneficial and supportive, Job perceived them as punitive, the very root of his despair. "I would rather be dead than endure more of these horrendous images you send me in dreams," he clamors to God.

This is an astonishing paradox. On the one hand, Job wants Hashem to guide him, and he so implores in daily prayers. Yet when Hashem provides him with precisely what he seeks, Job perceives this provision as the worst punishment he could have been dealt. Job's deeply conditioned mind does not have the resources to handle the powerful feelings that are emerging into his consciousness, or to accommodate the new possibilities or understandings that are awakening in him. He has not yet gained access to that state of consciousness that is open, accepting, and welcoming of the new—a psychic state unfettered by prejudice, tradition, or preconceived mental constructs. Yes, Job sought Hashem's support—but only if it was delivered in keeping with the everyday beliefs of ordinary people, which he had embraced since his childhood. For God's voice to be recognized as such, a miracle was needed, such as a speech from a burning bush. Then His counsel would have been welcomed and, indeed, venerated. If, however, God speaks to Job in a dream that is intense and evocative of powerful feelings, then the dream is taken as a bad experience, a punishment without real meaning. Job might have lived more than 2,500 years ago, but his attitude toward dreams—particularly disturbing ones—is, unfortunately for most of us, quite contemporary.

God had, in fact, provided Job with the keys to his salvation as well as to the resolution of his distress, but Job remained blind to them. He was stopped by the most powerful obstruction to healing work that exists: mental conditioning. He was, essentially, behaving like one of those physicists at the beginning of the twentieth century who claimed that all there was to know about the physical world had already been learned, and that physics as a field of scientific inquiry was therefore finished.

So when God, in His unwavering support of the healing process, presented to Job the images and the wisdom he needed to overcome his affliction, all Job saw was condemnation and oppression. For him, death was preferable to anything else that had been presented to him thus far. God had indeed spoken and had revealed His healing message, but Job remained impervious to its truth.

Eight

Job Awakes To Life And His Power

As the story unfolds, the struggle between feeling (Eros) and thinking (Logos) continues to intensify, becoming ever more acute. Job clamors for love and mercy, while his friends continue to take the side of the offender, the force Job believed had wronged him. To Job's dismay, his friends are unable to disregard his words and simply say: "This man is so hurt, so overwhelmed, that what he needs is to be loved. Let him scream his lungs out, let him yell and curse; it is cathartic. We shall not stand in judgment; the screams and curses of a wounded man are never to be taken at face value." Quite to the contrary, Job's friends continue to take personal offense at Job's statements, and the process runs steadily downhill from there on.

Logos Persists in His Attack on Eros by Demeaning Job's Plea for Love and Kindness

Bildad of Shuah spoke next. He said:

Is there no end to these words of yours,
    to your long-winded blustering?

Can God deflect the course of right
   or Shaddai falsify justice?
If your sons sinned against him,
   they have paid for their sins...(8:1-4).

Bildad is right when he asserts that God is truth and cannot depart from that truth. The problem is that while Job is experiencing his revelation of truth, neither he nor Bildad accepts what this truth implies. Job and Bildad are situated on opposite sides of the same paradigm: Job blames God for his miseries and rebukes his friends, while Bildad supports God and blames Job. Job feels wholly undeserving of the punishment that he has endured, while Bildad maintains that if Job and his children have been punished, it is because they had sinned; hence their punishment was deserved and appropriate. Bildad recognizes the natural order of things but cannot accept that God is amoral. Instead, he clings tenaciously to his belief that God is both merciful and just, and that whatever befalls us is deserved, regardless of whether this is evident to us or not.

...so you too, if so pure and honest,
   must now seek God, plead with Shaddai.
Without delay he will restore his favor to you,
   will see that the good man's house is rebuilt.
Your former state will seem to you as nothing
   beside your new prosperity.
Believe me, God neither spurns a stainless man,
   nor lends his aid to the evil (8:5-7, 20).

For conventional people like Bildad, who scrupulously follow traditional religions, the answer to life's adversities is simple: If punishment comes your way, you must necessarily have sinned and offended God. So Bildad counsels Job to return to Hashem and beg forgiveness. All we need do is repent, and wait patiently for His restoration. It sounds like a piece of cake. But for many afflicted with illness, however, this approach usually has little merit. Can we seriously be expected to tell people who come to us in search of guidance that they have fallen ill because they have sinned? Should we encourage them to repent, to mend their ways, and to implore God Almighty for forgiveness? And if they do repent, will their health and wellness necessarily be restored? Like Job, these people want real answers. Many are already unhappy even with the white lies their physicians shower upon them. They want to know the truth about their medical conditions, about their physicians' diagnostic and therapeutic capabilities, about healing and repair, and about people's ability to savor each and every one of life's irreplaceable moments.

Bildad's reasoning, not surprisingly, then, falls on deaf ears. Rather than reassuring and comforting Job, this reasoning makes him angry, defiant, and ironic:

Indeed, I know it is as you say:
    how can man be in the right against God?
If any were so rash as to challenge him for reasons,
    one in a thousand would be more than they could answer.
His heart is wise, and his strength is great:
    who then can successfully defy him? (9:2-4).

Then Job drops the ironic mask:

But am I innocent after all? Not even I know that,
    and, as for my life, I find it hateful.
It is all one, and this I dare to say:
    innocent and guilty, he destroys all alike.
When a sudden deadly scourge descends,
    he laughs at the plight of the innocent.
When a country falls into a tyrant's hand,
    it is he who blindfolds the judges.
    Or if not he, who else?
And if I am guilty,
    why should I put myself to useless trouble?
No use to wash myself with snow,
    or bleach my hands pure white;
for you will plunge me in dung
    until my very clothes recoil from me.

Yes, I am man, and he is not; and so no argument,
 no suit between the two of us is possible.
Nonetheless, I shall speak, not fearing him:
 I do not see myself like that at all (9:21-24, 29-32, 35).

"Lies on top of more lies," Job shouts at his bewildered companion. "What you are rationing out is the same old story: Be good and obedient, be submissive and pious, and you shall be rewarded. The question is, when and by whom? Moreover, how is it that other people—the tyrants who reject and belittle Hashem—lead such bountiful lives? When will their punishment come?"

Unable to believe what God has done to him, and appalled at His callousness, Job responds to Bildad in a way that widens the gulf between himself and God as well as between him and his friends. But now, Job is beginning to see God's deepest truth: His actions have no discernable pattern. Job discovers that life, God's creation, is totally divorced from any human law and morality. Whatever it is that rules life has nothing to do with what we believe to be good or righteous. God does not seem to care whom He hurts. Job, having seen God's true face, is overwhelmed, just as all others who have glimpsed it have been. Now, Job feels fearfully exposed and at the mercy of an unspeakable powerful force—one utterly independent of humankind's fears, inadequacies, limitations, and, yes, prayer.

When we move from the world of rational constructs to that of intuitive revelations, we inevitably experience a collapse of our value systems. Nothing makes sense or assuages our soul. Our disappointment is immense, and the wounding runs deep. What can we do in moments such as these but become despondent and cynical? Job, however, does something even more logical: He goes directly to the source of his oppression and demands accountability.

At the same time, we can discern however, another shift in consciousness in our protagonist. Job, who in the beginning felt wronged and forsaken by his God, is starting to have some doubts about himself: "But am I innocent after all? Not even I know that, and as for my life, I find it hateful." Initially, he was convinced of his innocence. Now, however, he is starting to equivocate and to reconsider. Yet immediately upon making the shift into this line of thought, he abandons it. He can't endure the new uncertainty. Not knowing if he was innocent or guilty is worse than either believing he was guilty or feeling victimized.

Despite the distress it causes him, however, Job's willingness to experience uncertainty represents an encouraging psychological progress. Less allied to his victim side and beginning to become less defiant of God and of His truth, Job is indeed growing, though in the short term his uncertainty heightens his despair. If he is not a sinner or a victim, how can he understand what is happening to him? Job's confusion, hopelessness, and pain are such that the only thing left for him to do is give free rein to his feelings, and he does. He clearly sees that the forces challenging him are too powerful to avert. So why hold back?

Since I have lost all taste for life,
    I will give free reign to my complaints;
    I shall let my embittered soul speak out.
I shall say to God, "Do not condemn me,
    but tell me the reason for your assault.
Is it right for you to injure me,
    cheapening the work of your own hands
    and abetting the schemes of the wicked?" (10:1-3).

In synchrony with all the events just described, something in Job's psyche begins a questioning of God that will become nothing less than a search for deeper understanding and resourcefulness. To begin with, however, Job feels like so many of us, that knowing why he had been taken ill, lost his children, and fallen victim to abuse will mitigate his despair.

Engaging our victimizer may not nullify all our pain and suffering, but it can help us frame our experience mentally, and integrate it more effectively. Victims of violent crime today are sometimes given an opportunity to confront their assailants through projects organized and overseen by the prison system. Directly confronting those who inflicted injury is found to help crime victims achieve emotional closure and find inner peace. The chance to tell their assailants about their injuries and suffering helped alleviate these victims' agony, and putting a face together with a heinous act makes them feel less vulnerable.

Job seeks to experience much the same rapprochement with God. His wounds have already been inflicted and their impact has been felt; nothing can change that. But Job feels that confronting his victimizer—especially being granted an opportunity to hear the reasoning underlying his punishment—will help him place these events in perspective and allow him to proceed with his life. He tells Hashem: "Do not condemn me, but tell me the reason for your assault," but in the same breath, the despair he feels makes him re-assert his stance:

...you know very well that I am innocent
    and that no one can rescue me from your hand.
Your own hands shaped me, modeled me;
    and would you now have second thoughts, and destroy me?
You modeled me, remember, as clay is modeled,
    and would you reduce me now to dust? (10:7-9).

Job is perplexed. "Was it possible that Hashem did not know I was innocent and beyond reproach? That could not be," Job answers himself. "Hashem is omniscient. But if He did know, how would He explain this tragedy? Where would its significance lie? Why would Hashem, who created and molded me from A to Z, want to destroy me now?"

In the throes of his despair, new strength emerges. There is defiance in Job's voice and he musters the courage to question Hashem's actions:

...you endowed me with life,
    watched each breath of mine with tender care.
Yet, after all, you were dissembling;
    biding your time, I know,
to mark if I should sin
    and to let no fault of me go uncensored.

Woe to me, if I am guilty;
   if I am innocent, I dare not lift my head,
   so wholly abject, so drunk with pain am I.
And if I make a stand, *like a lion you hunt me down*,
   adding to the tale of your triumphs.
You attack, and attack me again...
The days of my life are few enough:
   turn your eyes away, leave me a little joy,
before I go to the place of no return,
   the land of murk and deep shadow,
where dimness and disorder hold sway,
   and light itself is like dead of night (10:12-17, 20-22).

We cannot help but appreciate the beauty of the poetry and the depth of feeling that Job expresses in these verses. We are moved by his hurt, his quest for dignity, and his yearning for just a few moments of inner peace. Job is nearing the end, he feels he is dying, and all he demands now is a brief respite from his suffering.

Developmentally, Job is at a spiritual crossroads. He has seen truth but he has not yet died for it. He is close, but he is not quite there. A fierce war is still being waged between Job's old psychospiritual patterns, which seek to remain within him, and the new ones that demand to emerge. Yet despite this tension and uncertainty, Job has passed a point of no return. There is no way for him to turn back to the ways of old. His fate is sealed, and "death" is imminent. All that remains is to determine when it will occur.

The Acceptance of Death Frees Us to Live

Like many health professionals working with people who are experiencing sufferings like Job's, I am often asked how I can keep doing it: "How do you manage to do this type of work and remain optimistic and enthusiastic about living? How do you avoid feeling depressed and helpless when you must confront so many dear people dying, and you can do so little to succor them?" Surprisingly, I do not pose this question to myself at all, because it does not match the feelings I commonly experience about the work I do. Contrary to what these questions suggest, I have found that my work has energized my commitment to, and appreciation of, living. Each of the people I encounter serves as a motivational influence that helps me engage life with more zest, less fear, and a heightened appetite. The recognition that life is indeed finite, that neither I nor anyone else can control its flow, and that I am a human being exposed and vulnerable to injury, works to strengthen my determination and keep my priorities straight. Immersing myself in the work I do reminds me of the truth of my existence and helps me stay on track. Facing mortality has forced me to engage my fears, and my unfounded beliefs, and it has challenged me to die to a conventionally muted life of eyes-averted repression. I have been pushed forward into new living and have not let fear overwhelm me and keep me repressed and therefore dead. The poet-priest Gerard Manley Hopkins has rightly said, "This seeing (visiting) the sick, endears them to us; us too, it endears."[5]

The onset of my own illness and the defiance and determination it awoke in me have, of course, planted this enlivening process even more deeply in me than is normal with health care practitioners. I distinctly remember how angry I was when I realized that I had come so close to living a dead life. By stripping me naked of my false securities, and my dependency and trust on benevolent parents, mentors, teachers, institutions of higher education, and deities themselves, the illness forced me to take my life in my own hands and give it the best I could. In the course of the struggle, two particular life-giving qualities have grown up in me: a genuine resolute confidence when confronted by serious challenges, and a realism about the awesome gift of living of which we are privileged to partake. I have been taught how to live on the edge, knowing that there may be no tomorrow.

This is why I maintain that, whenever we accept death and integrate it into the fabric of our being, we become free to live. Everything becomes heightened and relevant. Time is indeed precious, and it is regarded with reverence. "Do you want to spend your time writing these lines, Jacob?" I ask myself in earnest. "If these were to be the last moments of your life, would you want to spend them this way? And what if you knew that all you had was one more year to live, would you spend it doing the work you do?" To ask such questions of ourselves is only to be realistic. These realities reflect truths about the world of God. To be oblivious to these realities, to be frightened by their implications, is to court empty living, disillusionment, and grief. To me, knowing and remembering what God's truth is all about entitles me to pursue vigorously what is meaningful and blissful. Overcoming my denial of truth did make me feel victimized for a while, and it also brought forth the anger and disappointment I felt when I realized how dumb and foolish I had been, and how close that foolishness had brought me to the end. In moments like these, I also railed the way Job did, against society, university, medicine, and even God. I could not believe they had all failed to advise me of the dangers inherent in the treacherous path I had taken. In fact, though, the anger and frustration we feel is truly toward ourselves and our disconnection from existence.

At this point in his story, Job is still unaware of this, so he blames God for viciously attacking him and inflicting so much hurt. Eventually, though, he and the rest of us will see the light, take our lives in our own hands and find the ways to true redemption.

Logos Does Not Relent. Too Much is at Stake, and He Persists in His Efforts to Counteract the Power that Eros is Beginning to Command in Job.

Job's friends are stubborn. They resist deviance from their normal notions and continue to insist that what Job has been saying about the divine order is nothing short of blasphemy.

Zophar of Naamath spoke next. He said:

Is babbling to go without an answer?
   will you jeer with no one to refute you?
These were your words, *"My way of life is faultless
   and in your eyes I am free from blame."*
But if God had a mind to speak,
   to open his lips and give you answer,

were he to show you the secrets of wisdom
　　which put all cleverness to shame—
　　you would know it is for sin he calls you to account.
For he detects the worthlessness in man,
　　he sees iniquity and marks it well.
And so the idiot grows wise,
　　thus a young wild donkey grows tame (11:1-6, 11-12).

Those who call themselves Job's friends harbor a remarkable amount of bitterness and spite in their souls. In the face of Job's plea for pity and compassion, his friends muster only disdain and ridicule: "What do you mean by your babbling? Who the hell do you think you are?"

Zophar of Naamath feels deeply offended by this creature who has had the chutzpah to stand up to assail the Holy One. "Own your fault," he says. "Flesh decays and is susceptible to damage. Nobody—and that means nobody—is faultless in the eyes of the Lord. Ask forgiveness."

Come, you must set your heart right,
　　stretch out your hands to him.
Renounce the iniquity that stains your hands...
Then you may face the world in innocence...
You will forget your sufferings,
　　remember them as waters that have passed away (11:13-16).

Like Job's other friends before him, Zophar of Naamath wants Job to return to the fold, to love God, and to acknowledge that His wisdom is so much loftier than our own that there is no point in even trying to comprehend it. Then, the bad dream will come to an end, and his life will continue unperturbed.

This unrealistic lack of empathy with Job and insistence on the conventional ideology of the day demand interpretation: What truly mattered to the friends was not ideology but rather the emotional perturbations Job's fate and reactions evoked in them. In psychoanalytic terms, the friends are trapped in denial and projection. Hence their persecution of their hapless friend. Job's predicament had shaken their faith in a merciful and just God. After witnessing the abominations He had inflicted on their friend, how could they continue to justify His behavior? Their faith was challenged and they began to have serious doubts about the fairness of the loving God upon whom they counted for guidance and direction. Unable to face this possibility, they think, "There had to be a good reason underlying God's harsh punishment of Job. He deserves to suffer until he repents."

Job's story, his shock, his protests, and his friend's attempts to evade painful truth are reminiscent of much of what we see and experience in medical practice. I recall how distraught I once felt upon encountering young patients who had been afflicted with cancer, or when cancers that had been in complete remission reasserted themselves in ways that traditional medicine could no longer address. These events challenged my faith in justice and in the power of the god of medicine I had so thoroughly embraced. How helpless I had felt under those circumstances, and how much I tried to cover up and evade that feeling.

I remember in particular a young woman with acute myelogenous leukemia whom I had guided toward complete clinical remission, and who was reaping the benefits of "my" accomplishment. She walked into the clinic one day for her monthly checkup, which included a bone marrow exam. She was looking well and was full of energy, and for a moment I was seized by a feeling of triumph. For once I had succeeded in taming this scourge; I had extricated it from this young person's body. But to my bewilderment and dismay, the bone marrow test showed a recurrence of the leukemia process. In a matter of days, this woman would find herself fighting for her life in the oncology ward.

The best way I can describe what I felt at the moment I saw her test was a sensation of having been slapped in the face and ridiculed. It felt as if the cancer were saying to me, "You stupid idiot! You thought you had me, didn't you? You thought you had succeeded in destroying me with your powerful weapons, your potent toxins. How naive and ignorant can you be? Do you not realize that I am indestructible, that I rise from the ashes stronger and even more resolute? Learn this once and for all: I am too powerful and too resourceful for you to vanquish!"

Later, through the terrible lens of my own illness, I looked back and saw how frightened I had been of cancer itself and, therefore, how much personal energy and power I had abdicated to it. This dread was a feeling many of my colleagues shared. Gradually, I discovered that the fear of cancer, of death, and of the uncertainty cancer generates was epidemic among us and that practicing oncology was, for many of us, a vicarious way of dealing with our own existential concerns. By fighting cancer and being part of the war against this disease, we were, in effect, attempting to win our own internal battles.

When we have not directly explored and resolved these fears and core psychospiritual concerns, however, it is easy to project them onto others, and to use others unknowingly for our personal ends. Perhaps the most aggressive oncologists are precisely those who are also the most frightened, insecure, and overwhelmed by the fears I have just described. Even if I am only partially accurate in this assessment, the problem remains: How can anyone who has not successfully come to terms with these critical areas of his or her own life adequately guide or comfort others who are necessarily trying to do so because their life-threatening illness forces them to?

Job is Awakening to the Realities of Life and Their Inherent Power. He Sees Through the Seduction that Logos has Placed in Front of Him and Does Not Swallow the Bait.

The friend's seductive offer—Job's admission of guilt in return for a restoration to prosperity—is rejected. Job replies with strength and some real logic of his own, one grounded in the felt truth of his lived situation:

Doubtless, you are the voice of the people,
　and when you die, wisdom will die with you!
I can reflect as deeply as ever you can...
A man becomes a laughingstock to his friends
　if he cries to God and expects an answer.
　The blameless innocent incurs only mockery.

And yet, the tents of brigands are left in peace,
　and those who challenge God live in safety,
　and make a god of their two fists!
If you would learn more, ask the cattle,
　seek information from the birds of the air.
The creeping things of earth will give you lessons,
　and the fishes of the sea will tell you all.
There is not one such creature but will know
　this state of things is all of God's own making.
He holds in his power the soul of every living thing,
　and the breath of each man's body.
But in him there is wisdom, and power too,
　and decision...
What he destroys, none can rebuild;
　whom he imprisons, none can release.
Is there a drought? He has checked the waters.
　Do these play havoc with the earth? He has let them loose (12:2-4,
　6-10, 13-15).

"I am neither mad nor mistaken," Job tells his friends, increasingly recognizing that neither goodness nor loyalty, neither devotion nor righteousness, is rewarded. All the good deeds he has done on behalf of the poor, the sick, and the needy have seemingly been for naught.

"God's world is indeed ruthless and amoral," affirms Job. "Good people are made to suffer ceaselessly while the wicked are rewarded and permitted to prosper. If you harbor any doubt about the veracity of what I say, ask any living creature around you; all will confirm it! Only man lives in denial of truth, drawing sustenance from an infantile interpretation of the world—an image that is destined to crumble as mine just did."

Job has discovered that good and evil, right and wrong, are just differing facets of the same whole—God's world—and this knowledge has left him at odds with the conventional beliefs of his society. Before he fell from grace, Job knew only God the merciful, but now he has discovered God the wrathful, and God the capricious—a deity that by turns creates and destroys, elevating us to the loftiest heights and then allowing us to plummet to unfathomable depths. Job has discovered the duality of the divine essence and is profoundly affected by that discovery. He sees himself at the mercy of a shadowy, spectral God, and he is resentful of his fate.

He robs the country's counselors of their wits,
  turns judges into fools.
His hands untie the belt of kings,
  and bind a rope about their loins.
He makes priests walk barefoot,
  and overthrows the powers that are established.
He robs the depths of their darkness,
  brings deep shadow to the light.
He builds a nation up, then strikes it down,
  or makes a people grow, and then destroys it (12:17-19, 22-23).

Job is discovering life's realities. To his dismay, life does not seem to proceed according to a rational, comprehensible plan. Job unmasks rhythms that he cannot understand but that seem to coalesce: Goodness is usually linked with evil, plenty is followed by scarcity, light springs forth from darkness and darkness follows light, success breeds failure, and failure engenders success. When we recognize these truths, we understand the real meaning of the notion that wisdom comes with age: The profound experiences that long-living can bring generate true knowledge of the way the world is. Job and his friends have been, so to speak, children, and his friends are trying to retain their infantile fantasies of life encased in rigid rationalizations, untouched by the enlightenment that comes from living one's hurts.

Job's Attunement to Feeling is More Persistent Now, and Hence He is Able to Avoid Succumbing to His Friends' Threats.

Now it is Job's turn to insist, and he does so by elaborating on the truth of his vision, pushing away with vigor his friend's vacuous pieties:

I have seen all this with my own eyes,
  heard with my own ears, and understood.

But my words are intended for Shaddai;
I mean to remonstrate with God (13:1, 3).

He further insists that his friends, the carriers of the conventional wisdom

...are only charlatans,
physicians in your own estimation.
I wish someone would teach you to be quiet
—the only wisdom that becomes you!
Kindly listen to my accusation,
pay attention to the pleading of my lips (13:4-6).

Job is adamant and will not yield to the forces of traditional living. He sees through society's hypocrisy, and the self-interests that underlie his friends counsel. He will not rest until he is granted divine audience, and he strongly berates his friends for their shady dealings with God and with him:

Will you plead God's defense with prevarication,
his case in terms that ring false?
Will you be partial in his favor,
and act as his advocates?
For you to meet his scrutiny, would this be well?
Can he be duped as men are duped?
Harsh rebuke you would receive from him
for your covert partiality.
Does his majesty not affright you,
dread of him not fall on you?
Your old maxims are proverbs of ash,
your retorts, retorts of clay (13:7-12).

The charges Job's friends have leveled against him have appalled him. Job knows his friends are lying and that, inwardly, they concur with what he says. "By raising these false accusations against me, you are offending the same God you claim to be intent on upholding," Job proclaims. "Hashem is the God of truth, and hence by lying you are violating His fundamental essence."

Job challenges his friends to prove with specific arguments that God is fair. Their invocation of a higher intelligence, of a divine wisdom, of things that lie beyond human comprehension, is unacceptable to Job. "God is in relationship with man, and we are His children," he tells them. "That is why He needs to communicate in ways that are comprehensible to us, His loyal servants."

No more prefabricated ideas handed down blindly from generation to generation. Job seeks instead contemporary answers—congruent with his experience and with his newfound understanding of the world. "This is what has happened to me, and these are my questions," he says. "So what are your answers?"

* * * * * * * * * * * * * * * *

Healthcare colleagues frequently say to me: "I want to spare my patients the pain of knowing their ultimate fate. Their disease is not responding to treatment, so why should I burden them when we can do nothing?" Very often, however, the patient is not the one who is being comforted. My colleagues are frequently defending themselves against the pain, guilt, and sadness they experience upon witnessing the deterioration of a patient for whom they care. Let us at least be honest and acknowledge whom we are really protecting and why, and then be open to what the patients may need. Ill people ask relevant questions that warrant honest and forthright answers. Surely they do not want to be bludgeoned with the truth, but neither do they want lies. Lying to them only fosters pain and mistrust, benefiting no one. "These are our questions," they say to us. "Can you give us your answers?"

Iyov, Job's Inner Warrior, Starts to Speak for Him Now. He Has Taken Charge of Job's Destiny and is Fostering Irreversible Change.

Silence! Now I will do the talking,
   whatever may befall me.
I put my flesh between my teeth,
   I take my life in my hands (13:13-14).

As Job reaches a zenith in his transformational journey, a new voice emerges from the depths of his soul—a voice able to recognize new realities and to assert truth. Job discovers that he has never really worshipped God, and that he has been untruthful both to himself and to others. He has been a liar, like his friends—a man who concealed his feelings as well as his motivations. The awareness appalls him, and yet it prepares him to become a true worshipper of God, a reflection of His divine image—in short, an honest man.

The driving forces of Job the victim, the wounded child, the heartbroken man, are dying in his inner universe. Once this dying is completed, Job will never again fall victim or, in turn, victimize. Instead, he will become a powerful, resourceful, and masterful human being. In these two verses we hear the voice of a new Job: Iyov, the warrior. Until now, like a wounded child, Job has expected God to save or restore him. Now, we hear this voice of a new man declaring he is taking care of himself. Having directly engaged the source of his agony, Job has become less fearful.

* * * * * * * * * * * * * * *

Virtually every patient who has heard me speak of the healing journey or of a process toward wholeness has inevitably posed the same question: How does one awaken the inner warrior amid the stress and threat of serious illness? There are no universally applicable, precise, or specific answers to this question. An infinite number of incremental paths do in fact lead to the emergence of what I am calling here "the warrior." In general terms, though, we can say that what one needs is to yield to the flow of life, to attune to the moment and what is happening in it. When sufferers can trust something within that knows how to surrender to the larger reality and connect with our inner wisdom, all becomes simplified and a rapid progress is set in motion.

Unfortunately, we are so conditioned to using only cognitive skills to solve our problems that such an attitudinal shift is very difficult to make. Only after we have exhausted all the rational resources available to us are we able to surrender to something new: our intuition, our inner guides. The moment we do yield, however, some mysterious power in us takes hold, and we begin to proceed in earnest. A voice emerges from within, lending us guidance and insight, and moving us forward with the new benefit of direct access to our resourcefulness and clarity. We recognize the voice as truthful by a variety of means. A great many of us will recognize its authenticity by experiences in our bodies: a vibration, an arousal of feeling, a quickening. We then undergo what the mystics call a cycle of death and rebirth, an experience in which an old order indeed recedes and a new one slowly and painfully emerges.

The Job we have known until now is edging even further toward death, and Iyov, the warrior, has already began to reveal himself. This revelation moves a person to feel, act, and behave so differently that the effect is uncanny. When a transformation such as Job's occurs, the person we have known has changed so much that we feel as if we are looking at someone familiar but also new. It is hard to remember the conventional, anxious, grief-stricken Job when Iyov speaks with such determined courage and clarity:

Let him kill me if he will; I have no other hope
   than to justify my conduct in his eyes.
This very boldness gives promise of my release,
   since no godless man would dare appear before him.
Listen carefully to my words,
   and lend your ears to what I have to say.
You shall see, I will proceed by due form of law,
   persuaded, as I am, that I am guiltless (13:15-18).

The Job who now speaks has new confidence that there is a chance his angst will be resolved. Indeed, we sense he is becoming resourceful and is growing capable of wellness through his newly acquired capacities. Job's strength has clearly emerged from his connection with what is necessary and meaningful to him. Speaking from an inner center attuned to his feelings and intuition, he seems to ask, "how can I go wrong now?"

Warrior-like, he is suddenly fearless:

Who comes against me with an accusation?
   Let him come! I am ready to be silenced and to die (13:19).

When we are ready to confront any accuser and even to die in the encounter, we have entered a state of expanded living. At precisely the moment we can accept being forever silenced, we have stopped all defensiveness and perhaps for the first time are able to say yes to both life and death, pain and joy, light and darkness. Fear recedes from our souls and someone more open, emotionally aroused, and spiritually enlightened can emerge.

Job's Warrior Has the Strength to Understand That, for Job to Complete his Transformation, He Will Need a Great Deal of Support from Friends and Family.

Job continues to address his friends.

But grant me these two favors:
   if not, I shall not dare to confront you.
Take your hand away, that lies so heavy on me,
   no longer make me cower from your terror.
Then arraign me, and I will reply;
   or rather, I will speak and you shall answer me.
How many faults and crimes have I committed?
   What law have I transgressed, or in what have I offended?
Why do you hide your face
   and look on me as your enemy?
you list bitter accusations against me,
   taxing me with the faults of my youth...
while my life is crumbling like rotten wood,
   or a moth-eaten garment (13:20-24, 26, 28).

Here, Job has begun his transition from death to rebirth, and he is determined to see the process through. Yet to do so he needs human support, so he implores his friends to stop criticizing him. Instead he exhorts them to ask him questions—questions to which he is all too eager to respond.

Job seeks to learn and to become wiser. He recognizes that he is not clearly innocent in what is happening to him, yet he does not understand how he has participated in this process. He knows that he has done no objective evil, and has caused no harm, so how can he explain his fate? He asks his friends for help in the hope that they might see in him answers that he himself cannot see.

So he asks them, "Have you seen me sin? How many crimes have you seen me commit? What laws have I transgressed, or in which way have I offended authority or God Himself?" The Sufferers at this stage seek answers that will restore some semblance of order to their world. Their lives have been thrown off course, and they are searching for someone to give them comprehensible clues that will restore their equilibrium.

In his heightened emotional state, Job slips easily from addressing his friends to addressing God. He returns to his pain, pleading for relief, for a suspension of his torment, if only because life is so short and we are never reborn to another life. Let life be lived without such torments, Job pleads.

Since man's days are measured out,
    since his tale of months depends on you,
    since you assign him bounds he cannot pass,
turn your eyes from him, leave him alone,
    like a hired drudge, to finish his day.
But man? He dies, and lifeless he remains;
    man breathes his last, and then where is he?
The waters of the seas may disappear,
    all the rivers may run dry or drain away;
but man, once in his resting place, will never rise again.
    The heavens will wear away before he wakes,
    before he rises from his sleep (14:5-6, 10-12).

Here, there is a hard realism. There is no more wishful thinking, no more thinking of the kind the old Job indulged at the beginning of the book. Any idea of reincarnation, for instance, is dismissed now that Job has encountered God's world: "Man, once in his resting place, will never rise again." Though later commentator-sages (people as limited, in their way, as Job's conventional friends) have tried to account for Job's apparently unjust misfortunes by making appeals to reincarnationism, the text clearly closes any such door. Ancient assertions, for example, that Job was the reincarnation of the soul of Terah, Abraham's father and an idol worshipper par excellence, would seem to the awakening Job mere fantasies: "Man will never rise again." Anxiety-ridden ancient scholars argued that Job's reincarnated soul had unfortunately brought considerable bad baggage with him from his previous passage through this earth, and this fact justified the horrible calamities that befell this pious man. A debit in the soul's moral account had to be paid. The awakening Job focuses on daily, ordinary realities of life but the ancient commentators' inventions seem only to reveal, once again, mankind's difficulties in accepting life as it is. Such shrinking from facts weakens the resolve and the defiance that we need to overcome obstacles seemingly unsurmountable. "If I do get a second, third, or fourth chance to repair my soul and redeem my bliss, what is the point of hurrying up, of fighting, exploring, learning, living?" Knowing and accepting that we go around only one time is indeed frightening, but when harnessed this knowledge will thrust us into ever-deepening appreciation of the miracle of our being, the life force within us and abroad.

Nine

Iyov Quickens Job In His Struggle With Logos

Despite flashes of a new, powerful energy, life seems to be slowly slipping away from Job and this realization returns to torment him (14:13-22). Yes, he knew he was mortal and that his life would one day end, but this is such an abrupt and unexpected ending. What distresses him most is the finality of it all: He cannot countenance the thought of never returning to this earth or to his family. Tormented now by the idea that death is irreversible and that the person he knew as himself would disappear forever, death's inexorability overwhelms him: for "once a man is dead can he come back to life? He is gone; you (God) mar him, and then you bid him go."

"I am too young to die," laments the sufferer. "There are so many things I want to do, so many dreams I have yet to fulfill. I was looking forward to being a grandfather, to a life of leisure with my wife. But none of this will ever happen. Instead, I have an incurable illness. Only a miracle will save me from certain death, and I have little faith that the dispenser of miracles will look upon me and take my plight to heart!"

Job understands intuitively that nature has mandated that he die, but what he does not yet know is that his death does not have to take a physical form. Because of his inner psychic conditions, something needed to die for him to burst into life, but in the language of the psyche, "death" signifies irreversible transformation rather than physical extinction. In Job's case, as in the case of many bodily sufferers, the transformation nature first demanded was psychospiritual. Before his outward tragedies revealed Job's appalling disconnection from feeling, his inner disease had been eating at him, clamoring for acknowledgement. Once the outward disasters struck, however, the stage was set for a resolution to take place. The moment Job dies, whether psychospiritually or physically, his disease state will indeed come to a halt, and life itself, the greater life within us and without, will then be able to continue unimpeded in its relentless search for the best means of achieving its ends.

Meanwhile, as all this turmoil and shifting of energies is happening in the unconscious realm of his psyche, Job's objective mind is attempting to do all it can to keep him physically alive. This mind simply can not believe that his wishes and hopes are to no effect and that no one can do anything to reverse his manifest fate.

* * * * * * * * * * * * * * *

The sufferer is full of anguish and needs to grapple with it as best he or she can. I had known Kathy for several years, but I had never seen the depth of anguish and despair she showed that morning in June.

"I am so f... angry at this awful disease," she clamored. "I am going to get rid of it all, can you hear me? I am getting rid of this cancer and nobody will stop me! I have made an inviolable commitment to staying alive, Jacob. You must understand this."

"Kathy," I replied. "I shall help you fulfill your wishes to the best of my ability."

"No, Jacob. No," she interrupted with force. "I don't want to hear this crap. I am tired of people trying their best and failing. You must promise me that you will keep me alive. Please, tell me that you will do it." As she shouted all that, she burst into the deepest cry I have ever witnessed, a cry that came directly from her wounded soul, and it bucked its way upward from her guts to her throat.

"I care very much for you, Kathy, and I shall continue working with you as I have done so far. You have already beaten some of the odds surrounding your prognosis, so why not keep an open mind and hope for more successes?"

"Oh Jacob, Jacob, Jacob. I feel such despair! I need more, much more than what you are offering me. I need assurances, promises that cannot be rescinded. You must help me with this. I need to see my son graduate from high school. He needs me there by his side, loving and supporting him. I must survive for that day."

"Yes, Kathy," I said calmly, "I promise you that I shall not give in to the negative thoughts or abandon you at anytime. I promise you that I shall fight at your side the best battle I know how to fight."

"Oh, my God...Oh my God..." she wailed in desperation. "I am so f... tired of this bullshit, these empty words. If you can't assure me that I will make it, then f... you. I'll find someone who can."

As she left my office, I felt an immense sadness—a hollow emptiness. She walked away carrying a heavy burden. That was the last time I saw Kathy. Six weeks later she was dead.

Despite the Profound Changes Beginning to Take Hold in Job's Inner World, Logos, as Represented by His Friends, Relentlessly Defends the Status Quo

Eliphaz of Teman spoke next. He said:

Does a wise man answer with airy reasonings...
Does he defend himself with empty talk...
You do worse: You flout piety,
    you repudiate mediation in God's presence (15:1-4).

We cannot help but be amazed at the vast breach separating Job's requests from his friends' responses, as if they were speaking different languages. Job speaks from his heart, understanding that his days are numbered and that every second counts. He wants his friends to take the pressure off him, to stop protesting his words. But they cling to their old perceptions. Whenever Job opens his mouth, his friends hear only insults and invective, betrayals of God's commandments, and repudiations of all that is truthful and just. "We must defend our beliefs and those of our forebears," they proclaim. "We are priests of a creed that must be preserved against these heretical statements at all costs."

Such unreasoning reasonableness must have a lot to hide. Job's friends can be seen as representative of that part of people that defend against having the repression and cruelty that reigns in their homes exposed and revealed. Such people have endured so much abuse during their own lives that there is no way they can allow others to expose their own abusers. After managing to rationalize their hurt for so long, how could they allow Job's pain to be acknowledged and redeemed?

Thus, Job's apparent arrogance infuriates Eliphaz: "Your own mouth condemns you, and not I; your own lips bear witness against you" (15:6). In verses 5 through 29 of Chapter 15, he repeats earlier arguments for repression: "Do you have a monopoly on God's wisdom to have such self-assurance? Control your feelings! You are hysterical and are being carried away by passion. Don't you see the evil inherent in that? Feelings, the fruits of Eros, cloud the mind, make you lose your balance and your predictability. Repent; recognize the truth," clamors Eliphaz. "You are an unclean sinner possessed by demons and this is your well-deserved punishment!" So does the psyche struggle to maintain old ways in the act of awakening (which, paradoxically, as we have seen, requires a death). The process of inner redemption depicted in *The Book of Job* parallels the way it actually unfolds in life: rather than a clean linear movement, there is a spiraling upwards, a recycling of material often many times, until a new stage or platform is gradually attained. And even then, there may be lapses, regressions, and a need to fight old battles.

While the initial reaction of many readers is to lay blame on Job's three friends for a good part of his despair, we may well ask, "Why did he have friends like these to begin with?" He was heavily identified with his rational, controlled, conventional side, so he naturally chose to befriend men of similar tendencies. His ongoing dispute with his friends is, from an intra-psychic point of view, a reflection of an on-going struggle between Logos, who until then dominated Job's psyche and ruled his thoughts and behavior, and a new and emerging force, Eros, who by her sheer presence in Job's consciousness seriously challenged the status quo. Job, who is partly numb and partly aware of what has happened to him, now seeks understanding and compassion, but he is asking the wrong people for it. His friends have not undergone the changes he had endured, so they cling stubbornly to their old perceptions and beliefs. So what is the point in asking them to provide something they could not give? Is this not a naive and misguided approach?

Yes, it is. Nonetheless, it illustrates how faulty and unfounded expectations create misery and disarray in our lives. What happened to Job was by no means trivial and inconsequential; his collision with God's world wreaked havoc on his home and on his very foundation as a person. But it was the other component of his experience, the component engendered by his friends' callous reactions to his plight, that distressed him more severely. Even though the events that had hit him earlier—the death of his children, the forfeiture of his wealth, and even the loss of his physical well-being—were catastrophic, he perceived them as belonging to a larger reality over which he felt he had no direct or immediate sway. But to be misunderstood in the here and now, again and again, and by his friends, is terrible.

For cancer patients, being diagnosed with the illness works in a similar fashion. For them, being diagnosed with cancer is something they usually can't relate to or comprehend, except as a product of complex factors that lie outside their sphere of volitional control. But does the diagnosis necessitate experiencing overwhelming despair, despondency, and a profound sense of hopelessness? Such reactions, in my estimation, are more often than not the products of a lack of social understanding, support, and appropriate guidance than of the medical events themselves. This is why any approach toward illness that does not heed how we and others respond to such experiences is limited and essentially ineffectual — a form of management that may well keep people alive, but that falls far short of promoting living.

Job's Warrior Slowly Gains Strength Again and Begins to Reorganize Job's Priorities.

As he suffers the torments of his "friends" once more, Job is drawn again to counterattack.

How often have I heard all this before!
   What sorry comforters you are!
I too could talk like you,
   were your soul in the plight of mine.
I too could overwhelm you with sermons,
   I could shake my head over you,
and speak words of encouragement,
   until my lips grew tired.
But, while I am speaking, my suffering remains;
   and when I am not, do I suffer any the less?
And now ill will drives me to distraction,
   and a whole host molests me...
In tearing fury it pursues me,
   with gnashing teeth.
My enemies whet their eyes on me,
   and open gaping jaws.
Their insults strike like slaps in the face,
   and all set on me together (16:2, 4-10).

Western men are known to be poor providers of emotional support. They know how to offer solutions, but often they do not know how to nurture. Such support derives from feeling, and, therefore properly belongs to the feminine realm of our psyches. Without a feminine aspect, these men can scarcely provide compassion. This is why the induction of our feminine attributes is so essential to the healing process: A mind disconnected from its heart is insensitive, ruthless, often brutal. Too many western physicians today are ineffective healers precisely because their feminine aspect, by and large, lies dormant.

Logos, who animates them and rules their actions, can explain, categorize, and analyze masterfully; he (Logos) can chart complex strategies and fashion intricate plans. But please do not ask him to soothe the wounds of the soul.

Physicians who are also what I will call true healers, by contrast, are human beings who can integrate both Logos and Eros. They assess a clinical situation with the same expertise as any traditional physician, but at the same time they remain attuned to the feelings and spiritual concerns of the people with whom they come in contact. They analyze clinical findings and integrate them within a fully human framework, one that promotes physical recovery while lending psychological, spiritual, and social support to the afflicted, their families, and their friends.

Job, supported by the strength of his feelings, turns away from his friends again and back to contemplating his own fate and God.

> Yes, God has handed me over to the godless,
> and cast me into the hands of the wicked.
> I lived at peace, until he shattered me,
> taking me by the neck to dash me to pieces.
> He has made me a target for his archery,
> shooting his arrows at me from every side.
> Pitiless, through the loins he pierces me,
> and scatters my gall on the ground.
> Breach after breach he drives through me,
> bearing down on me like a warrior.
> I have sewn sackcloth over my skin
> and rubbed my brow in the dust.
> My face is red with tears,
> and a veil of shadow hangs on my eyelids (16:11-16).

Job's account of his most recent actions and pain touches our hearts. When tragedy first struck, he bemoaned his fate but continued to bless the Almighty. Now, he vents his resentment with God and with human beings. More eloquent than ever, having been able to integrate some of his feelings and articulate them more forcefully, Job's unblinking tone in this passage implicitly acknowledges that what happened to him was indeed part of the process of living. "I have eaten from the tree of knowledge of good and evil, and have became conscious," Job seems to be saying. "No longer can I go back and feign unconsciousness. All that has befallen me has undoubtedly happened, and I am appalled by it."

The Value of Self-Reflective Consciousness

I am frequently asked the following questions, in various ways, by patients struggling with the psychospiritual upheavals brought about by cancer: "What is the value of a self-reflective consciousness? What do we gain, as creatures, from knowing that we know? What is so terrific, for example, about being aware that we are vulnerable to illness or that we shall eventually die? Isn't ignorance bliss, and if so, why would nature have evolved such a perplexing function? It could not be mainly to torment us with negative information, existential anxieties and worries—or could it?"

Obviously, neither of the speculative answers posed in the last two questions above is correct. Reflective consciousness has enormous consequences and benefits us on a personal, collective, and even a planetary scale. Without reflective consciousness, the world with all its colossal beauty and mystery would be virtually non-existent, and there would be no reality we could speak of. Moreover, reflective consciousness introduces a force into nature that accelerates, in unimaginable ways, the speed of evolutionary change. Changes in our bodies, our minds, our society, and our relation to nature that could have taken millions of years to unfold can now blossom in a single lifetime. Sophisticated technology opens up wonderful possibilities, allowing the development of medical and psychological sciences invested in the prevention, detection, and treatment of all illnesses. It also makes possible the establishment of those sophisticated systems of communication, education, and vital support that continue to enhance our capacity to survive the difficult challenges life presents to us. Moreover, without reflective consciousness, we would never be able to create or experience the exquisite music, poetry, paintings,

states, and buildings that are the ornaments and pleasures of humanity. I would not be writing this book, you would not be reading it, you
and I would not even know who we are. Reflective consciousness
makes us human and introduces into life the greatest support known
to enhance a species' chances for well-being.

Despite its remarkably beneficial effects, however, reflective consciousness also lends itself to misuse, and therefore fosters disorder
and chaos. It can also burden us with knowledge and information that
is hard for most of us to accept. No wonder the emergence of this
faculty (eating from the fruit of the Tree of Knowledge, as discussed
in Genesis 3:6) has been paradoxically perceived by so many religious
traditions as a fall from naive grace, an expression of humans'
transgression of the divine injunction (original sin), for which, "for-
tunately," we are all still paying. The dawn of reflective consciousness,
after all, introduced the knowledge that we are mortal, and this monumental event caused us to become aware for the first time that we
have feelings, distressing ones in particular: fear (of injury and death)
and pain and shame (of our emotional nakedness). Each human being
must move from infancy into childhood and then through the many
developmental sequences life demands from us, experiencing pain at
every one of these difficult transitions. But we also come to know that
even under the worst of circumstances, we have the capacity to undertake a conscious process to enhance our chances for survival, and
this is the most reassuring and comforting knowledge there is. It is not
that we can or will always accomplish our particular ends, but at least
we can have the satisfaction of having tried, and having been given a
reasonable chance to succeed.

Frequently, when I encounter people for whom reflective consciousness may still feel like a punishment, I think part of their distortion of
reality stems from their belief that so much of what we can consciously
know cannot be effectively changed, and if so, why know it? While
some fundamental realities brought forth by self-awareness cannot be
changed—like all creatures we, too, are vulnerable to injury and mortality—we can change the way we perceive, integrate, and respond to
these realities and to the feelings these realities evoke. Regardless of
the collective conditions we experience, we can use self-awareness to

accept what cannot be changed, and strive vigorously to create whatever attitudes or practical measures can enhance survival and inner harmony.

A young patient with whom I had been working for several months crystallized the practical meaning of these ideas for me. This man was afflicted by several moderately severe medical ailments, as well as a chronic depressive state punctuated by episodes of hopelessness. He felt emotionally depleted, dejected, and helpless. He saw himself merely going through the motions of life, alienated from it and unable to experience happiness and true fulfillment. I encouraged him to grow and reconnect to his feelings and also to make efforts to become closer to family members. This emotional opening up had not worked very well for him until one day, when he visited the family of his best friend. This large family—people living together in a trans-generational fashion—whose home was always open to others, and whose attitude was warm, welcoming, and nurturing, embraced him. He felt heightened and energized there. The loving contact from people, in particular the youngsters, did magic for his mental state and his sense of self. Shortly afterward, he went through a true mystical experience that showed him this was exactly what his soul needed. Then, his capacity for self-awareness allowed him to place this information in a context of practical understanding. He became aware of how the fatigue, depression, and alienation that had shrouded him for so many years could lift almost completely when in the proper psychosocial milieu. Now that he knows (and knows that he knows) he can move on with determination and confidence, or, he also knows, he may loosen his grip on knowledge and self and fall back to old ways and states. At the very least, however, having the new self-awareness allows him to consider options and facilitate the outcome he has yearned for and sought for so long.

* * * * * * * * * * * * * *

Like this patient Job's struggle continues. He must use his increasing self-awareness to find a path that is right for him. He searches for some inner wisdom that will eventually redeem his pain and restore his dignity, and he is convinced that sooner or later this wisdom will come.

This notwithstanding, my hands are free of violence,
  and my prayer is undefiled.
Cover not my blood, O earth,
  afford my cry no place to rest.
Henceforth I have a witness in heaven,
  my defender is there in the height.
My own lament is my advocate with God,
  while my tears flow before him.
Let this plead for me as I stand before God,
  as a man will plead for his fellows.
For the years of my life are numbered,
  and I shall soon take the road of no return (16:17-22).

"Because I have a witness in heaven, my defender is there in the height," asserts Job. He knows that the resolution of his drama can come only from the issuance of divine guidance and insight from within him. Until that time, however, his pain and agony are unremitting. Job is also newly aware that with every day that passes, his life has been foreshortened. He now understands mortality, and he is trying to enhance his life and render it richer ("For the years of my life are numbered, and I shall soon take the road of no return.") He wants to overcome his trials, transcend that which obstructs him, and move on. Once mortality is acknowledged, life becomes increasingly focused and more purposeful.

Yet his pain and despair keep resurfacing and overwhelming him. He cannot help but give new voice to his profound anguish and resentment:

I have become a byword among the people,
  and a creature on whose face to spit.
My eyes grow dim with grief,
  and my limbs wear away like a shadow.
Come, then, all of you: Set on me once more!
  I shall not find a single sage among you.

My days have passed, far otherwise than I had planned,
    and every fiber of my heart is broken.
Night, they say, makes room for day,
    and light is near at hand to chase the darkness.
All I look forward to is dwelling in Sheol,
    and making my bed in the dark.
I tell the tomb, "You are my father,"
    and call the worm my mother and my sister (17:6-7, 10-14).

Although Job has become progressively stronger, he is still periodically overcome by sadness and despair. His feelings are anything but stable, and interspersed with the times when he feels secure and powerful are moments when he feels utterly lost and forsaken. His eddying psychological process is much like those of the cancer patients I attend.

Once again, Job is devastated not only by the objective disasters that have befallen him, but also by his inability to handle the feelings that intermittently flood his psyche. His repeated collapses make him dependent, vulnerable, and even more desperate. Neither his wife nor any of his closest friends know how to support him during these terrible moments, and he is overcome once more by a sense of utter hopelessness, rapidly losing faith in himself and in life.

Sensing Eros' Powerful Advance, Logos Escalates His Attacks by Threatening Job With the Harshest of Punishments.

Once more, the melee resumes when another friend tries to enforce the insights of a narrow, feelingless Logos.

Bildad of Shuah spoke next. He said:

Will you never learn to check such words?
    Do you think we shall be slow to speak?
Tear yourself to pieces if you will,
    but the world, for all your rage, will not turn to desert,
    the rocks will not shift from their places.
The wicked man's light must certainly be put out,
    his brilliant flame cease to shine.

Disease devours his flesh,
   Death's First-Born gnaws his limbs.
He is torn from the shelter of his tent,
   and dragged before the King of Terrors.
Driven from light into darkness,
   he is an exile from the earth...
A fate like his awaits every sinful house,
   the home of every man who knows not God (18:1-2, 4-5, 13-14,
   18, 21).

Bildad is taken aback and then infuriated by Job's diatribe. He can't understand Job's ill will toward him. He and the others have been showering Job with wisdom and illuminating his path to salvation, and in return Job only berates them. There is only one possible explanation for this aberrant behavior: Job has gone mad. "Tear yourself to pieces if you will, but the world, for all your rage, will not turn to desert." But it is actually the conventionally minded Bildad who is removed from reality. We are reminded here of a sequence from the French film *Rape for Love*, wherein a mother, having learned of her daughter's rape, counsels her daughter to put the incident aside. She advises the girl not to pursue her assailants but rather to go on with her life as if nothing had happened. The daughter is appalled by her mother's response, much as Job is shocked by his friends' reactions to him. The daughter cannot believe that her own mother would fail to support her at such a critical time. To make matters worse, the mother finally becomes angry and blames her daughter for the rape. "Had it not been for the way you carry yourself," she states, "the rape would never have occurred!"

Would a mother have responded in this way if she too had not been raped, figuratively or otherwise, and had never allowed herself to confront her own assailants? In all probability, she had also been taught to remain silent, to forget her transgressors, and to go on with her life as though nothing had transpired. Evidently, her inability to take care of herself and assert her rights prevented her from supporting her daughter in her hour of need.

Bildad is trying an old trick on Job—one that has been used for centuries with excellent results. He is trying to intimidate Job by recounting for him the horrors that await him if he fails to mend his ways and return to God's fold. Job, however, has grown immune to such threats. He has learned to see through these stories and will no longer allow his naive inner child to succumb to them.

Ten

Logos Is Finally Dethroned

Job Understands Now That the Answers to His Plight Will Have to Come From Within, From His Spirit, the Source of All.

Once more, Job defends himself and his inner Eros. He says,

Will you never stop tormenting me,
  and shattering me with speeches?
Ten times, no less, have you insulted me,
  ill-treating me without a trace of shame.
Suppose that I have gone astray,
  suppose I am even yet in error:
it is still true, though you think you have the upper hand of me
  and feel that you have proved my guilt,
that God, you must know, is my oppressor,
  and his is the net that closes around me (19:2-6).

Job's agony reaches a new apex. He is convinced God betrayed him and shattered his life, and that his wife and friends, not fewer then ten times, have been blind, insensitive, and callous to his despair. Job beseeches his friends to bypass tradition. "Don't become fixated on whether I am mad or guilty," he says. "Don't you feel anything for me? Please stop playing God! I have enough with one. He is ruthless, awesome, and powerful enough for any mortal to contend with. Don't add salt to my injury, don't collude with Him. Recognize life for what it is; acknowledge God's darkness. I am not saying He is not also the light you suggest He is, but rather that He is orders of magnitude more than what you allow Him to be. Know that God Almighty is my destroyer and victimizer, the hand that strangles my resolve and my hope."

Underlining, once more, his inability to make his friends understand, Job complains that he can't ever obtain a hearing from God.

If I protest against such violence, there is no reply;
    if I appeal against it, judgment is never given (19:7).

Job who craves insight and direction, is still dominated by his old beliefs and ideologies and cannot yet fully acknowledge God's truth. He hoped that his protestations to God would cause the heavens to part and that God's sonorous voice would burst forth and dictate to him exactly what *he* sought to hear. Instead, an inner voice responded, "This is reality, Job; life strikes you and silence follows. There is no divine Father overseeing His prodigal sons. You are alone, and there is no one who can redeem your pain." Job still can't totally accept that no answers lie outside him. All he knows is that the outer world has not delivered the knowledge that he needs but, as he will come to understand in time, that world cannot deliver what it does not have.

Meanwhile, no matter where he turns, he finds a human hand derailing his efforts to escape his earthly hell. Even Job's servants dismiss him now, paying no heed to his wishes. He becomes a powerless man, ridiculed and shunned by all.

My kindred and my friends have all gone away,
    and the guests in my house have forgotten me.
My servant does not answer when I call him,
    I am reduced to entreating him.

To my wife my breath is unbearable,
  for my own brothers I am a thing corrupt.
Even the children look down on me,
  ever ready with a jibe when I appear.
...those I loved best have turned against me (19:14, 16-19).

Here Job gives expression to all the desperation humanity harbors
in the depth of its soul. It is desperation born from coming to know
life's ruthless side and from seeing that, regardless of how we act in
life, we will still fall prey to nature's mischief. Job's pain has become
so acute that he now asks for support and sustenance from anyone
who is willing to listen. Job's despair needs an outlet. More than ever,
he needs real compassion.

Pity me, pity me, you, my friends,
  for the hand of God has struck me (19:21).

Remarkably, though, part of Job is still assured of his innocence and
convinced that, when all is said and done, God Almighty will indeed
take his side. So with convincing assertiveness, he proclaims.

This I know: that my Avenger lives,
  and he, the Last, will take his stand on earth.
After my awaking, he will set me close to him,
  and from my flesh I shall look on God.
He whom I shall see will take my part:
  these eyes will gaze on him and find him not aloof (19:25-27).

In the same breath, Job also threatens his unsympathetic friends:

You, then, that mutter, "How shall we track him down,
  what pretext shall we find against him?"
may well fear the sword on your own account.
  There is an anger stirred to flame by evil deeds;
  you will learn that there is indeed a judgment (19:28-29).

"These deeds of yours, this cruelty, this inhumane behavior will not
go unheeded. You shall pay for your abomination with blood!" Thus
Job lets his friends know his thoughts.

Logos, Sensing that His Battle with Eros is About to be Lost, Invokes in His Defense the Idea that Eros's Gains are Only Fleeting.

Zophar of Naamath spoke next. He said...
Do you not know, that since time began
    and man was set on the earth,
the triumph of the wicked has always been brief,
    and the sinner's gladness has never lasted long?
His sons must recoup his victims,
    and his children pay back his riches.
Since he once destroyed the huts of poor men,
    and stole other's houses when he should have built his own,
since his avarice could never be satisfied,
    now his hoarding will not save him...
On him God looses all his burning wrath,
    hurling against his flesh a hail of arrows.
The heavens lay bare his iniquity,
    the earth takes its stand against him (20:1, 4-5, 10, 19-20, 23, 27).

What Zophar is saying is insightful but not soothing to Job. Human justice is indeed transgenerational. The children and grandchildren of the righteous and the wicked will endure the consequences of their parents and grandparents' actions. But this is of no solace to a man convinced he has been wronged by God. Moreover, Zophar had no proof of Job's wickedness; therefore, his admonitions are empty and misguided. Rather than being motivated by honesty, Zophar is moved by his inability to dispute the incontrovertible truth of the world's lack of perfect justice, which Job has argued and exposed. Zophar has seen some wicked people live long, prosperous lives, and he has seen pious people be, in the current vernacular, "trashed." It would have been preposterous for him to insist on denying the undeniable. So what does he do when challenged? He promises Job punishment even beyond the grave. Zophar, with the intellectual enthusiasm of the system builder, elaborates by saying that God will bring down even the wicked who escape torment here and now in death and final judgement. Sooner or later the ax falls, and everything works as it should. "Don't you realize that the other wicked men will be stricken? Life is orderly, flows according to doctrine, and we can all rest assured and be happy," Zophar tells Job.

* * * * * * * * * * * * * * * *

When two conflicting inner worlds such as Logos and Eros collide with one another, nothing short of a miracle will bring their conflict to a halt. Here is the dance of opposing forces that repel and attract each other at the same time. What is logical to Logos is cruel to Eros. What is beautiful to Eros is threatening and chaotic to Logos, and so the dance continues. Job cries out for mercy and compassion; Zophar, with lawyerly logic stands up only for what seems conventionally right and moral.

The idea of an ongoing intra-psychic battle between the forces of our own Logos and Eros may seem unreal to most of us. In fact, it is something of which we are seldom consciously aware, either in our objective or our subjective lives, but it is a battle to which we all contribute and of which we all partake. When crucial dimensions of the psyche have evolved separately, as they have in most of us, they do not easily integrate their functions within the totality of psychic life. This internal struggle is nothing more than part of the psychic adjustment needed to coordinate competing forces invested with critical functions.

Bill's story reveals the profound schism that often exists between Logos' and Eros' reaction to life and illustrates how this schism surfaces, if allowed to, at moments of crisis. A man in his late 40s with disseminated lung cancer (the disease had spread to several parts of the body in addition to the lung), Bill was diagnosed a few months earlier with brain metastasis (the spread of cancer cells to the brain tissues). He was treated with a novel radiotherapeutic approach consisting of large doses of radiation energy administered directly to the site where the tumors were growing. This type of treatment can be administered without great danger only when the number of tumors in the brain is small and when they are well circumscribed. The treatment was temporarily successful, but after a few months new and multiple tumors appeared in both cerebral hemispheres. Bill's radiation oncologists recommended whole-brain radiation. Initially, Bill resisted the doctors' recommendations, but after a while he understood their rationale and agreed to the treatment. He realized there were no reasonable alternatives at this juncture and that without these treatments the quality of his life would suffer. After starting the treatments, Bill felt an urgent need to see me. There was something perturbing his emotional stability that made the experience of the treatment particularly distressing.

"How are you feeling?" I asked Bill as soon as he settled in his favorite chair.

"Okay," he replied in his usual matter-of-fact way, but before I could say anything, his eyes welled up, and in a choked voice, he exclaimed. "I feel so violated, so intruded, Jacob. The smell of burning flesh coming out of the machine each time I go for treatment torments me. It makes me feel as if I were frying my brain. I can't believe I am doing this to myself!"

"Try to let your feelings come out, Bill," I encouraged him. "Remember that your feelings have always truth..."

"Why did I agree to participate in such a barbaric experience? Can you explain this to me? Why did I consent to have my brains fried and my healthy tissues damaged wantonly with total disregard for suffering?"

"You are quite right in feeling so distraught," I reassured him. "When the medical treatments are seen from the perspective you have raised, they are indeed primitive and injurious."

"It is so humiliating and painful to see the radiation treatment personnel be so oblivious of what they are doing to me and of what their actions cause me to feel," he insisted.

"Yes, Bill, that is precisely why I am encouraging you to honor and respect your feelings, to validate them and to stand up for that part of you that feels so ripped by the brutality and callousness of this treatment approach."

"But if I give free rein to my feelings", retorted Bill, "then how can I go on with the radiation treatments? I will have to stop them immediately. It would be unconscionable to continue them."

"No, Bill, that is not so. To respect your feelings does not mean that you have to abide by their dictates."

"So then, what am I to do? How am I to resolve this awful dilemma?"

"It is in the clarification of your purpose that you will find resolution to this conflict. It is true that the treatments to which you have agreed injure your normal cells and that you must be sensitive to the violation of the human body that occurs each time you subject it to this therapeutic onslaught, but did you have a choice? Is it reasonable that for the benefit of your whole person, you have agreed to tolerate damage to some of your parts?"

"You know," Bill confided, "it is a relief to know that my feelings are indeed sensible. I never thought of the idea of giving them voice and due regard. I know very well that rationally and objectively I need to do what I am doing. I know that from a logical point of view there is no alternative, and yet, I would have never anticipated the profound dejection and feelings of violation the treatment elicited. Evidently, there are parts in me that perceive and feel differently about the same event. It is a remarkable realization."

"Welcome to the world of the many selves," I responded encouragingly. "I am glad that you found solace to your despair"

Bill looked back at me, a half-smile insinuating itself through the right side of his face, and said, "Life is so strange and humorous, Jacob. While in the midst of this turmoil and despair, I met a woman. We went out last night, it was so refreshing: no cancer, no radiation, no fear. Just laughter, funny stories, and the joy of human fellowship."

****

Zophar's emotional detachment serves only to catalyze and further magnify Job's anguish. Again, shocked that his feelings are unheeded and his character besmirched, he protests:

Listen, only listen to my words;
   This is the consolation you can offer me.
Let me have my say;
   you may jeer when I have spoken.

Do you think I bear a grudge against man?
Have I no reason to be out of patience?
Hear what I have to say, and you will be dumbfounded,
will place your hands over your mouths.
I myself am appalled at the very thought,
and my flesh begins to shudder (21:2-6).

Job is growing weary of sermons. He has heard these empty voices
and their distortions of the truth once too often. He has uncovered
something different from what his friends can offer him. "I am not
speaking just for the sake of speaking," he tells them. "My words are
full of meaning. I too would like to believe my insights to be of no
import, but I cannot. I have seen life's face and can no longer seek
solace in my childhood fantasies. Come back to the facts," he insists,
"and tell me..."

Why do the wicked still live on,
their power increasing with their age?
The peace of their houses has nothing to fear,
the rod that God wields is not for them.
They end their lives in happiness
and go down in peace to Sheol.
Yet these were the ones who said to God, "Go away!
We do not choose to learn your ways.
What is the point of our serving Shaddai?
What profit should we get from praying to him?"
Do we often see a wicked man's light put out,
or disaster overtaking him,
or all his goods destroyed by the wrath of God?
(21:7, 9, 13-15, 17).

Job's challenge to his friends is monumental, his revelations of truth
brutal and forthright. his friends feel disarmed and exposed. When the
truth is insisted upon, there is nothing they can say in response to what
they themselves have experienced and have known all too well. In
reality, good people suffer as much, if not more, than evil ones. They

are more innocent, more open, even more naive, and hence less prepared to handle some of what life holds in store for them.

Job, seeing that his friends are starting to waver, takes up another
of their false justification and continues the onslaught:

God, you say, reserves the man's punishment for his children.
No! Let him bear the penalty himself, and suffer under it!
When he has gone, how can the fortunes of his House affect him,
   when the number of his months is cut off? (21:19, 21).

"The idea that the descendants of the wicked are punished for the
sins of the fathers is abhorrent," Job remarks to his friends. "The
whole idea is not just and I shall not abide it. Let the wicked bear the
brunt themselves, as it should be. I want murderers to feel punishment
on their own flesh."

Job's eyes are open wide enough now for him to admit implicitly
that nature is indeed relentless in pursuit of balance and eventually
finds a way to restore it, though it cannot always follow any of humankind's timetables. An unworkable system, the text hints, invariably breaks down and undergoes revision, but only in its own time.
Such a vision cannot for the moment console Job. He must still rub
his own face in the truth of the facts his life has forced him to see so
clearly, the truth of the here-and-now world. His speech describes a
terrible vision of a world full of apparent injustice, an amoral world
where some live and die well and happy and others never have so much
as a single good day.

And again: One man dies in the fullness of his strength,
   in all possible happiness and ease,
with his thighs all heavy with fat,
   and the marrow of his bones undried.
Another dies with bitterness in his heart,
   never having tasted happiness.
Together now they lie in the dust
   with worms for covering (21:23-26).

It is a world also where the wicked apparently escape any earthly punishment, whatever may be their fate in a hereafter. Job mocks the words of Zophar, offering the consolation of some far distant other-worldly justice at the day of Judgment:

The wicked man is spared for the day of disaster,
  and carried off in the day of wrath?
But who is there then to accuse him to his face for his deeds,
  and pay him back for what he has done,
when he is on his way to his burial,
  when men are watching at his grave.
The clods of the valley are laid gently on him,
  and a whole procession walks behind him.

In frustration, he flings back his friends' pious, easy, conventional answers:

So what sense is there in your empty consolation?
What nonsense are your answers! (21:30-34).

Job's discovery of life's terrible injustice overwhelms him. "We all die," he says, "and once dead we are indeed equal. But how unjust is that which precedes it!" The idea that wickedness is being spared for the day of disaster, that day when Hashem's justice is to be proclaimed throughout the four corners of the globe, is revolting to him and affords him no consolation.

Job is starkly clear about the apparent amorality of existence. But the momentum of feeling that has brought him to such truth has pushed him beyond a point of no return. Now he will have to seek a resolution by marching forward, in time to confront the source from which all of life's forces emanate. Job is preparing himself to meet his Maker, the creator of all things.

* * * * * * * * * * * * * * *

Every day, the physician witnesses human suffering and has an opportunity to help the distraught, questioning, bewildered, and even the guilt-ridden with the struggle for healing and meaning that the dark side of God's world excites. Job is not only the patient, he is also the patient's family, lover, friend, and colleague. It had been more than two weeks since I last saw Marian. She was at the time mourning the death of her beloved daughter and had come to share her sorrow and her despair with me.

"The memories of her suffering torment me," she exclaimed as soon as we sat down. "Her last few years were truly hellish, agonizing. It breaks my heart to remember."

"Yes, Marian," I responded caringly, "Rachel suffered a great deal. It was truly painful to witness her anguish."

"I can not tell you, Jacob, how guilty and burdened I feel. I can not stop hearing her painful moaning and sensing her despair each time I walk by her bedroom. Had I known what pain the chemotherapy treatments caused her, I would have never consented to them."

"It must have been excruciatingly painful to see your daughter endure so much," I replied compassionately.

"She was so adamant, so determined not to know. Do you remember how angry she would get whenever anyone tried to pierce her denial or attempted to undermine her resolve or hope? 'Mother,' she would implore me ever so often: 'Please, promise me, no more treatments ...You won't let them hurt me...!' So what was I to do but to take over her medical care and with the help of her physicians orchestrate her treatments? I did such a lousy job, though. I hurt my baby so much."

"No, Marian, you did not hurt your daughter at all," I counseled her. "In fact, you helped her immensely. You allowed her to do what she wanted so badly to do, which was, in fact, to try to fight the disease with everything that chemical medicine could offer, without her constantly acknowledging the disease she was fighting. You gave her a structure on which she could support her natural psychological ambivalence. You helped her fulfill her heartfelt wishes."

"But how can you say that I helped her, Jacob, when her life was so miserable and afflicted by so much despair?"

"In her disease process and treatment, she lived her best, the best she could, with your help. It is only for a short time, while you now mourn the loss of your beloved child, that everything seems senseless and purposeless. How else could a loving, caring and devoted mother feel? It is an inevitable period to endure and eventually past through."

"I wish I could clearly remember what was meaningful for Rachel," she whispered back. "I am sure it would comfort me and soothe my soul. I hope I soon find the clarity of mind that will help me understand what this was all about.."

"Remember, Marian," I interceded, "Rachel was well aware of what was going on in her body. Her denial of the knowledge about her condition was a choice she made to avoid something she knew could interfere with her life. As you recall, she needed to fight fiercely against hopelessness and also against giving in. She wanted to make a statement for herself and for us all that living is indeed transcendental and meaningful. Thanks to you, she was able to live as much like a healthy girl as possible, while fighting her disease with determination and commitment. By willingly taking on the difficult mantle of superintendent of therapy, you allowed her to fulfill her yearnings for survival, and also to find meaning in her suffering. Rachel is an angel among us, whose awful pain and insistence in living to the end teaches us to appreciate with wonderment the gift we have been granted, and to draw sustenance from her devotion to the maintenance of her own life."

"Thank you, Jacob. When I hear you speak this way, I feel better, clearer. My turmoil seems to ease. Who was the poet who said, 'The thunder of my tormenting thoughts resonates somewhat farther away'? Yes, Jacob, I can feel it again in my soul: my baby is indeed an angel among us."

Job's Warrior Now Unfolds His Standard. The Ruling Order Crumbles and, While Chaos Reigns in the Land, a New Order Starts to Surface.

In Chapter 22, Eliphaz once again insists on asserting conventional reasonableness, but Job ignores this repetition. He simply sticks to his protest, his questioning, and his search for ultimate answers:

Job spoke next. He said:

My lament is still rebellious,
  that heavy hand of his drags groans from me.
If only I knew how to reach him,
  or how to travel to his dwelling!
I should set out my case to him,
  my mouth would not want for arguments.
Then I could learn his defense, every word of it,
  taking note of everything he said to me.
If I go eastward, he is not there;
  or westward—still I cannot see him.
If I seek him in the north, he is not to be found,
  invisible still when I turn to the south.
And yet he knows of every step I take!
  Let him test me in the crucible: I shall come out pure gold
  (23:1-5, 8-10).

Job sees himself as a seeker on a journey that runs through all the earth. Symbolically, he is trying to penetrate a world from which all things emanate and to decipher the principles that sustain it. If he achieves this, he will be able to place what had happened to him in some proper context. His hurt would still then abide, he thinks, but in some way he will be justified. "If I only knew how to reach Him," he proclaims. Then, as quickly as this confidence has surged up, it recedes:

But once he has decided, who can change his mind?
  Whatever he plans, he carries out.
No doubt, then, but he will carry out my sentence,
  like so many other decrees that he has made.
That is why I am full of fear before him,
  and the more I think, the greater grows my dread of him.
God has made my heart sink,
  Shaddai has filled me with fear.
For darkness hides me from him,
  and the gloom veils his presence from me (23:13-17).

Doubt takes possession of Job's psyche. "Once He has decided, who can change His mind?" he repeats obsessively to himself. "God will not redeem me." Job is caught in a ripple and needs to let go of the inner conflict of reason, the binary games of "yes" and "no." Despite his remarkable progress in many key areas, Job's persistent inability to connect with God's wisdom causes him to regress psychologically and to fall victim to the fallacy of the intellect, that dimension of the psyche that promises us more rewards that it can possibly deliver. By letting his frustration and doubts seduce him back into his rational fortress, Job forces exhaustion and further disillusionment on himself. So the more he tries, the less he succeeds.

Paradoxically, what Job needs to do to fulfill his wishes and expectations is simply do nothing. If he ceases to fight the current and aligns himself with life's flow, something magical and unexpected may happen. The gates of heaven might well open up and a channel may connect him directly with the understanding he seeks. What Job has so energetically yearned for might then reveal itself spontaneously and effortlessly.

As a step in this direction, Job needs to relinquish the notion that he can force nature to accede to his demands. He has to accept that he can't force God's hand, regardless of how much he is suffering or how deeply wronged he feels. Suffering, to his chagrin, is not an experience that moves God or successfully redirects His attention. Job must see clearly at last that the world in general (as opposed to its appearances in his early personal experience) is not the simple, just, and happy place he once thought it to be, and that his friends' conventional Logos still pretend it to be. At last, after so much shuffling and cycling back and forth between protest and a search for human reasonableness in the world of God, Job shows in a precise but dark panorama that the world is what it is: no more and no less.

The wicked move boundary marks away,
    they carry off flock and shepherd.
Some drive away the orphan's donkey,
    and take the widow's ox for a security.

Beggars, now, avoid the roads,
  and all the poor of the land must go into hiding.
Fatherless children are robbed of their lands,
  and poor men have their cloaks seized as security.
Others of them hate the light,
   know nothing of its ways,
   avoid its paths.
When all is dark the murderer leaves his bed
   to kill the poor and needy.
All night long prowls the thief,
   breaking into houses while the darkness lasts.
Is this not so? Who can prove me a liar
   or show that my words have no substance?
   (24:2-4, 9, 13-14, 16, 25).

Job's vision of this truth finally shatters his efforts to integrate reality with his *philosophical status quo ante*. He is telling it as it is, and his statements are incontrovertible. "The world is fraught with darkness," he asserts. "It is the mother of all the murderers, adulterers, criminals, and tyrants that roam its vastness...True", he says, "during daytime all is quiet and orderly, but when night falls, witness the emergence of the evil that can overtake men's souls."

Job ends his vision by issuing a powerful challenge. "If what I say is shown inaccurate, I am ready to relent to you, but first prove my words empty as I have proven yours to be false."

The polarization between Job's position and that of those who approach the world through their Logos is further dramatized in Chapter 25. With each moment that passes, Job becomes more convinced of his innocence, while Bildad grows increasingly convinced of his guilt and tells him, once more, to submit unquestionably to God.

His breath made the heavens luminous,
   his hand transfixed the Fleeing Serpent.
All this but skirts the way he treads,
   a whispered echo is all that we hear of him.
   But who could comprehend the thunder of his power? (26:13-14).

We are reminded that God reigns through fear and terror. No living creature has evaded this wrath. Compared to nature's fury, nothing we can conjure amounts to anything.

Job spoke next. He said:

To one so weak, what a help you are,
    for the arm that is powerless, what a rescuer!
What excellent advice you give the unlearned,
    never at a loss for a helpful suggestion!
But who are they aimed at, these speeches of yours,
    and what spirit is this that comes out of you? (26:1-4).

"Will you ever realize that I am a ruined man?" Job is forced, once again, to ask his friends whose commitment to Logos will stop all protest and questioning. "Don't you see that I need help and encouragement?"

A large part of *The Book of Job* details in this battle between Logos and Eros, friends full of platitudes and Job's wish for friends with heart. We may well ask why Job did not simply stop this after a few repetitions, and cast his friends out of his home. Clearly, he must unconsciously have agreed with some of their assessments, and he must have really had to struggle to overcome them in successive trials of strength. At one level, Job has been on both sides of an inner conflict, which the text illustrates in the repeated dialogues with the three friends, and he has been slowly and painfully making his way through it. Moreover, from a psychosocial perspective, Job, as emblematic of the human sufferer, has naturally been seeking external validation for his feelings. His exhortations against God would have been meaningless in private. Without witnesses to register his words and actions, his rebellion would have had no effect. He needed an audience to oppose him, to resist him vigorously, and, ultimately, to yield to him.

At Last, the Battle is Finally Over. Logos is Now Dethroned, and a More Blended and Integrated Psychospiritual State Emerges.

And Job continued his solemn discourse. He said:

I swear by the living God who denies me justice,
    by Shaddai who has turned my life sour,
that as long as a shred of life is left in me,
    and the breath of God breathes in my nostrils,
my lips shall never speak untruth,
    nor any lie be found on my tongue.
Far from ever admitting you to be in the right:
    I will maintain my innocence to my dying day.
I take my stand on my integrity, I will not stir:
    my conscience gives me no cause to blush for my life (27:1-6).

Job knows clearly now that for him to accept that he deserved what happened to him would have been an act of great cruelty against himself, an abuse to the heart. He will stand his ground and not falter no matter what, and he will again and ever more firmly, teach the others what reality is.

No: I am showing you how God's power works,
    making no secret of Shaddai's designs.
And if you all had understood them for yourselves,
    you would not have wasted your breath in empty words
    (27:11-12).

"Hashem is both light and dark. He rewards, punishes, and loves us unconditionally, while at the same time He doesn't care about us at all." God does not abide by mere human rules. No matter how you behave in the world, you will be rewarded or punished but you will never know why or when. "It is all senseless. This is the way it is, and you are simply unable to see it."

Zophar, in turn and once more, affirms the old conventional view of God's legalistic ways (27:13-24). "Here is the fate that God has in store for the wicked. A sword awaits his sons." But Job's understanding stands and its underlined meaning ("I am showing you how God's power really works") asserts convincingly his ultimate clarity about the primacy of fact over rationalization.

PART III

*THE REWARDS OF SURRENDER: WISDOM,
POWER, AND INTEGRATION AWAKE IN JOB*

Eleven

Job Begins To Appreciate Life From A Richer Perspective

The establishment of Eros as a ruling force in Job's psyche has opened up the gateways to understanding and transformed him from a knowledgeable and erudite man into a sentient and intuitive human being capable of connecting with his inner wisdom. Suddenly, as Job's thoughts, images, and dreams are moored to feelings and imbued with a purpose and meaning they lacked before, Job moves from a world of abstraction and swift rationalizations to a world of connectivity and lived reality. He is able to appreciate the richness of his inner world and the complexity of its workings.

Having access to our inner Eros allows us to stop groping around the world blindly, confused and utterly disconnected from our sources. We begin, instead, to learn mystically and intuitively about our awesome gifts. This access will eventually also permit us to trust what we so discover, and to heed that discovery. We are no longer blindfolded people following empty and uprooted thoughts, but rather warriors able to follow the dictates of our loving hearts. This surrendering to the wisdom of the body—the messages we receive continuously through our feelings, images, and sensations—opens the gateways to deeper realization and healing. We finally realize that the body is an exquisitely sensitive instrument, finely tuned to the countless messages it receives from within and without, attempting to guide our journey through life with accuracy and knowledge rooted in fact.

The culmination of the long battle we witnessed in Part II, and the establishment of a new order that includes and integrates the forces of Logos and Eros, leads us to anticipate the prompt appearance of deep understanding in the life of Job and all others who, like him, have been this fortunate. The vast knowledge they now touch was not unavailable or hidden from them before, as is evident in Chapters 2 and 7. It is only now, however, that this information is appreciated as a reflection of parts of themselves. By listening to his inner world, Job has earned the right to mine the depths of his personal and collective unconscious, and there discover awesome and vibrant truths.

What people feel when they first enter the realm of their unconscious, and their awareness moves beyond the confines of their objective world, is precisely expressed in metaphor when the poet declares:

Man makes an end of darkness
   when he pierces to the uttermost depths...
   in places where there is no foothold,
   and hangs suspended far from mankind (28:3, 4).

Through the piercing of the veils that separate us from the unconscious world (our darkness), we come in touch with our wisdom and our essence. There we discover that...

Silver has its mines,
   and gold a place for refining.
Iron is extracted from the earth,
   the smelted rocks yield copper.
That earth from which bread comes
   is ravaged underground by fire.
Down there is a path unknown to birds of prey,
   unseen by the eye of any vulture;

a path not trodden by the lordly beasts,
   where no lion ever walked.
Man attacks its flinty sides,
   upturning mountains by their roots,
driving tunnels through the rocks,
   on the watch for *anything* precious.
He explores the sources of rivers,
   and brings to daylight secrets that were hidden.
Perdition and Death can only say,
   "We have heard reports of it" (28:1-2, 5, 7-11,22).

Once we penetrate the great void and become accustomed to its stark vastness, we sense the presence of an awesome and mysterious force there, one able to answer the most difficult questions. We assume this force to be God's, so we ask:

...tell me, where does wisdom come from?
   Where is understanding to be found? (28:12).

At last, after a seeming endless wait, we hear a gentle but unmistakably clear voice that tells us assertively that the road to wisdom

...is still unknown to man,
   not to be found in the land of the living.
"It is not in me," says the Abyss;
   "Nor here" replies the Sea.
It cannot be bought with solid gold,
   not paid for with any weight of silver,
nor be priced by the standard of the gold of Ophir,
   or of precious onyx or sapphire (28:13-16).

What this inner voice is telling us is hard to accept. How can we acknowledge the existence of, let alone trust, a faraway and unknown wisdom, when all that has guided our lives thus far belongs in the land of sensorial living? While part of us has no alternative but to persist, probing for rational leads, hoping that sooner or later we will uncover the knowledge we so desperately seek, our more intuitive parts thrust us forward in search of the larger truth. With excitement and great anticipation, we ask again:

But tell me, where does wisdom come from?
  Where is understanding to be found? (28:20).

Silence follows, however, and after an interminable pause we hear
  the voice telling us:

It is outside the knowledge of every living thing...
God alone has traced its path
  and found out where it lives.
(For he sees to the ends of the earth,
  and observes all that lies under heaven.)
When he willed to give weight to the wind
  and measured out the waters with a gauge,
when he made the laws and rules for the rain
  and mapped a route for thunderclaps to follow,
then he had it in sight, and cast its worth,
  assessed it, fathomed it (28:21, 23-27).

Finally, and to our utter delight, an epiphany takes place and we receive the answer we so diligently sought:

"Wisdom? It is fear of the Lord.
Understanding?—avoidance of evil." (28:28).

Powerful revelations have emerged now from the unconscious world. "To fear God," we understand, means respecting the natural order of things and relinquishing arrogance and pretense when dealing with nature. Job's earlier story can be summed up in this pregnant phrase, for all Job's painful sufferings (including those forced on him by his "friends," or by society afterward) come from a lack of acceptance of the ways of the cosmos. This intolerance of life is a direct consequence of his inability to handle emotion. This is why Job could not avoid experiencing what happened to him as evil. How could he, if he had no capacity to integrate the despair certain life events provoke? Now that he is beginning to understand the awesome truth, and he is learning how to address his feelings constructively, he can conform to the larger reality within and without, and avoid evil. He now appreciates life's myriad expressions and is freer from denial and repression. As he becomes acutely aware of the effects that his actions have on himself, on his loved ones, and on his community, he understands that his behavior really matters, and this awareness encourages him to become fully invested in sustaining his life.

While the ways of the psyche include moments of sudden revelation that are singularly numinous, acceptance of what has been revealed is often difficult as is learning to use it practically. Accepting these revelations is like trying to alter the course of a large boat. It can be done, but not quickly. So Job turns from the wisdom he has heard, lapses back into regret at all he has lost, and laments his present condition:

Who will bring back to me the months that have gone,
    and the days when God was my guardian...
when Shaddai dwelt with me,
    and my children were around me;
when my feet were plunged in cream,
    and streams of oil poured from the rocks? (29:2, 5-6).

No one will do this for Job, and thank God for that. Job's righteousness is too tempting for Satan, and to recreate the conditions that led to his precipitous fall would certainly be disastrous. Job remembers now the fame and esteem he once enjoyed and hungers again for that kind of validation, but this is to no avail. He who was once a widely respected teacher, and a leader among his friends, has seen his self-esteem plummet and his requests for encouragement and support from his friends be fruitless. Hence, as no one comes forth to reassure him, he does so himself and, remembering, declaims:

In a lordly style, I told them which course to take,
    and like a king amid his armies,
    I led them where I chose.
My praises echoed in every ear,
    and never an eye but smiled on me (29:25, 11).

It is rather distressing to see again how the goodness that once suffused Job's existence lulls him back into believing he is exempt from suffering and turmoil. Hanging onto this naive assumption yet one more time, he states:

...because I freed the poor man when he called,
   and the orphan who had no one to help him.
I was eyes for the blind,
   and feet for the lame.
I used to break the fangs of wicked men,
   and snatch their prey from between their jaws.
So I thought to myself, "I shall die in honor,
   my days like a palm tree's for number.
My reputation will never fade,
   and the bow in my hands will gain new strength"
(29:12, 15, 17-18, 20).

Job had unfortunately convinced himself that he had found the way to circumvent nature's ruthlessness, and to live a life devoid of misery and loss. This illusion, however, was so much at odds with reality that the only course remaining to him was downhill. And downhill he went—but he went so far down that it felt as if he had fallen into a bottomless abyss. Now he knows that these were fantasies—the mental delusions of a naive person who is being scorned even by the children of people who he once considered inadequate and unworthy to be hired as his shepherds, people who had to scrounge out a desperate living in the hills and caves.

And now I am the laughingstock
   of my juniors, the young people,
whose fathers I did not consider fit
   to put with the dogs that looked after my flock.
...they made their dwellings on ravines' steep sides,
   in caves or clefts in the rock.
You could hear them wailing from the bushes,
   as they huddled together in the thistles (30:1, 6-7).

Amazingly, Job was more innocent and naive than the young children of the weak and homeless he had scorned. They had been forced at an early age to face life's realities and had lost their innocence young, while prosperous Job had managed to cling to his naiveté well into adulthood. It should not surprise us, then, to see Job branded the village idiot, a man whom everyone ridicules. Job had proved the point sustained by all those whose presence he so disdained: Goodness doesn't pay off. There is no reward for loyalty and righteousness.

Their children as worthless a brood as they were...
are the ones that now sing ballads about me,
   and make me the talk of the town!
To them I am loathsome, they stand aloof from me,
   do not scruple to spit in my face (30:8-10).

Job is angry at the children for making fun of him, but what else can he expect? He perceived himself as a loser after his fall, so everyone else naturally followed suit. The way we perceive ourselves powerfully influences the way we are perceived by others. "If you see yourself as a victim, expect victimization," says the rule. If we pretend to be martyrs, we should expect martyrdom. What is most remarkable, however, is that we still act surprised when our lives work out in this predictable way. "I can't understand," exclaimed Job, "why I am being treated this way," and in a long rehearsal of his affliction and of his former virtuous acts and habits, he presses again his appeal for answers.

I cry to you, and you give me no answer...
Yet have I ever laid a hand on the poor
   when they cried out for justice in calamity?
I have become the jackal's brother
   and the ostrich's companion.
My harp is tuned to funeral wails,
   my flute to the voice of mourners (30:20, 24, 29, 31).

We are remarkably slow to understand the messages our unconscious world shows us. Job, who has been through a long and tortuous journey, is beginning to see the light and to experience the wisdom revealed. Nonetheless, he is still unable to see his own shadow. This is why, as he connects with the inner self, he uses the opportunity to press his innocence even harder, hoping perhaps for an acknowledgment of God's wrongdoing:

Now, what shares does God deal out on high,
    what lots does Shaddai assign from heaven,
if not disaster for the wicked,
    and calamities for the iniquitous?
But surely he sees how I behave,
    does he not count all my steps?
If he weighs me on honest scales,
    being God, he cannot fail to see my innocence.
Have I ever seen a wretch in need of clothing,
    or a beggar going naked,
without his having cause to bless me from his heart,
    as he felt the warmth of the fleece from my lambs?
·Have I raised my hand against the guiltless,
    presuming on my credit at the gate?
If so, then let my shoulder fall from its socket,
    my arm be shattered at the joint.
God's terror would indeed descend on me;
    how could I hold my ground before his majesty?
(31:2-4, 6, 19-23).

Cycling and recycling through the psychological process of his personal liberation, Job once more returns to earlier stages, and reminds God again of all the good deeds he has done on behalf of the poor. His life was truly beyond reproach. So how could Hashem fail to consider the type of person Job had been before dispensing His punishment? In such repeated cycles, particularly in the long middle section of *The Book of Job*, the work imitates, and evokes, the turnings and returnings that are typical of all organic growth, especially the evolution of consciousness both in the individual and in humankind as a whole. Among psychotherapists, the patterns of patients' progress are proverbial: "two steps forward and one step back" and of repeated "working through" (the image is one of turning a difficult screw with repeated efforts of the wrist, hand, and arm) of old and new psychological material. This repetitive process goes on, until, finally, the old inner ways are largely worn away and new realizations become mainly dominant. But, as we all know, regressions can occur at even advanced stages—indeed, *The Book of Job* opens with the apparent successful temptation of God Himself, not once but twice. The circling of Dante's exploration in his descent into Hell and the symmetrical upward windings round and round through Purgatory to Heaven also imitate this same psychospiritual process of revolution. So do Job's repeated encounters with his friends, and his later backslidings mirror the uncertain though decisive, progress of the psyche.

Job once again appeals for an audience with God, a confrontation, a way out of seeking explanations by himself. "Most likely, I will not agree with the explanations God has to offer," he murmurs to himself, "but at least the guessing game will be over, and I shall be able to move on. Until then, I am at the mercy of my vivid imagination and feel oppressed and restless. Can someone help me? Can someone teach me how to find Him and His wisdom? Can someone show me the secret way to His palace?"

I have had my say... now let Shaddai answer me (31:35).

Twelve

God Speaks Through the Voice of Elihu

Iyov, the warrior, is a key psychological resource for healing. His emergence prepares the way for Job to hear truth and receive divine revelation. Elihu now appears in the text as another friend of Job, but he represents the wise, enlightened teacher who will serve as a conduit for the expression of Higher Wisdom. Through Elihu, who symbolizes Job's own ability to uncover truth, Job will open to new frontiers of knowledge and understanding, and be further inducted into higher states of consciousness.

Throughout his ordeal, Job has staunchly maintained his innocence and resisted his friends' attempts to sway him. His three friends spoke three times each, nine speeches altogether, and then they abandoned their efforts. One more effort is made, and this one is the real thing—the voice of Higher Wisdom channeled through a capable vessel. Elihu, the fourth man, delivers the tenth and climactic speech. Having witnessed what he sees as Job's contempt toward God intensify, Elihu is filled with animus: He fumes with rage against Job for thinking that he was right and God was wrong; he was equally angry with the other

three friends for giving up the argument and thus implicitly admitting
that God could be unjust (32:2,3).

Thus Elihu son of Barachel the Buzite spoke next. He said:

I am still young,
  and you are old,
so I was shy, afraid,
  to tell you what I know.
I told myself, "Old age should speak,
  advancing years will utter wisdom."
But now I know that it is a breath in man,
  the inspiration of Shaddai, that gives discernment.
Great age does not give wisdom,
  nor longevity sound judgment.
And so I ask you for a hearing
  now it is my turn to tell what I know (32:6-10).

Job has been seeking a hearing with Hashem, and that is what he
gets in the person of Elihu. Yet at first he can't perceive it as such. Job
is still looking for a burning bush, for something dramatic and miraculous, to bear witness to God's presence. But "Eli-hu," the bearer of
divine wisdom, stands directly before him. In Hebrew, *Elihu* is the
conjoining of the two words: *Eli*, which means *my God*, and *Hu*,
which means he, hence *my God, he is!* When Elihu speaks, therefore,
God Himself is speaking through him.

Like Job, all of us, including my patients, are frequently blinded to
the wonderful sources of wisdom and support that surround us (in
our spouses, children, friends, and others). We spend years, even decades, searching for these sources elsewhere. At last, when our minds
open up to the truth, we look at our circumstances and frequently find
what we so intently searched for everywhere but at home.

*Higher Wisdom Rebukes Job's Friends' Rigid Positions and Also Job's
Assertions of Innocence.*

There was a time when I hoped for much from your speeches:
  I gave your reasonings a ready hearing,
  and watched you choose your words.

I gave you all my attention,
   and I can say that no one gave Job the lie,
   not one of you disproved his statements.
So do not dare to say that you have found wisdom,
   or that your teaching is from God not man.
I am not going to follow the same line of argument;
   my reply to Job will be couched in different terms.
For I am filled with words,
   choked by the rush of them within me.
I have a feeling in my heart like new wine seeking a vent,
   and bursting a brand-new wineskin (32:11-14,18,19).

"I thought you insightful and wise," Elihu tells the three sages in these words, "but I misjudged you. You know nothing of God's nature or of the way in which He works, and your ignorance is damaging."

Emphasizing that his understanding of Job's suffering differs from that expressed by the three friends, Elihu prepares the stage for his powerful revelations by stating that the raw, unadulterated truth, the world according to God, will now be revealed:

Now, Job, be kind enough to listen to my words,
   and attend to all I have to say.
...my heart shall utter sayings full of wisdom,
   and my lips speak the honest truth.
How could you say in my hearing—
   for the sound of your words did not escape me—
"I am clean, and sinless,
   I am pure, free of all fault.
Yet he is inventing grievances against me,
   and imagining me his enemy.
He puts me in the stocks,
   he watches my every step?"
In saying so, I tell you, you are wrong:
   God does not fit man's measure (33:1, 3, 8-12).

"How can you be so naive as to maintain that you are clean and sinless?" Elihu/Hashem[6] asks Job. "Certainly I am aware of all those deeds you have done for others, but I am also aware of what those deeds bespoke: You were fearful of my wrath, for example, and ironically fearful of precisely that which has befallen you! Your exemplary behavior thus did not stem from any attunement to life's grand complexities (so often symbolized in nature—a crystal, a leaf, the course of the sun, the stars) but was rather a byproduct of your small anxieties and pedestrian concerns. I was not impressed by all those sacrifices, I can tell you.

"And there is the darker side, too: Can you recall the murders you have committed in your sleep? Don't think for a moment that I knew nothing of them. And what of the lies and adulterous relationships in which you have engaged so profligately and the perjury you have committed day after day within the sanctum of your inner world? And can you recall the repression and torture to which you subjected your enemies in your daydreams? Perhaps others were fooled, but not me. I know well your complexity, including your pretense of simplicity and innocence.

"All of nature seeks a dynamic balance of its forces and you must do the same: When I say 'God does not fit man's measure,' I mean that life and nature and you yourself are mysteries to be discovered and then the parts harmonized as best one can. No more blindness, Job. Become God-like in seeking your whole Self."

* * * * * * * * * * * * * * *

I have been working with a man who, like Job, believes himself good, honest, moral, and pious. His brightness, he thinks, leaves no shadow, and he feels he is a man incapable of voluntary wrongdoing. God and other people must surely look on such a man with delight and favor. In fact, however, the man has only the most formal relations with people. He has been divorced twice, and he is left to face the ordeal of his illness and treatment with no one to love or support him. Ironically, his unwillingness or inability to acknowledge those hidden parts of himself that are not perfect is the cause of his aloneness. He is unable to say, for example, "*I am scared of intimacy, I feel insecure in social situations, I believe there is something rotten in me that I do not want others to see*," and so forth. He is someone who cannot accept his psychological limitations and in particular his capacity to abuse or cause injury and hurt to others. Naturally, in relationships with others, such people do not conceive that the pain and distress others may experience with them is in many ways linked to their own behavior. They deny the other person's feelings, project blame outwardly, or simply claim that because their actions were well-intentioned, their conscience is clean.

The human psyche, in its relentless pursuit of balance, cannot tolerate such disequilibriums. It searches for creative ways to compensate for them. Ideally, people whose psyche follows this path (we can call them the "Innocents") recognize their condition and learn to undo some of the damage they inevitably cause. Denying their own vulnerability and repressed fury, they project these traits outwardly. They are responsible for the failures of relationships. And others are all too often caught up in the transaction: Angry at the Innocent's lack of candor and vulnerability, driven to fury, they become the very projections of the innocent's shadow: critical, short-tempered, irrational. Until these people can successfully retrieve the energetic field they have projected onto others and liberate those others from the need to enact what they themselves have not been able to acknowledge, there will be no peace. At most, there can be a psychological pseudo-balance. This occurs often when the spouses and children of such people manifest deep insecurities and uncertainties about their own value and importance. Confronted with a spouse or parent that is all good, right, and righteous, they label themselves as the opposite, and they often end up behaving that way. Someone has to balance the energy of nature.

According to Jung's psychological rule, psychic material that remains concealed from our conscious awareness will manifest itself in our lives as fate.[7] Jung alludes here to the existence of a system of inner forces seeking balance and wholeness. Behaviors that may be harmful to an individual do equilibrate something in society that is out of harmony. Accordingly, when examining the life of any individual, we must also examine the lives of all those who are intimate with that person if we want to have an accurate perspective. It is not that a person's children, spouse, relatives, and friends are themselves innocent bystanders to what happens to them, or that they are mere victims of the psychological limitations of those around them. In fact, it is quite the opposite. We are all masters of our lives, and it is incumbent upon us to transcend the restrictions and challenges life places in front of us to the best of our capacity. But as long as there is denial of our complex richness (like nature's own) all our lives will be strongly influenced, and even determined, by invisible forces we feel we cannot control.

Such has been Job's fate until now, and to avoid a similar fate we must know, and then integrate, all the dimensions of our own psychic lives. In fact, each of us is a family of internal psychic beings that need validation, tolerance, and creative blending. We are physical/instinctual beings concerned with survival, sexual and sensual beings who need to create and procreate, emotional beings responding to inner and outer stimuli with diverse feelings, speaking beings who can communicate and cooperate with each other, mental/intellectual beings who have the awesome attributes of thinking and self-awareness, and spiritual beings whose lives have meaning and who can appreciate a transpersonal and transcendental reality. When such complexity is acknowledged and balanced, the human being arrives at a habitual state of love, compassion, and immense tolerance, an energetic state of being human that is unconditional and capable of embracing all of God's creation. Within such psychological balance, all that we are is accepted and appreciated in its proper place, and we become the directors of an inner orchestra that is fully integrated and can produce the most beautiful and breathtaking music we shall ever hear. The experience of this inner harmony is part of what the ancients meant when they spoke of the heavenly "music of the spheres."

* * * * * * * * * * * * * * *

Elihu continues:

Why do you rail at him
    for not replying to you, word for word?

God speaks first in one way,
   and then in another, but not one notices.
He speaks by dreams, and visions that come in the night,
   when slumber comes on mankind
   and men are all asleep in bed.
Then it is he who whispers in the ear of man,
   or may frighten him with fearful sights,
to turn him away from evil-doing,
   and make an end of his pride;
to save his soul from the pit
   and his life from the pathway to Sheol (33:13-18).

The multiplicity of God's being (and hence of nature and of the psyche) implied in the strikingly simple assertion "God does not fit man's measure" has as a necessary corollary the notion that God's communication with man takes place through multiple means. Job has not been listening with all his capacities. "Are you merely an objective being void of an inner life?" inquires Elihu/Hashem. "Are you purely a product of your sensations? Don't you have dreams, intuitions, and feelings? I express myself in the external world; you can see my handicraft all around you. But my home, my holiest of holies—these you can find only deep within you. So waste no more time, Job. If you indeed want to find me, look inside. Don't let fear deter you from journeying therein. The sooner you do so, the faster you will discover that I am there waiting for you."

"You have bitterly claimed that I have failed to answer your prayers and invocations. This is not so. Can you remember last night's dream, and your dreams of a week or a month ago, and even those you experienced before tragedy befell you? Do you remember how many times I warned you of the distress that plagued your inner world and how vividly I illustrated the dangers that lurked there? Who do you think fashioned those dreams and imbued you with those insights? Yet despite my efforts, all you found appropriate to do was offer sacrifices for the sins you feared your children might have committed. Not once did you look into your heart and see that it was you who was straying from my path."

"Listen to me, Job; calm yourself. When you speak so loud, you can't hear my voice or heed my counsel. You are no more what you assume yourself to be than I am what you would like me to be. So listen attentively and learn!"

* * * * * * * * * * * * * * * *

To be detached from our dreams is akin to being blind, deaf, and mute, all at the same time. Our dreams, which are indeed the royal road to our unconscious, give honest insight into the foundation of our being in the world: our psyche. Through our dreams we can learn about the hidden forces that drive our daily lives and what our total personality needs. Just as we can make no assessment of the well-being of the physical body by a strictly sensorial inspection, making an assessment of the status and evolution of the psyche by relying exclusively on the answers that the rational mind can give to our questioning and probing is also inadequate. To understand the workings of our psychic world, we need to contact our dreams, our intuitive insights, and our imagination.

Once we become aware of how critically important our dreams are to full living, any previous idea that we could lead a truly healthy and wholesome life based only on sense data and reason falls by the way. With dismay and amazement, we discover that the beliefs we held about our health and well-being were partial and inaccurate—the artificial creations of our intellectual self meant to protect us from truth. Similarly, we realize that to be good, obedient, and proper toward authority figures (be they parents, political, religious, or medical figures) beyond childhood does not protect us from the ruthlessness of living, or from disease or death. Then our posturing about how righteous we are ceases immediately. In these moments of deep revelation, we feel exposed and vulnerable to God's scorching light. This is why, when we learn with Job to appreciate the meaning of Elihu's first speeches (that God speaks to us and guides our healing efforts through our dreams and intuitions), all else Elihu says from then on has a special sense. When Elihu speaks, he speaks of, from, and to the inside of us. Even when some of his words superficially resemble those of the other three friends, "ignorant and misguided by cruel men," from Elihu's mouth even these statements are full of deeper meaning, and Job understands them as such; so should we.

Elihu turns to Job again and, noticing his pain, he says:

With suffering, too, he corrects man on his sickbed,
  when his bones keep trembling with palsy;
when his whole self is revolted by food,
  and his appetite spurns dainties;
when his flesh rots as you watch it,
  and his bare bones begin to show;
when his soul is drawing near to the pit,
  and his life to the dwelling of the dead (33:19-22).

"Human suffering does not keep me from teaching or from attempting to heal the world in which you live," asserts Elihu/Hashem. "Suffering cures your ills even in your sickbed. If suffering is what it takes to accomplish my ends and nothing else will do, then suffering it shall be. Yet I am anything but ruthless. I am more accurately defined as determined and relentless. How many times did I warn you of your plight? How many signs did I send you? And what of all the precognitions that were intended to alert and advise you of your impending fate? All were ignored, summarily dismissed as detritus from your daily life, to be disposed of as quickly as possible. Don't you have any recollection of all my efforts on your behalf?"

Then there is an Angel by his side,
  a Mediator, chosen out of thousands,
to remind a man where his duty lies,
  to have pity on him and to say,
"Release him from descent into the pit
  for I have found a ransom for his life" (33:23,24).

"Please, Job, pay attention to your angels[8], those wondrous creatures I have created to serve as intermediaries between your world and mine. Because I am too powerful, too raw, and at times too overwhelming for you to perceive directly, they are the entities who make it possible for our worlds to blend together. Without them, chaos would reign forever in your universe." From a psychological standpoint, what Elihu tells Job is that he must open his mind beyond mere rationality to messages from his unconscious and all its contents, in particular its Higher Wisdom. Job must learn to allow these messages into his conscious awareness, to listen with an inner ear and see with inner eyes what this mediating function in himself can say to him. The results can be transforming. As William James noted, *"there are men who are born once and then there are the twice born.".*[9] Through the operations of the angel, our lives can be renewed and restored to wellness.

...his flesh recovers the bloom of its youth,
   he lives again as he did when he was young.
He prays to God who has restored him to favor,
   and comes, in happiness, to see his face.
He publishes far and wide the news of his vindication,
   singing before his fellow men this hymn of praise,
"I sinned and left the path of right,
   but God has not punished me as my sin deserved.
He has spared my soul from going down into the pit,
   and is allowing my life to continue in the light."
All this God does
   again and yet again for man,
rescuing his soul from the pit,
   and letting the light of life shine bright on him (33:25-30).

"When man strays, I bend over backward to help him see his error," proclaims Elihu/Hashem. "He may at times experience great suffering. Yet it is precisely this suffering that acts as man's saving grace, that allows him to embrace his freedom. It is not the only path I have made available for man to reach wholeness," He insists, "but it is certainly the one most commonly traveled."

Job has finally found his way into the great unconscious, where he is connecting with Higher Wisdom. Yet trusting what he learns is still difficult. The drama of self-redemption continues. Indeed, when wisdom derives from a mortal source, why should it be heeded? Job evidently remains incredulous, and Elihu must call him back from his wandering doubts.

Job, give me your attention,
  listen well; keep silence: I have more to say.
If you have anything to say, refute me,
  speak out, for I would gladly recognize your innocence.
If you have not, then listen:
  keep silence, while I teach you wisdom (33:31-33).

With an implicitly growing acceptance of the wisdom of Elihu/ Hashem, Job keeps silent, refocused, as his teacher continues. Such silent receptiveness is an essential practice for the evolution of spiritual wholeness. We learn to be quiet and thereby open to bigger truths than our personal intellects or society's various voices can describe.

Elihu continues his speech. He says:

You men of wisdom, listen to my words:
  lend me your ears, you learned men.
Let us discover together where justice lies,
  and settle among us what is best.
Now Job has said, "I am in the right,
  and God refuses to grant me justice.
The judge who judges me is ill-disposed,
  and though I have not sinned, my wounds are past all cure."
Listen then to me, like intelligent men.
So far is God removed from wickedness,
  and Shaddai from injustice,
that he requites a man for what he does,
  treating each one as his way of life deserves.
God never does wrong, do not doubt that!
  Shaddai does not deflect the course of right.
If you have any intelligence, listen to this,
  and lend your ear to what I have to say.
Could an enemy of justice ever govern?
  Would you dare condemn the Just One, the Almighty,

who can tell kings that they are good for nothing,
   and treat noblemen like criminals,
who shows no partiality to princes
   and makes no distinction between the rich and the poor,
all alike being made by his own hands?
You may say, "They have so turned from him,
   and so ignored his ways,
that the poor have cried out to him against them
   and the wailing of the humble has assailed his ears,
yet he is unmoved, and nothing can touch him;
   he hides his face and nobody can see him."
But nonetheless he does take pity on nations and on men,
   freeing the godless man from the meshes of distress (34:1, 2, 4-6,
   10-12, 16-19, 27-30).

"You men of wisdom have proven yourselves to be imprudent and unwise," asserts Elihu/Hashem. You have failed in your attempt to enlighten Job about the misery that surrounded him. Why did this happen? Why were you unable to offer my servant guidance and support? It is because you responded out of fear and sheer ignorance. Your grave mistake was to suggest that I operate out of capricious choice, dogmatically, rather than in response to each one's way of life.

"I, Hashem, the overseer of the universe, could not operate out of choice or capriciousness; this would make the world far too erratic and cause profound dislocations in the way life flows. To the contrary, I respond reliably, faithfully, and consistently in accordance with my stated precepts.

"Have you seen anything in nature that functions capriciously? Everything that is inborn to humankind operates in keeping with predetermined and precisely defined patterns that lie largely beyond the realm of volitional control. My servant Einstein could not have put it more lucidly when he stated, 'God does not play dice with the cosmos.'

"The world in which you live is not unpredictable at all because my actions are not determined by choice. Please understand this if you want to appreciate my reality: I have no choice in what I do. I, the supervisor of the universe, am both responsive to and dependent on what you do. The problem you face in understanding my acts is that you have superimposed human standards on them, and in so doing have sown grave misunderstanding."

* * * * * * * * * * * * * * * * *

As we have seen, when Elihu/Hashem speaks to Job, he is reflecting the realities of the world within, a world in which the conventional morality that supports objective, social life does not necessarily apply. This is why, regardless of what we may have been forcing ourselves to enact objectively, it may not be perceived in the same vein when scrutinized internally. For example, motivation is critical in analyzing the moral basis of an action. We may make a show of being humble, only to save our pride; we may give alms, only to show our wealth; we may do good not from love of it but out of fear or social conformity or ignorant habits. In this regard we may find that people who seem objectively good and righteous to others may be correctly perceived from an internal standpoint as insensitive to others and cruel to themselves. This is why Elihu/Hashem can question Job's behavior and suggest that *"Job drinks scurrility like water and keeps company with evildoers marching in step with the wicked"* (34:7,8). If Elihu/Hashem were to speak about Job's objective life, the social mask he wears for others, then these statements would be as vicious and misguided as those of Job's three friends. But here they are accurate, because Elihu/ Hashem is reflecting the world of inner truth he so eloquently endorsed when reminding Job how Hashem spoke to people in dreams and through frightening sights, to turn them away from evil-doing and to make an end of their pride (33:15-17).

From the standpoint of psychology, including the psychology of our higher nature, Hashem takes the form in Elihu of Higher Wisdom. This is an internal system of supervision and regulation that coordinates the psychic life of each of us. This system is innate and integral to our wellness and reflects an inner reality that we are constantly being prompted to experience and engage. "God," from this point of view, represents the highest capacity that has emerged as man's psychological complexity has increased through time.[10]

Once a person can appreciate that his or her psychic life is indeed supervised from within by a Higher Wisdom, Elihu's words to Job in verse nine become clear: "How can you say it is useless for man to try to please God?" If God is ever-present, and the parameters for His supervision and regulation are predictable and stable, then we may anticipate how the supervisory function will proceed most of the time, and it would be important to "please God." In the same vein, and as long as we don't superimpose a moralistic perspective or a human timetable for "God's" enactment of His supervisory and regulating functions, all shall remain well, and we can easily accept the validity of Elihu's description of Hashem as always "just."

Finally, the last verses of this chapter reveal the key to psychospiritual redemption—our capacity to repair our soul. Verses 30-33 tell us that God responds with compassion to an honest acknowledgement of wrongdoing, and He offers immediate comfort and solace.

But nonetheless, He does take pity on nations and on men,
    freeing the godless man from the meshes of distress.
If such a man says to God,
"I was led astray, I will sin no more.
If I did wrong, tell me about it,
    if I have been unjust, I will be so no more—
in such a case do you think he ought to punish him,
    you who reject his decisions? (34:30-33).

Job and His Friends are Naive About Their Impact on Higher Wisdom

Elihu continues his relentless questioning of Job, challenging his assertion that God is independent of humankind and hence unaffected by his deeds. He says,

Do you presume to maintain that you are in the right,
    to insist on your innocence before God,
even to ask him, "How does it affect you,
    what harm has it done you if I have sinned?"

Well then, this is how I will answer you,
   and your friends as well.
Look up at the skies, look at them well,
   and see how high the clouds are above you.
If you sin, what do you achieve against him?
   If you heap up crimes, what is the injury you do him?
If you are just, what do you give him,
   what benefit does he receive at your hands?
Your fellow men are the ones to suffer from your crimes,
   humanity is the gainer if you are good.
How idle to maintain that God is deaf,
   that Shaddai notices nothing!
You even claim, "He does not see me:
   my cause is exposed before him, and yet I wait and wait."
Or even, "His anger never punishes,
   he does not seem to know of men's rebellion" (35:2-8, 13-15).

"How innocent you must be to cling to your belief that I am auton-
omous of you," replies Elihu/Hashem. "How can I oversee your world,
my creation, and remain independent of your acts? If I see your every
action, how could your deeds fail to affect my responses? But these
actions do not change me, instead they change the fate of humanity.
Whatever happens to me in response to your actions is ultimately
expressed in you," says Elihu/Hashem. "I pass it on; nothing remains
with me. If your acts evoke my mercy, then your world is filled with
joy; if your acts inspire my wrath, then you experience my punitive
hand. This is how it is, and there is no way you can change it."

   With the incisiveness that characterizes a wisdom undeterred by
pretense and false posturing, Elihu explains Job's despair.

...when Job opens his mouth, it is for idle talk:
   his spate of words comes out of ignorance (35:16).

Ignorance can be devastating to our health and well-being. It de-
prives us of the right attitude we need to cope with life and its hazards.
God's world seems unforgiving to those who remain blind and innocent. Ignorance of the world's potential hurts may be bliss during

childhood, but it is a state we must transcend if we are to avoid the devastating psychological consequences that await us later on when we are not handled so gently by life.

Job Has Completed a Critical Sequence of Psychospiritual Unfolding and Now Has the Resources to Find out the Meaning of What Happened to Him and Why it Had to Happen.

Elihu is preparing to reveal to Job the truth underlying the events that have affected him so profoundly. It is not what Job had hoped to hear, but it will restore meaning to his world. Job is instructed to look with an inner eye and see underneath the appearances of events. What is said from now on is symbolic of our inner life and the only way to our real happiness, which is spiritual. Like many splendid teachers, in times past and after, Elihu speaks figuratively in defense of "God's" justice, but what is meant is psychological: Disconnection from Self is the cause of what we call sins; ignorance of Self runs us into the wall of disaster.

Elihu went on speaking. He said:

What I say contains no fallacies, I assure you,
    you see before you an enlightened man.
God does not spurn the blameless man
    or let the sinner live on in all his power.
He accords justice to the poor,
    and upholds the good man's rights.
When he raises kings to thrones,
    if they grow proud of their unending sway,
then he fetters them with chains,
    binding them in the bondage of distress.
He shows them all that they have done,
    and all the sins of pride they have committed.
He whispers a message in their ears,
    urging them to amend themselves.

If they listen and do as he says,
  their days end in happiness,
  and their closing years are full of ease.
If not, then a thunderbolt destroys them,
  and death comes on them unawares.
Yes the stubborn who cherish anger,
  and when he shackles them, do not ask for help:
they die in their youth,
  or lead a life despised by all.
The wretched, however, he saves by their very wretchedness,
  and uses distress to open their eyes (36:1, 4-15).

"I am not the way you see me, but I am exactly as I said I would be," says Elihu/Hashem in his commanding voice. "If you perceive only the obvious, then you will see things as you see them now. Yet that is but one aspect of my world, and it is a minuscule one. It is neither what sustains nor what supports all that I have created. If, however, you look deep within the recesses of your soul, you will know that those who seem to be thriving on the outside (as you once did) are full of cruelty and repression on the inside (as you once were). In like manner, you will know that those who suffer, who are reviled by all and perceived by others as lesser, can eventually attain enlightenment and inner peace (as you are now experiencing). All those years you were good—or, rather, fearful of being bad—you were never with me. You were ridden with worry and anxiety; you could not hear or be close to me. It is only now, by virtue of all the painful things that have happened to you, that we are beginning to blend and that you are becoming whole.

"As you open to the richness of the world I have created, you will see that it indeed operates in total congruency with the principles I handed down to my servant Moses in Sinai.[11] This is the meaning of your suffering: You were alienated and detached from me. Sooner or later you would have to become unsettled, and then you would come back to me. This is the nature of a loving, and caring 'supervisor,' to be yearning for your return, waiting for you to be ready.

"Do you remember the many things you were passive about? True, your generosity toward the poor, the ill, and the dispossessed was commendable. But most if not all of that stemmed from fear of your own nature. You knew quite well what you held within and the acts you were capable of committing. Your passivity, your fear, and your arrogance injured many, primarily you. That is why you could never be free enough to know me, to live fully in the luminous inner world I bequeathed to you."

Elihu goes on to explain, once again symbolically, just how Job's detachment from inner life led him to experience the terrible sufferings he has recently endured.

Once you lived in luxury unbounded,
 with rich food piled high on your table.
But you did not execute justice on the wicked,
 you cheated orphaned children from their rights.
In future beware of being led astray by riches,
 or corrupted by fat bribes.
Prosecute the rich, not merely the penniless;
 strong-armed men as well as those who are powerless.
Do not trample on those you do not know
 to install your relations in their place.
Avoid any tendency to wrong-doing,
 for such has been the true cause of your trials (36:16-21).

Here Elihu is like an interpreting Rabbi, or any other kind of gifted and forceful preacher, repeating well-worn doctrinal platitudes but leaning forward as he does so, gazing into Job's eyes, insisting with every intonation on the deeper subjective meaning. This call to special attention echoes in repeated statements: "What I say contains no fallacies. I am an enlightened man." Out of this insistence, the true meaning emerges: If you want to understand and to find harmony, stop searching for answers outside yourself. Rather, look toward your inner family, your inner children, your elders and parents, brothers and sisters. How have they lived in your home? Have they been nourished, cared for, attended? Or have they felt like orphans wanting for care and compassion? And what of your inner garden, the one I gave you to keep and cultivate? Have you tended it, or have you allowed its flowers to wither and die? Were you distracted from self-awareness by riches? Did you lose yourself by being impressed by strength and kinship?

"Remember, Job: As long as you see only the outside world and believe it is the only world that counts, you will miss most of me and forever remain vulnerable to my fire. My divine creation—the world of your senses—is itself nothing less than a mirror image of the world within, a reminder of inner forces, inner laws, and inner powers. See this world in a symbolic light." Elihu goes on to describe this world.

...the greatness of God exceeds our knowledge,
  the number of his years is past computing.
He it is who keeps the raindrops back,
  dissolving the showers into mist,
And who can fathom how he spreads the clouds,
  or why such crashes thunder from his tent? (36:26, 27, 29).

The description continues in Chapter 37.

Listen, oh listen, to the blast of his voice
  and the sound that blares from his mouth.
He hurls his lightning below the span of heaven,
  it strikes to the very ends of the earth.
After it comes the roar of his voice,
  the peal of God's majestic thunder.
He does not check his thunderbolts
  until his voice resounds no more.
No doubt of it, but God reveals wonders,
  and does great deeds that we cannot understand,
When he says to the snow, "Fall on the earth,"
  or tells the rain to pour down in torrents,
he brings all men's strivings to a standstill
  so that each must acknowledge his hand at work.
God breathes, and the ice is there,
  the surface of the waters freezes over.

He weighs the clouds down with moisture,
  and the storm clouds radiate his lightning.
He himself guides their wheeling motion,
  directing all their seasonal changes:
they carry out his orders to the letter
  all over his inhabited world (37:2-7, 10-12).

Such verses symbolize the power, majesty, complexity, and order of
the Self—our inner richness and our inner wisdom. All that has been
described as taking place thus far in *The Book of Job* now reaches its
climactic revelation. When we are witnesses to the revelation of truth
(divine truth) it is as if we had walked through a door that, once passed
through, closes behind us permanently, preventing us from turning
back. There is an irreversibility associated with genuine personal transformation, and this explains why one of the most frequent comments
I hear from people thrust into a healing journey is "My bubble has
been burst and there is no way to reverse this. I can't go back to the
way I lived before." This is why Elihu tells Job emphatically,

Listen to all this Job: no backsliding now!
  Meditate on God's wonders.
Can you tell how God controls them
  or how his clouds make the lightning flash?
Can you tell how he holds the clouds in balance:
  a miracle of consummate skill?
Tell me what to say to him:
Can my words carry weight with him?
  Do man's commands reach his ears?
There are times when the light vanishes
  behind darkening clouds;
then comes the wind, sweeping them away,
  and brightness spreads from the north.
God is clothed in fearful splendor:
  he, Shaddai, is far beyond our reach.
Supreme in power, in equity,
  excelling in justice, yet no oppressor—
no wonder that men fear him,
  and thoughtful men hold him in awe (37:14-16, 19-24).

We can sense here the psychospiritual stage of the final dying of Job's naive child, the one who feared "God," in the sense of the great reality within which we live, and who perceived himself as a victim of His wrath (37:24). Job is now in what the sages described as "the alchemical vessel," completing his rebirth.[12] He is preparing to receive the raw, primordial force of the inner and outer divine directly, this time without benefit of intermediaries. Elihu/Hashem has symbolized Higher Wisdom, speaking to Job from outside himself. Elihu had the resourcefulness to be such a conduit; Job did not. He could not grasp the divine essence directly until he died to his old self, and only then did a new being emerge—one capable of containing Higher Wisdom. Now there will be no need for filters, for buffers, or for interpreters. Now Job is to hear and see God firsthand, from within, uniting with essence. Job has transformed completely, and is awestruck by feeling the power of God moving in the vastness of his hitherto lonely inner universe.

Thirteen

God the Creator/ Destroyer Speaks Directly to Job

During the initial stages of his journey, Job was able to access the closest layers of his personal unconscious. He discovered some answers there, but nothing he found was strong or encompassing enough to suit his needs for ultimate answers and peace. Later, he entered the farther layers of the unconscious and connected with Higher Wisdom there, but whenever he tried to repeat this experience at will, he failed. Finally, when Elihu/Hashem progressively revealed God's truth to him, Job's psyche was inducted into a higher and transcendental level of consciousness. As the intermediary stops speaking, God erupts into words from the heart of Job's inner turmoil and begins to pose questions to him:

Where were you when I laid the earth's foundations?
　Tell me, since you are so well informed!
What supports its pillars at their bases?
　Who laid its cornerstone

when all the stars of the morning were singing with joy,
and the Sons of God in chorus were chanting praise?
Have you ever in your life given orders to the morning
or sent the dawn to its post...
Have you journeyed all the way to the sources of the sea,
or walked where the Abyss is deepest?
Have you been shown the gates of Death
or met the janitors of Shadowland? (38:4, 6, 7, 12, 16, 17).

Whenever I introduce patients to healing work, I alert them to the dangers and perils they may encounter there. "All your life will come up for review and consideration," I remind them. "Your marriage, your work, the many choices you have made in your life, all will be re-evaluated, and summarily re-assessed by your own mind. Are you prepared to confront your inner demons, the psychic configurations that have remained relegated to the recesses of your unconscious for all these years? Are you ready to take off the masks you wear for protection and look at your naked face?" Unfortunately, most people who express a desire to enter into a healing journey do not realize what this entails. I ask these people to be aware that knowledge can burn them, force them to act, entertain possibilities that may run counter to their pragmatic and objectivistic lifestyles. "What will happen if you discover that your marriage is stale and deadening?" I ask these patients. "Would you let go of it? And what if your heart tells you to leave your work and your home? Would you do it? And if you are not prepared to entertain any of these possibilities, then why know?"

These warnings anticipate the remarkable shift in consciousness and energy flows that all those immersed in healing work notice as their process deepens and they experience the revelations of truth. Until then, these sufferers occupied the developmental place of victims, pointing their accusatory fingers to God and posing challenging questions to Him. Now, however, it is Higher Wisdom who is asking them the challenging questions. Having their ignorance and detachment from life fully exposed, their psyche is flooded with a ton of queries. "Where were you when the disease was developing?" their inner voices ask them. "Why did you not see the lump on your neck faster? How did you not know about the turmoil and the inner distress surrounding your existence? How could you have been so naive to believe yourself invulnerable to the disease you investigated and treated each day of your life?" and so forth.

Of the many questions posed to me as my journey unfolded, and the one I had to address almost immediately, was whether my marriage had contributed to the illness I developed. At the time this perturbing question was formulated, I was in a no-man's land of uncertainty, scared and evaluating every facet of my life for insight and clarity. It was hard to entertain this possibility, and it was particularly disconcerting for my wife, who for many months did not know what was happening to me and where I was going next. Because of this difficult time, however, I have learned that while reviewing life's commitments can be traumatic, it ends up promoting health and wellness. My explorations confirmed that my marriage was not only not contributing to my illness, but that it was one of the key foundations supporting my health. So it was that my healing journey opened in me gateways to deeper love and even more respect for the woman with whom I have already shared more than thirty years of my life, and furthermore, our relationship burst into an ever-deepening communion and intimacy. Today, our marriage is filled with love, genuine friendship, excitement, and an increasing appreciation for the joys and pleasures we bring each other. To question my marriage was at first a frightening part of my journey through illness, but the enhanced clarity and insight into what we have, and the further transformation of our love, were beautiful aspects of the greater rebirth I experienced.

* * * * * * * * * * * * * * * *

As "God" continues to reveal to us His creation, we are lifted to a perspective on the vast richness and sublimity of the inner life.

Have you ever visited the place where the snow is kept,
    or seen where the hail is stored up,

which I keep for times of stress,
 for days of battle and war?
From which direction does the lightning fork
 when it scatters sparks over the earth?
Who carves a channel for the downpour,
 and hacks a way for the rolling thunder...
Can you guide the morning star season by season
 and show the Bear and its cubs which way to go?
Have you grasped the celestial laws?
 Could you make their writ run on the earth?
Do you find a prey for the lioness
 and satisfy the hunger of her whelps
when they crouch in their dens
 and lurk in their lairs? (38:22, 23, 32, 33, 39, 40).

The revelation is continued in Chapter 39.

Do you know how mountain goats give birth,
 or have you ever watched the hinds in labor?
Who gave the wild donkey his freedom,
 and untied the rope from his proud neck?
Can the wing of the ostrich be compared
 with the plumage of the stork or falcon?
Are you the one who makes the horse so brave
 and covers his neck with flowing hair?
Do you make him leap like a grasshopper?
 His proud neighing spreads terror far and wide.
Exultantly he paws the soil of the valley,
 and prances eagerly to meet the clash of arms.
He laughs at fear; he is afraid of nothing,
 he recoils before no sword.
Does the hawk take flight on your advice
 when he spreads his wings to travel south?
 (39:1, 5, 13, 19-22, 26).

Our first glimpse of the deeper layers of our unconscious world
forces us to understand earlier disconnection from inner reality and

the absurdity of our previous self-righteousness and rigidity. As we contemplate more of God's creation, we more fully appreciate the mysteries of the unfolded psychic world both within us and around us. This experience imbues us with great joy, serenity, and a feeling of deep connection to nature, in particular to our creative nature. When this occurs we are, in fact, entering the transpersonal dimensions of the psyche, and we stand before the palace of the All. As we venture into this uncharted domain, we begin to understand through our feelings and our intuition rather than through cognition alone. We suddenly find ourselves privy to truths that have been part of humankind since the inception of our kind. We are unmasking the secrets underlying human existence, the very laws of creation, and evolution. Reality expands dramatically, and our perspective shifts from the personal to the universal life.

Job has penetrated a dimension of consciousness in which we all unknowingly partake and by which we are all influenced. The forces he has encountered from the beginning of his story, and most clearly in this section, touch his daily life but do not seem to have a personal origin. He is, in fact, tapping what Jung called the collective unconscious, an arena that feels, at first, alien to Job's objective mind. Its dynamics reflect, to his surprise, realities of a spiritual nature rather than the myriad common occurrences to which he normally responded in the course of his daily life. It is only here, in the transpersonal and not within the confines of his objective existence that he, at last, will be able to find the answers to his existential concerns and the resources with which to engage his real life crises.

In the psychospiritual domain Job has now entered, there is no secret that cannot be uncovered or wisdom that cannot be tapped. In this place, we feel as if we have been given access to all the genes that comprise the human genome, including the ones that could create and shape life almost at will. Once Job penetrated such layers of universal knowledge, the powerful resources to which he has been given access are infinite. This is why it is imperative that people who venture into these realms be well prepared, lest they misuse the information.

As Job learns to decipher the archetypal code that sustains life, he begins to understand how his world came into being, and to understand the principles that govern its unfolding. He is beginning to understand the existence of layers of reality that are neither objective nor subject to personal wishes or societal dictates. His is instead a more encompassing reality, one that overshadows and overrides all he has heretofore tried to control volitionally.

As Job's journey continues, he experiences a rekindling of some knowledge he had, unfortunately, long forgotten.

Does the eagle soar at your command
  to make her eyrie in the heights?
She spends her night among the crags
  with an unclimbed peak as her redoubt
from which she watches for prey,
  fixing it with her far-ranging eye.
She feeds her young on blood:
  wherever men fall dying, there she is (39:27-30).

In the midst of Job's mystical experience, he is reminded that, despite the awesome creativity and resourcefulness of his human psyche, he and all other human beings are still members of the animal kingdom, a vast community of beings in continual exchange and interconnection with each other. Within the context of this kingdom, what is necessary and pleasurable for human beings is frequently displeasing and threatening to other living entities. And what is food for an eagle's young may be pain and agony for the children of the fallen human being. By the same token, what we usually call disease is at times an effort by other living organisms to find sustenance in us for their growth and survival. We are warned not to abstract ourselves from these realities or from life's larger picture. Once, many years back, during his first thirteen years of life, Job knew of this and lived in attunement with nature. But when he became a conventionally socialized adult, he grew too cerebral, and he became detached from life and lost sight of these basic truths. The consequences, as we have seen, were profound and terrible.

Hashem, denying Job the time to integrate the vast amount of knowledge He has just delivered to him, presses forward.

Is Shaddai's opponent willing to give in?
Has God's critic thought up an answer? (40:2).

When the compartments that separate us from our inner worlds and our creative power collapse, we first feel embarrassed by the vastness of our ignorance and the recognition that, despite our ripe age, we are still operating with the mentality of a six-year-old child. So in moments like these, the best we can do is simply say, as Job did:

My words have been frivolous: what can I reply?
I had better lay my finger on my lips.
I have spoken once. . .I will not speak again;
I will add nothing (40:4-5).

Job has learned truth, and he is humbled by it. His response to Hashem is no longer the cry of a man rent by a wrathful God, nor is it the protest of one who has been overwhelmed by a whimsical and capricious deity. Rather, it is the response of a human being who has witnessed God's mystery and has emerged awestruck.

Yes, it is true that Job still feels devastated. But something magical has nonetheless occurred. Job has undergone an alchemical process, a metamorphosis, and from the vantage of a new selfhood he appreciates ordinary and transordinary life in its totality.

The Book of Job now flows forward with some of its most arresting poetry—images of monster-size created beings, symbols of God's strength and, more pointedly, of his enormous potential for the destructive.

Hashem gave Job his answer from the heart of the tempest. He said:

Brace yourself like a fighter,
now it is my turn to ask questions and yours to inform me.
Do you really want to reverse my judgment,
and put me in the wrong to put yourself in the right?

Has your arm the strength of God's,
   can your voice thunder as loud?
Now think of Behemoth;
   he eats green stuff like the ox.
But what strength he has in his loins,
   what power in his stomach muscles!
His tail is as stiff as a cedar,
   the sinews of his thighs are tightly knit.
His vertebrae are bronze tubing,
   his bones as hard as hammered iron.
He is the masterpiece of all God's work,
   but his Maker threatened him with the sword,
forbidding him the mountain regions
   where all the wild beasts have their playground.
So he lies beneath the lotus,
   and hides among the reeds in the swamps.
Should the river overflow on him, why should he worry?
   A Jordan could pour down his throat without his caring.
So who is going to catch him by the eyes
   or drive a peg through his nostrils?
Leviathan, too! Can you catch him with a fishhook
   or run a line around his tongue?
You have only to lay a finger on him
   never to forget the struggle or risk it again!
   (40:6-9, 15-21, 23-25, 32).

He continues this description in Chapter 41:

When roused, he grows ferocious,
   no one can face him in a fight
Who dare open the gates of his mouth?
   Terror dwells in those rows of teeth!
From his mouth come fiery torches,
   sparks of fire fly out of it.
His nostrils belch smoke
   like a caldron boiling on the fire.

Strength has made a home in his neck,
   fear leaps before him as he goes.
When he stands up, the waves themselves take fright,
   the billows of the sea retreat.
He churns the depths into a seething caldron...
He has no equal on earth...
He looks the haughtiest in the eye;
   of all the sons of pride he is the king (41:2, 6, 11, 12, 14, 17, 23, 25, 26).

In Chapters 38 and 39, God the creator spoke to Job and introduced him to the mystery inherent in creating something from nothing. Now, Hashem shows Job an aspect of Himself and reality that is diametrically opposed to that of the creator: God the destroyer/liberator, a force that can crush and devastate, making ordinary people feel as if evil had struck them headlong. God, however, describes such forces as what they are: both powerful and vital. To ordinary people they may seem abominable, as elements to be rejected and destroyed in turn. To God, however, they are of benefit both to His creation and to its living creatures. This is the power and meaning of the awesome presence at this climactic moment in the story of Behemoth and Leviathan.

Jacob Discovers the Creative/Destroyer Force Within

Until the summer of 1983, I perceived myself as a successful man whose future was secure and free of trouble. I have often wondered what would have happened if I had been visited then by an "angel of God" who, addressing me, would have said, "Jacob, you are an insensitive, cruel, dishonest, and childish fool." Most likely, I would have reacted with righteous indignation to his offensive remarks and said, "How do you dare to smear my impeccable reputation? Why do you insult me for no reason?" And yet, this angel would have been speaking the truth. In the years since, I have often wished that someone more enlightened than I would have come forth and exhorted me to pay more attention to my inner world, warning me of the many dangers lurking ahead. Yet I know that had I encountered such a person, I would have ridiculed and dismissed his or her advice. In my clearest moments, I know for certain that only an event of the magnitude of my cancer diagnosis could have moved me from my entrenched position. Nothing else would have served.

I still remember vividly my awakening into the world of dreams and inner imagination during the spring of 1984 (six months after my diagnosis of lymphoma). I had then my first moving dream. Initially, I experienced it as foreboding, utterly distressing to my sense of well-being. Over the years, however, my explorations of the dream revealed truths of such magnitude that I cannot help but feel this dream was indeed healing, a dream that announced the emergence of a transformative force within me: the destroyer/liberator, that thrust me out of childhood's innocence and into the turmoil of adulthood's awesome, albeit hard, beauty.

I walk out of my house and step into my car, parked in the open garage. As I am about to drive away, a blond, blue-eyed, athletic man opens the passenger door and sits by me. I am startled by his presence. I have never seen this man before, and something about him frightens me and makes me very uncomfortable. I realize that he represents trouble, and also that he is determined to stay with me.

I drive to an office building of sorts (I believe it is a consulate or embassy), where I am supposed to retrieve important documents. I get to one of the offices, the intruder by my side, and request the papers. As I wait, the man pulls a machine gun from underneath his jacket and proceeds to take the office employees as hostages, demanding all the money stored in the office's vault. I am petrified, terrified, but I don't know what to do. I fear being perceived as an accomplice and that my reputation will be ruined forever. While these thoughts race through my mind, the man begins to shoot wantonly, and I see a number of the people in the office falling dead or seriously injured. Chaos and confusion break out, and I run for my life to get away from the murderer. I manage to escape and feel somewhat relieved.

The scene shifts and now I am in a travel agency, buying a one-way ticket to a foreign land. Following this, I find myself seated in a restaurant having lunch with Benny, an old friend from high school. I can't remember what we talk about, but it certainly is not about the events I witnessed that morning. Suddenly, the murderer appears and sits down with us at the table. Nobody says anything, but I know by his looks that he is saying to me something like, "Did you really think that you could get rid of me, little boy? You must be kidding!" I am oppressed by his presence and overwhelmed with fear.

The three of us are all now at my house and I am in the kitchen. The television is on, and we are all listening to the news. The anchorman describes a massacre that took place that morning and gives a detailed description of the murderers. Benny, my friend, is glued to the television set, and he realizes as he listens that the description given of the assailants fit me and the man who joined us at the restaurant. He stands there in front of the TV dumbfounded, and I realize that my well-kept secret is out and that I have no other choice but to kill the murderer who has brought so much chaos into my life. Nobody will ever believe that I had nothing to do with the atrocities he committed. I will be seen as a murderer. I pull a gun from somewhere and aim it at the real murderer. He looks at me with disdain and says: "You will never dare to shoot me. You are a coward, you will chicken out."

"I won't," I reply, and proceed to pull the trigger. To my dismay and his amusement, there is no bullet in that chamber of the revolver, and nothing happens.

The murderer laughs and ridicules me, saying "you see, I told you. You do not dare to kill me." I feel indignant, take aim a second time, pull the trigger, and hear a very powerful explosion that fills the room with smoke. When the smoke dissipates, I see that the bullet has shattered the man's head and that he lies motionless on the floor. In the background, I hear the sounds of police sirens approaching my home. I know they are on their way to apprehend me. I feel greatly relieved. I know that I shall have to pay for my acts, and that I will surely go to jail. I also know that it will be for a short time, and that once out, I shall be free from this murderer and from his appalling acts.

The richness and wisdom displayed by the dream's imagery still leaves me awestruck. This dream illustrates with wonderful insight what the cancer diagnosis did to my psyche. The threat posed by the intruding, cold-blooded murderer symbolizes the way I felt after discovering I had cancer: exposed, frightened, and vulnerable to destructive forces that I neither recognized nor could immediately control. These forces seemed evil, wreaking havoc on my reputation and on the social and professional image I had built for myself over many years. These were forces I wanted to escape but did not know how.

The diagnosis of cancer made it impossible for me to continue pretending that all was well inside me. After all, if I was healthy inside, how did I manage to develop a life-threatening illness? Similarly, and after seeing the images projected by my dream, how could I continue claiming I was an honest, law-abiding citizen of unblemished reputation? The cancer and the murderer within had burst my denial of truth and were even shattering my whole world. Both illness and dream figure were symbolic of the destroyer within, a force that can burst our innocence and cause the collapse of our infantile ways.

On the other hand, and as I gradually came to understand as I analyzed the dream by myself and with the help of others, the cancer in my neck and the murderer in my dream were also symbols of liberation. They liberated me from the delusion, detachment, utter foolishness, and gross misunderstanding of the world of God that I had carried for so long. Like Job, when faced with misfortune I, too, initially swore by my innocence. "The murderer and I have nothing in common," I would declaim to whomever wanted to listen. "All appearances to the contrary are mere coincidences." This seemed true, but the psyche and its dream were not convinced. How could I be an innocent bystander of a psychic configuration that emerged from the depth of my own unconscious? How could I feign innocence of the doings of my own creations? The dream was mine, all its images were mine, and every aspect of it came from me and symbolized part of myself.

When the murderer challenged me to overcome his oppression and destroy him, he became, in fact, my Liberator. If I could muster the courage to stand up to him, I would move to a higher level of development. The moment I could pull the trigger and shatter the murderer's head, I would in effect become a murderer, too. Thus, I would own my destructive side, at last, and be forced to accept and live with full knowledge of it. In the process, I would liberate myself from the inner conflict between my innocent side, Everything's-All-Right, and Mr. Murderer. I would assume full responsibility for my acts and, to put it simply, grow up. In the dream, I knew that my actions would be judged negatively by society, and that the ruling order would not tolerate my bypassing its regulations and taking the law into my own hands. Nonetheless, I was determined not to waver. My innocence had been pierced, and there was no going back. This dream of mine enacted the ancient myth of death and rebirth: Jacob, the innocent and idealistic child, was to die, and Israel, the man who fought the angel of God, was being born. From the time I analyzed the dream, my understanding of life changed drastically, and never again would I return to the childlike and limited perception of things that dominated the first 37 years of my life.

By threatening my life, cancer and the birth of the murderous man inside me made me appreciate life's finiteness. I discovered that regardless of what I did, I would not be able to overcome this truth, or avoid its consequences. Such realizations liberated me from the oppression that conventional responsibilities, societal and professional obligations, conditioned responses, and other automatisms exerted over my life. Rules and beliefs that I had had since childhood, and that were still directing my comings and goings, had to be examined critically. For the first time, I was forced to take my life in my own hands and experience the mastery and the strength that such a step entails. In this process, one clarification bred another. It became evident that nobody, regardless of what they promised, would fight as hard or care as much as I would for my survival. I could not, therefore, allow conventional or even unconventional restrictions and ideas to compromise my chances for success. This is not to say I thought I could do whatever I pleased. After all, I was and am still part of a society and am bound by the same unchangeable principles universally recognized as essential for psychological balance and wellness. Nevertheless, beyond these limits, I could try anything. The experience of cancer and my dream liberated me from the empty concerns about other people's opinions and judgments. They forced me into an awareness of reality that awakened me to the new challenges and thrust me into a life free from fear and paralyzing uncertainty.

* * * * * * * * * * * * * * * *

As we examine parts of Chapters 40 and 41 of *The Book of Job*, we can see that God is teaching Job that His destructive aspects loom larger than anything the rational mind can conjure. "My powers know no peer on earth and must be approached with great care," Hashem warns his loyal servant. "Otherwise they may burn and kill you."

Job is learning that God's world is one sustained and characterized by harmony and balance, but this equilibrium is dynamic, a crashing and mighty symphony. "In the absence of any modulation," Hashem remarks in passing, "creativity, productivity, and expansion are not necessarily wholesome processes. When totally unchecked, they run counter to life. That is why my destructive components, symbolized by Behemoth and Leviathan, are needed to keep the world in balance."

Job understands now that his conventional morality, religious beliefs, and psychological conditioning concealed these truths from him, keeping him vulnerable and weak beneath any appearance of prosperity or success. Hashem, however, never concealed anything. It was rather Job's self-imposed worship of a narrow and socially imposed rationalism that kept him blind and detached from truth.

"Can you understand now why one of my names is Shaddai?" Hashem asks.[13] "Didn't I command my world to cease creating itself from the very beginning? This is also one of the reasons I command you to observe the Sabbath. Contrary to what most believe, my directive for the Sabbath is not to rest from work, because I never tire, but rather to rest from creating—an act that allows destruction and restoration to take place in my universe, permitting balance to prevail."

As individuals, we live a biological existence that precisely mirrors the world of spirit Hashem here reveals. Health, our most precious treasure, is nothing more than the product of the balance between the anabolic and catabolic processes of our body, the constructive and destructive aspects of our biological essence. Disease results, therefore, from a perturbation of this balance, when either too much construction or too little destruction has taken place or vice versa.

In fact, the disease we call cancer illustrates this principle quite well. Cancer is a disorder caused by the accumulation of cells that have lost their capacity to mature and die (deficient destruction). What such a process of excessive construction or creativity does to the human body is terrible. This is why chemotherapy and radiation therapy, two destructive forces (Behemoth and Leviathan), are used to control this serious derangement.

The general need for "death" to sustain and promote life is yet another example of the critical relationship that exists between the universal creative and destructive forces. If all that Hashem created was to be born but never die, life as we know it could not exist. Thus, death is essential and meaningful. That the individual, or even humanity in the aggregate, rarely accepts this fact, feels overwhelmed by it, and tries to deny or to reverse it, is another story. God never promised us a world in which Leviathan and Behemoth would not destroy all that was in need of destruction. He couldn't have promised us such a world, because it would have run contrary to all that supports and energizes His universe.

When God hears some of us promoting, in His name, a world without loss, disease, or death, He knows us to be false prophets—people who at best misunderstand His message. This is why Job's friends were false spokesmen of the divine order and why Elihu alone reflected God's truth (32-37). What God is saying in these vital chapters to Job and to us is, above all: "Remember, that I *am* your creator and your destroyer. I *am* the totality of everything. Precisely because I am both creative and destructive am I wholesome and holy. I am always just because my purpose is to balance and harmonize your universe. When parts of me create too much, then other parts destroy a little, and vice versa. This way, the universe is always in balance or in the process of becoming balanced.

"Hear more of my message: Whatever happens to you that seems painful is a product of disequilibrium and internal strife. I do not choose or select these things; they are part of my reality. On occasion, my creative sides may get carried away, as do my destructive sides. In the end, however, balance prevails in my universe.

"Whether I become too creative or destructive, however, is also a function of what you do. After all, I gave you free will, didn't I? Sometimes, as a result of your biases and prejudices, you try to change the order of things and render my world all good, never recognizing the disequilibrium you are thereby creating and leaving me no alternative but to react with force. When this happens, my response is so devastating that you feel torn asunder. I hope you have learned your lesson well, and for My sake remain true to this knowledge!"

Job's encounter with Hashem has indeed sealed the end of his innocence. God, Job's Higher Wisdom, has revealed secrets of such magnitude that whatever might have remained of Job's old beliefs finally crumbles, and Job witnesses truth and is forever transformed by it. No longer is he aloof and childlike. He knows too much now, so he is able to comprehend the deeper meaning of things. In his new existence, nothing is trivial or excessive. Nothing needs to be added to or taken away from life.

Job's mind now begins to perceive the interrelatedness and interdependence of all that surrounds him. He marvels at the complexity and wonder that this coherence bespeaks. With the humility and deep appreciation of someone who has been blessed with insight, Job answers Hashem and says.

I know that you are all-powerful:
  what you conceive, you can perform.
I am the man who obscured your designs
  with my empty-headed words.
I have been holding forth on matters I cannot understand,
  on marvels beyond me and my knowledge (42:2-3).

As Job's understanding deepens and as he becomes more attuned to life's rhythms, he begins to feel better. Job understands that what has happened to him was neither avoidable nor a product of God's wrath. He still feels pained by what has transpired, but no longer is he oppressed by it. He feels wounded but not helpless. In short, Job is sad but not defeated. He has seen the light and is able now to bathe in its primal splendor.

When we encounter nature in its fullness and uncover the awesomeness of living, when we discover the beauty, the power, and the mystery that surround us, our ordinary, day-to-day concerns seem so frivolous as to be stripped of meaning. Once we are truly aware of what we are, of the miracle of life, and of the transcendent harmony of creation and destruction, all else assumes its proper place.

Our fears recede now, and the oppression that has bound our hearts lifts. Never again will we be victims, helpless creatures at the mercy of our demons. We are instead Warriors, magicians fully endowed with the personal resources we need to experience life in its fullness. Freer and more open to all, Job's tone softens, and in the last verses deepens, and we hear his calm wisdom as he says to Hashem:

I knew you then only by hearsay;
   but now, having seen you with my own eyes,
I retract all I have said,
   and in dust and ashes I repent (42:5-6).

His newfound understanding has redeemed his suffering and helped him find a total peace. Job has accepted God and the world, and from this surrender to truth he can go forth into tomorrows filled with love, compassion, and a true holiness far beyond the cultic posturing with which *The Book of Job* began.

Fourteen

Job Has Became a
Wholesome Man

As we reach the conclusion of Job's journey, our beings are once again heightened by the profound wisdom the text reveals. After completing His answer to Job, Hashem unexpectedly addresses Eliphaz of Teman:

> "I burn with anger against you and your two friends" he said, "for not speaking truthfully about me as my servant Job has done. So now find seven bullocks and seven rams, and take them back to my servant Job and offer a holocaust for yourselves, while Job, my servant, offers prayers for you. I will listen to him with favor and excuse your folly in not speaking of me properly as my servant Job has done." Eliphaz of Teman, Bildad of Shuah and Zophar of Naamath went away to do as Hashem had ordered, and Hashem listened to Job with favor (42:7-9).

With burning anger in His voice that reveals His own Eros, Hashem accuses Job's friends of not speaking truthfully about Him. Why would He do this to people who have upheld His tradition and said all the "right" things? Evidently because they misunderstood His directives. Hashem is indeed the epitome of justice, but His justice is not meted out in human terms, nor does it require dogmatic enforcement. Accordingly, in the absence of definable evidence of wrongdoing, men are presumed innocent and deserving of accountability and due process. Job's friends vigorously attacked Job's integrity and innocence while lacking proof he had done anything wrong. Their rationale, based only on simplistic dogmatic beliefs about God's justice, encouraged bigotry and oppression. Indeed, it is this pretense of thinking we know God in our terms that is the basis for all religious repression and fundamentalist wrath. People have been violated, abused, tortured, and ruthlessly burned throughout history in the name of the "just" God of mercy and of loving kindness.

Had it not been for Elihu's intervention, Job might have very well been lynched by the righteously indignant crowd incited to action by the accusations leveled on him by his three best friends. "If you couldn't see what Job had done wrong, then why did you condemn him?" God asks the sages. "It makes no difference to Me that you were intellectually correct in assuming that some general, abstract, and pious justice exists. This mere notion, this half-understood conventional teaching, did not give you the right to abuse and condemn Job. Neither general nor specific dogmas about the divine are worthy; they are offensive and denigrating to Me."

Job's ideas about God, by way of contrast, were also inaccurate, but his actions never maligned God's essence. He could not see that he had done anything wrong, and he steadfastly maintained his innocence, believing his plight to be a huge mistake. This didn't offend God or raise His ire; all it did was expose Job's naiveté and ignorance. Moreover, as soon as Job received divine insight, he immediately acquiesced and said:

My words have been frivolous: what can I reply?
I had better lay my finger on my lips.
I have spoken once I will not speak again;
more than once I will add nothing (40:4-5).

Ignorance, we are being shown, attracts God's wisdom and divine consciousness; it is the mother of our enlightenment. False righteousness, to the contrary, provokes God's wrath.

In verse eight, Hashem proceeds to give the clue for the resolution of Job's misfortunes. "I have asked him to pray for you and I will listen to his prayers with favor." Then, in direct and unambiguous fashion, Hashem restored Job's fortunes, because he had prayed for his friends (42:10).

This praying is evidently an event of paramount significance. It implies that Job has reached a state of inner integration, which allows him to accept and even love those who have been crudely insensitive to his plight. When he prays for his friends, his home (that is, his inner home) miraculously ceases to be divided. No doubt, his human psyche still contains polarities, with inner forces existing independently of each other. But no longer is he in any fundamental sense psychologically fragmented. Instead, Job has been able to evoke a superior function in himself that can oversee and direct inner forces, one that is capable of synthesizing opposites while allowing them to coexist under a single roof. It is this higher level of functioning that is symbolized by Job's lost fortunes being not only restored but doubled:

> Hashem blessed Job's new fortune even more than his first one. He came to own fourteen thousand sheep, six thousand camels, a thousand yoke of oxen and a thousand she-donkeys. He had seven sons and three daughters; his first daughter he called "Turtledove," the second "Cassia" and the third "Mascara." Throughout the land there were no women as beautiful as the daughters of Job. And their father gave them inheritance rights like their brothers. And all his brothers and all his sisters and all his friends of former times came to see him and sat down at table with him. They showed him every sympathy, and comforted him for all the evils Hashem had inflicted on him. Each of them gave him a silver coin, and each a gold ring (42:11-15).

These final passages imply the emergence of a new world order, a new whole man. They suggest that as long as one is psychologically split and compartmentalized, one will experience at most only half of life's richness. Formerly, Job had indeed led a most agreeable life, but it was still only half of what living could be—one devoid of passion or any other profound emotion. It was good, yet bland and uninspiring. When we are psychologically cleft, it does not matter how many gifts we amass; we still reap our rewards from only half of life's diversity. In the end, we have an abundance of sameness, which only makes us feel stale. It is precisely this feeling of staleness that drives us to work harder to collect more goods, more money, more fame, or more of whatever it is we are after, not realizing that in the end we will still be only half alive, only half fulfilled, and unable to find inner strength.

When Job attains enlightenment and embraces life as life is, when he integrates Eros and Logos and the light and dark sides of his nature, the fusion of those two inner worlds is symbolized in number as a two. Job's possessions are doubled to dramatize his numerological move from a one toward a two, a being who integrates his two worlds into a cohesive whole. This enriching inner integration is also symbolized by Job's giving equivalent inheritance rights to both daughters and sons. His feminine essence is now forever welcomed in his home. Naturally, he has a stronger masculine aspect—that is to say, seven sons and three daughters—but the feminine element in him is now seen as worthy of equal reward, appreciated as something beautiful and rich.

> After his trials, Job lived on until he was a hundred and forty years old, and saw his children and his children's children up to the fourth generation. Then Job died, an old man and full of days (42:16, 17).

The final two verses of *The Book of Job* suggest that Job went on to become an ever more resourceful and capable human being. In his unified twoness, he lives to be 140, twice the ordinary biblical man's age of seventy—the proverbial three scores years and ten. And in this redoubled life he flowers and differentiates, ever more accepting, and open to his vast inner and outer family of four (two and two) generations. No longer did Job need to be good, honest, or righteous; for that matter, he did not need to be anything. He was just Iyov, a free spirit—a man who was capable of immense compassion, who was able to love and give unconditionally, and who therefore exuded a radiance that suffused his life as well as the lives of all those whom he touched.

The Mystery of Healing

One of the secrets of our undertaking to do healing work on ourselves is that it never fails to render constructive results. Each and every person who undertakes it invariably emerges feeling more resourceful and powerful. It is a highly reassuring fact, even if each of us faces eventual physical decay, that our psychospiritual unfolding is an unlimited and ever-expanding process. To know that the greatest joy of elderhood can be freedom from the fear of injury, decline, and death, is healing in and of itself, and it complements the realization that life is indeed finite.

Such an awareness renders invalid any perception that life can ever be terminal and restores meaning and sacredness to the totality of human existence. In the absence of such psychological development, the decline that all beings must endure, and the social dependency that this decline frequently imposes, are dreadful and most unattractive. From a purely evolutionary point of view, the intuitive knowledge of our physical decline mandates the development of attributes that make this decline manageable. It is the freedom from fear that I alluded to in the previous paragraph that allows us to understand and accept the incontrovertible reality of our physical existence and that prepares us for its natural unfolding.

People who are free from fear, and hence from the drives of their psychic shadow, need to project less negative or trivial psychological energy toward the world, and they are able to give more love, caring, and compassion to others, and to draw nearer to them. Whenever we are in the presence of such a people, we are moved to assist, support and love them. It is what all human beings wish and need for their elderhood, yet it is experienced by only a few. These elusive qualities cannot be purchased, regardless of how much money, fame, or public recognition we draw to ourselves during our lifetime. They are instead a natural outgrowth of our psychospiritual development—exterior attributes that from the very beginning were enfolded within the totality of our psyche and that provide the ingredients needed to travel successfully through God's creation.

We must remember that no human being can be exempt from pain and misery. The conditions that surround our material existence makes it impossible for any of us to avoid experiencing injury and bad feelings—hurt, shame, sadness—and discovering how vulnerable we are to the actions of nature, and more specifically to the activities of our own nature. Living creatures endowed at birth with inborn "desirable" patterns of behavior, who invariably experience the emergence of reflective consciousness, cannot avoid feeling the pains associated with the involuntary and unconscious collisions of these patterns with the greater world. How can infants know not to put their hands in the fire and be burned by it? How can they know not to cross the street and be hit by an oncoming car? How can they avoid the many threats and injuries associated with living? The process of psychospiritual unfolding involves a progressive and irreversible loss of innocence. These losses are, on the one hand, desirable occurrences, essential for the sustenance of the individual's life, and yet they will simultaneously be perceived as injurious and the cause of severe mental anguish. It is easy to see how nobody can escape either colliding with God's world or experiencing the consequences that such collisions produce. But when we come out of them more resourceful and freer, we have inched ourselves closer to wholeness and to the state of blissful existence that life has also enfolded in potential for us. We must all move forward with courage and hope toward a life ever more supported by the timely unfolding of all the wonders and richness that lie dormant within the recesses of our sacred hearts.

EPILOGUE

THE MYSTERY OF TRANSFORMATION:
FROM FEAR TO AWE AND BEYOND

The Book of Job serves as literary testimony to the profound change in human understanding that took place within the psyche of a singular western man 2,500 years ago. Today, the same process of psychospiritual change seems to be unfolding in an ever-larger number of people who, like Job, end by reaching fulfillment, inner peace, and wholeness.

Until this remarkable change in understanding took place, we were living in psychospiritual childhood, a stage of psychic life dominated by a "Supreme Ruler" who was always right. While in this stage of existence, our reality was always split into halves, and everything was deemed either good or bad, right or wrong, superior or inferior. In this world, our miseries were always the product of our sinfulness—either personal sins or those of our brethren—and if neither had been sinning, then one could always invoke original sin. Humans were thus forever repenting and asking for forgiveness from their Father in heaven.

The Book of Job, however, introduces a new type of human being: one unwilling to accept punishment for sins never committed. Job is someone who, when affected by life in ways that seem unjust to him, is relentless in the defense of his innocence and persistent in his demand for accountability from none other than God Himself. This new type of person defines a stage of human development one can describe as psychospiritual adolescence, a period in which a significant shift in understanding occurs, but within the same old framework. Now, instead of seeing himself as a sinner who is deserving of the calamities that befell him, Job sees himself as a victim of a ruthless and amoral God.

This evolution in understanding and perspective, while benefiting Job by making him feel better about the disasters that befell him, does not foster healing. Job still feels wounded and exposed, terrified at what this conscienceless God might do to him next, and lacking any clue as to how to avert a recurrence of his misery. All this still makes him feel weak and at the mercy of an overpowering force that lies beyond his control.

But Job understands that if he is to find serenity in this world, he needs a new way of looking at things. Changing polarities within the old paradigm from good boy to rebel can take him only so far, and it isn't far enough. The time comes for the old paradigm to be transcended and for a new one to emerge. Job prepares to surrender to life and to experience an irreversible and essential transformation.

Then, as Job cedes volitional control of his healing journey, he enters the deeper layers of his unconscious, wherein he penetrates God's palace. There, he uncovers the secrets of creation and evolution, the foundations of health and disease, the meaning of death, and a host of other truths, and this knowledge leaves him awestruck. Job finds meaning in all things surrounding him, and as his journey moves into its final stages, a transformed man emerges—one capable of experiencing the world differently, appreciatively, constructively.

Life will go on in all its daily routines, of course, but Job's response to it has become refreshing and new. He is not suddenly deprived of all sorrow, nor has he become free of injury and all fear. Such could never be the resolution for his suffering, because it is contrary to his very human nature. Rather, Job will now respond in a transformed way to the challenges life presents him. In his new state of awareness, Job no longer will feel victimized, hopeless, or forsaken. He may not like life's pains, and he may be distraught by them, but he has learned to accept them and flow forward with them.

From the perspective of such a psychospiritual understanding, Job's story finds a meaning that is consistent with any religious or philosophical approach. This meaning accepts and validates the finiteness of our earthly existence, the uncertainty surrounding our life and that of our loved ones, and the relativity of our perceptions. It also accepts the understanding that in addition to a biographical history, we partake of a collective (archetypal) reality that influences our life and, to a significant extent, determines its unfolding. The knowledge that life is sustained by nature's balancing and healing forces and by biophysical and psychospiritual complements and symmetries, rather than by moral and behavioral codes created by humans, is also revealed.

Once men and women accept and integrate these truths, everything else falls into place for them and the world begins to make sense. This new perspective is immensely valuable to us, because it fosters (a) our *awakening* from slumber; (b) the emergence of new and unexpected *resourcefulness*; (c) the fulfillment of our *privilege to choose* between alternatives; (d) the eradication of our excessive innocence and naiveté;

and (e) the manifestation of our *capacity to embrace and savor each of life's irreplaceable moments.* On the other hand, this understanding burdens us with the knowledge that we will experience pain, decline, and death and, furthermore, it reaffirms our conviction that no matter what we do, such fates cannot be eluded.

When we approach the story of Job from this general perspective, we discover its pregnant mystery, cohesiveness, and magnificent beauty. Job's ignorance, aloofness, and disconnection from feeling caused profound disequilibrium in his world. Job was not to blame for this; it was the way he had been conditioned to approach the world. Life, however, cared not how Job had been educated or what he had been taught. It simply needed to bring Job back to the center of it and ensure inner harmony, and nothing would stand in its way.

On a personal level, Job had no ethical responsibility for the tragedies that overtook his existence. From any objective and rational perspective, he had clearly done all he had been advised to do to avert misery. Yet this did not stop the tragedies from happening or exclude him from the collective realities into which he had been born. When we become alienated from collective truth, the world becomes incomprehensible to us. Moreover, our obliviousness to the forces that move the human collective makes us highly vulnerable to their power, and places us at the mercy of energies that can demolish our creations.

Had Job been less ignorant and more evolved, he would have been better able to handle the challenges he confronted and would have been less overwhelmed by his emotions. Moreover, when afflicted, he wouldn't have interpreted his fate as punishment or as proof of his inadequacy, but rather as a manifestation of life's design moving through his feeble and mortal body.

As time passed and as Job became more alert and conscious, he began to understand what had happened to him, and he began to feel stronger and more potent. He was a man who had taken his life into his own hands. The more connected to inner truth he became, the more confident he felt. Now he could repent for his denigration of Higher Wisdom, not out of guilt or moral remorse, but rather in acknowledgment of his profound ignorance: "My words were frivolous." Job speaks here neither as a defeated man nor as a bystander of life who has no participation or resource. He is neither a victim nor a sinner unaware of his transgressions. Instead, he is a wise man who is acknowledging how ignorant and blind he was and, more important, how ignorant and blind he remains.

Job now is a man who can depend totally on himself to heal and repair the wounds of his body and soul. He does not abdicate this responsibility to external authorities or to superior forces. This does not mean, however, that Job denies them or dismisses their power. Quite the contrary, he acknowledges his encounter with Higher Wisdom as the enactment of divine essence both within and without. Job discovered the existence of inner guides and teachers, inner support, and resourcefulness—all of which allowed him to engage the challenges of life with joy and enthusiasm.

As Job stopped being a victim, he realized that the calamities he had experienced were, in fact, the remedies for his illness rather than the illness itself. His tragedies were part of nature's efforts to restore balance rather than the product of a wrathful and vindictive God. Mind you, he did not like the therapy he was receiving. The remedies perturbed him and even overpowered his sense of stability. But he ultimately came to understand their purpose while still being able to appreciate them for what they were: tough, painful, and unavoidable.

As meaning was restored to his life, Job's experiences took on a new quality. Free from victimization, from feeling sorry for himself, from shunning life, he behaved from then on like a warrior. Iyov had been reborn, and from that moment life could become a sweeter and more exciting adventure.

We can easily imagine how, when years later new calamities perturb his calm, Job's response to them will be different. He will know to take these events in stride and not be compelled to sit in the ashpit and bemoan his birth once more. He will not play the victim. This time he will look within immediately, confident that Higher Wisdom will deliver the guidance and support for which he yearns. Despite a human tendency to regress and slip back into unconsciousness, Job will now know unequivocally that Higher Wisdom is never dormant and, to the contrary, is relentlessly pursuing the fulfillment of its wholesome ends. These, he has learned, include commitment to the healing of man's wounds and to the preservation of his life, and this knowledge will always deeply reassure the humbled soul of Job.

AFTERWORD

Nearly twelve years have passed since my diagnosis that morning. I am no longer a scientist/physician in a leading university, nor a happy and secure man whose life is predictable or under volitional control. Instead, I see myself more like a surfer, one who uses his skills to negotiate the powerful waves and currents that life presents to him. As this twelfth year comes to an end, I sense that my unfolding as a physician/healer is coming to a new, critical stage, but I also know that whatever images and ideas I am now consciously holding about the precise meaning of these impressions are at best superficial and probably inaccurate. This fact, rather than depressing me, fills me with a sense of curiosity and eager anticipation.

It is not important for me now to know precisely what I shall be doing next year, or for me to anticipate the specific events that may affect my present life. Instead, what I hope for is the presence of mind to acknowledge whatever comes into my existence, and to have the flexibility and resourcefulness to engage it constructively.

I am learning to enjoy the dance of life and to respond to its changes in rhythm and flow. I have fallen in love with living, and time has become of the utmost importance to me. I try not to take anything for granted, and I listen attentively to the wonderful music of the spheres. My body is indeed my sanctuary and greatest ally, and I dedicate a good part of my time to supporting its wellness. This is not to say that I am separate or distinct from it, but rather that I, as a self-conscious being, can feel it, and nurture it reflectively. In a way, I perceive myself as a custodian of an invaluable treasure (no money can buy health) that needs to be guarded diligently from the threats and challenges inherent in living.

Of the many benefits I have derived from the healing experience, one of the most gratifying has been the freedom to love and to tolerate both myself and others. This freedom makes my experience of the world rich, diverse, and magical. The impulse to judge and be severe with people has receded in my life, giving way to deep appreciation and openness. The world is indeed my oyster, a place for wonderment and delight.

Few things surprise me now, but I am continually amazed by the mystery surrounding my own existence and that of all those I love and come in close contact with. When it comes to spiritual perceptions and to feelings, nothing is at it seems, and while accepting that there is no absolute clarity about what is real has been difficult at times, on the whole it has more often been very refreshing.

I am still perturbed when I encounter a sufferer for whom I can discern the path to a redemption, but for whom I cannot do much. I am learning, however, to respect human individuality and innate capacity, to be less invested in changing people's life, and to be in turn more gentle and encompassing of each person's rhythms and flow.

I have not yet integrated some areas of my own life and I suspect there are a few others (perhaps many others) I have not even begun to discover. Although the feelings reflecting my inner life are usually comforting and harmonious now, I am ever less prone to be lulled into forgetting my blindness and my need to push forward into deeper learning and consciousness. The key difference in my perspective today is that this knowledge of my limitations does not oppress me that much. It just alerts me to the degree of my unconsciousness, and it helps me to be more watchful and less aloof. Life has consequently become less of a conflict (it is hard to be in conflict when there are no major discrepancies between what is and what one believes is supposed to be) and less distressing, and its episodic challenges and unusual rhythms seem frequently quite humorous. I have learned to take myself much less seriously, although I am quite serious about what I have just said.

I am pleased and delighted to have been able to share some of my experiences, thoughts, and feelings with you, and I hope you find them challenging and helpful. The future feels bright, and I hope we meet again soon, as we travel the world searching for understanding and deeper awareness of the mystery that we are.

APPENDIX I

THE MYSTERY OF NUMBER

Seven sons and three daughters were born to him. And he owned seven thousand sheep, three thousand camels, five hundred yoke of oxen and five hundred she-donkeys, and many servants besides (1:2-3).

Little in the story of Job seems accidental or random, including the numbers. Each number is a symbolic representation of a deeper and more meaningful reality. All the numbers in Chapter 1 have a common denominator: They all add up to ten or its multiples (seven + three = ten; five hundred + five hundred = one thousand; seven thousand + three thousand = ten thousand). Why not five sons and three daughters or four thousand sheep and five thousand camels? Because Job's is a story of wholeness—of the process whereby we reach integration and numerologically become a ten, the numerical symbol of perfection and completion that has remained a constant in western culture. Ten has even been used most recently to symbolize perfect/complete physical beauty and gymnastic performance. This is only one instance of how the meaning of the story is also encoded in its numerology.

When we encounter Job for the first time, he is in a virginal state, exhibiting the attributes of the child/fool, which is to say that he is then in his first stage of psychospiritual development, or, a "one." He is also a man whose world is split in two and who manifests only the side of light and goodness. Symbolically, this is why his darkness takes on so much power and erupts so forcefully into the fore of his awareness. Life does not tolerate polarizations of this nature for long. When darkness is concealed from view, it becomes demonic and erupts with overwhelming force, leaving us convinced we have been stricken by Evil itself. But it is not evil or anything of the sort Job is experiencing; instead, it is life attempting to balance and repair the wounds of the soul. Only years later can we fully understand that what we originally perceived as destructive was in fact liberating—the light of darkness bringing forth truth and honest revelation.

By contrast, toward the book's end, Job reaches maturity and is now a warrior—an empowered and fully endowed man. He is someone who has attained wholeness and has indeed become a ten. When we become a true ten, we have gained access not only to all the forces and attributes of spirit but also to a function that knows how to make use of these attributes effectively. To become a ten, we must have lived and experienced both the wonders and the horrors of God's world. A ten is an individual who is capable of masterfully handling the mystery of life and living.

That the story of Job illustrates our path to wholeness is further confirmed by the numerological value of Job's name itself. In Hebrew, our hero is called Iyov (spelled Aleph, Yod, Vav, and Bet). Aleph is the first letter in the Hebrew alphabet and has a numerical value of one; Yod is the tenth letter and is worth ten; Vav is the sixth letter and is worth six; and Bet is the second letter and is obviously worth two. Thus the numeric value of Job's name is nineteen, which, in turn equals one + nine = ten.

Iyov therefore contains within his name the code defining his essence. He is a man whose very destiny is to be whole and integrated. This, of course, was by no means a certainty; for all we know, it was an effort that might have failed. Nonetheless, Iyov's mission was enfolded in him from the start. Iyov was a ten—or, better still, a nine plus one. As such, he not only had all that was needed to be whole, but he also possessed what makes the whole function in an integrated fashion. If he had been merely a nine, he would have been like an orchestra of virtuosos capable of unique expression but lacking a conductor to blend their music. This is why I say that ten is so much more than nine even though it contains no new number (zero by itself has no numerical value). What it does contain is that special function that allows for the emergence of harmony and balance in the world.

The other key numerical symbol in *The Book of Job*, which also serves as an organizing, structural principle, is seven. One of its most prominent appearances, appropriately enough, is in Chapter Five (ten divided by two), verse nineteen (one plus nine = ten).

Six times he will deliver you from sorrow,
  and the seventh, evil shall not touch you (5:19).

What did the author mean when he stated that "six times he will deliver you from sorrow"? He refers to the despair we experience as we go through the six developmental gateways—infancy, childhood, adolescence, early adulthood, mid-life, and late adulthood—in our quest for maturation and differentiation. When traversing these six gateways, we become progressively freer and more serene about the world we live in. Once we traverse the seventh and final gateway (elderhood), fear has dissipated from our soul, and freedom rules our home.

We must understand that the passage through the gateways of development is essential to the balance of our inner universe. We must be cognizant, as well, that each passage is fraught with tragedy, misery, distress, bewilderment, and pain. Yet each transition moves us closer to that place within in which we attune ourselves to truth and from which life flows unimpeded. When we traverse the last threshold, evil (disarray, turmoil, conflict, and darkness) is no longer effective: *"Evil shall not touch you."*[14]

These verses remind us that God supports our efforts to grow and develop. They are intended to rekindle our trust in God's ability to carry us through trying times of sadness and loss. Six times we shall be delivered, even though we frequently feel exasperated and trapped in our agony.

Eliphaz's higher self encourages Job to do something that is difficult to accomplish when we are stuck in the ashpit: Trust life and the healing process. *"Illness and misery,"* he says, *"can't last forever, and hence resolution must be forthcoming. It is only when we can't cross the gateways that despair overcomes us and disease permeates our universe."*

These transitions are transcendental, the author implies. Human life as we know it is a continual miraculous and awesome process of maturation and unfolding, beginning with the fertilization of the ovum by the sperm and ending with our return to the dust or primal matter whence we originated. There is no part of the living experience that is not sustained and promoted by this large process. Our health, love, family, society, and country all depend on the appropriate unfolding of developmental sequences contained in our genetic and psychic blueprints. This is why any disturbance of or interference with the maturation process causes our personal world to become unstable and prey to injury and disease.

The Book of Job has forty-two chapters, and each new gateway comes forward every six chapters. In Chapter nineteen we read for example:

Ten times, no less, you have insulted me, ill-treating me without a trace of shame (19:3).

Here, we are in the time immediately following Job's passage through the third gateway of his psychospiritual development (adolescence). The numerology (our old number nineteen) emphasizes that we are in a critical stage. Job is rebellious and defiant of authority, but he is not yet very resourceful.

"I have endured as much as I can and now I am fed up with you," he tells Hashem. "Enough is enough! At first, I kept my hopes up and believed that sooner or later something good would happen. I felt that perhaps in time I would understand my torment and find inner peace, but this is not what took place. I trusted your justice and fairness, but all I received in return were insults and injuries. Ten insults are more than I can handle. I am fed up with you and your behavior. I have come to the end of my rope and am unwilling to take it any more."

Job had to endure ten insults (a sort of perfected set of insults) before he could muster the energy to confront his tormentor. Just as it took ten plagues to soften Pharaoh's heart before he allowed the Jews to leave Egypt, so too did it take ten insults for Job to acquire the courage to take on God, his perceived oppressor. Five times was clearly not enough, and neither was eight; ten was what he needed. Somehow, Job needed to experience pain and agony precisely that number of times before he realized that it was necessary for him to confront his abuser.

In the beginning, Job thought that what was happening to him was a freak occurrence, a cosmic mistake that would soon be corrected. He therefore continued to believe in God's justice and to wait for a miracle to happen. The more he tried to justify God, however, the more offended he became. At the end, he realized that he was wrong and that there was no divine justice—or, better still, that divine justice was not what he had thought it would be. God, after all, was not made in man's image.

APPENDIX II

THE BOOK OF JOB

THE BOOK OF
JOB
I. PROLOGUE

Satan tests Job

¹1   There was once a man in the land of Uzᵃ called Job: a sound
²,³ and honest man who feared God and shunned evil. Seven sons
and three daughters were born to him. And he owned seven
thousand sheep, three thousand camels, five hundred yoke of
oxen and five hundred she-donkeys, and many servants besides.
This man was indeed a man of mark among all the people of the
⁴   East.ᵇ It was the custom of his sons to hold banquets in each
⁵   other's houses, one after the other, and to send and invite their
three sisters to eat and drink with them. Once each series of
banquets was over, Job would send for them to come and be
purified, and at dawn on the following day he would offer a
holocaust for each of them. "Perhaps," Job would say, "my sons
have sinned and in their hearts affronted God." So that was what
he used to do after each series.

⁶,⁷ One day the sons of Godᶜ came to attend on Yahweh, and
among them was Satan. So Yahweh said to Satan, "Where have
you been?" "Around the earth," he answered, "roaming about."
⁸   So Yahweh asked him, "Did you notice my servant Job? There
⁹   is no one like him on the earth: a sound and honest man who
¹⁰ fears God and shuns evil." "Yes," Satan said, "but Job is not
¹¹,¹² God-fearing for nothing, is he? Have you not put a wall around
him and his house and all his domain? You have blessed all he
undertakes, and his flocks throng the countryside. But stretch out
your hand and lay a finger on his possessions: I warrant you, he
will curse you to your face." "Very well," Yahweh said to Satan,
"all he has is in your power. But keep your hands off his person."
So Satan left the presence of Yahweh.

1 a. Probably in the south of Edom. b. i.e., of Edomite or Arab territory to the east of Palestine.
c. The angels who make up his Council.

¹³ On the day when Job's sons and daughters were at their meal
¹⁴·¹⁵ and drinking wine at their eldest brother's house, a messenger
came to Job. "Your oxen," he said, "were at the plow,with the
donkeys grazing at their side, when the Sabaeansᵈ swept down
¹⁶ on them and carried them off. Your servants they put to the
¹⁷ sword: I alone escaped to tell you." He had not finished speaking
when another messenger arrived. "The fire of God," he said,
"has fallen from the heavens and burned up all your sheep, and
¹⁸ your shepherds too: I alone escaped to tell you." He had not
finished speaking when another messenger arrived. "The Chal-
¹⁹ adaeans," he said, "three bands of them, have raided your camels
and made off with them. Your servants they put to the sword: I
alone escaped to tell you." He had not finished speaking when
another messenger arrived. "Your sons and daughters," he said,
"were at their meal and drinking wine at their eldest brother's
house, when suddenly from the wilderness a gale sprang up, and
it battered all four corners of the house which fell in on the young
people. They are dead: I alone escaped to tell you".

²⁰ Job rose and tore his gown and shaved his head.ᵉ Then falling
²¹ to the ground he worshiped and said:

"Naked I came from my mother's womb,
    naked I shall return.
Yahweh gave, Yahweh has taken back.
    Blessed be the name of Yahweh!"

²² In all of this misfortune Job committed no sin nor offered any
insult to God.

¹2 Once again the Sons of God came to attend to Yahweh, and
² among them was Satan. So Yahweh said to Satan, "Where have
³ you been?" "Around the earth," he answered, "roaming about."
So Yahweh asked him, "Did you notice my servant Job? There
is no one like him on the earth: a sound and honest man who
⁴ fears God and shuns evil. His life continues blameless as ever; in

1 d. Predatory nomads. So are the Chaldaeans of v. 17. e. Mourning ritual.

vain you provoked me to ruin him." "Skin for skin!" Satan re-
5 plied. "A man will give away all he has to save his life. But stretch
6 out your hand and lay a finger on his bone and flesh; I warrant
7 you, he will curse you to your face." "Very well," Yahweh said
to Satan, "he is in your power. But spare his life." So Satan left
the presence of Yahweh.

8,9 He struck Job down with malignant ulcers from the sole of his
foot to the top of his head. Job took a piece of pot to scrape
himself, and went and sat in the ashpit. Then his wife said to him,
"Do you now still mean to persist in your blamelessness? Curse
10 God, and die." "That is how foolish women talk," Job replied.
"If we take happiness from God's hand, must we not take sorrow
too?" And in all this misfortune Job uttered no sinful word.

11 The news of all the disasters that had fallen on Job came to the
ears of three of his friends. Each of them set out from home—
Eliphaz of Teman, Bildad of Shuah and Zophar of Naamatha—
and by common consent they decided to go and offer him sym-
12 pathy and consolation. Looking at him from a distance, they
could not recognize him; they wept aloud and tore their garments
and threw dust over their heads. They sat there on the ground
beside him for seven days and seven nights. To Job they spoke
never a word, so sad a sight he made.

II. THE DIALOGUE

A. FIRST SERIES OF SPEECHES

Job curses the day of his birth

¹3 In the end it was Job who broke the silence and cursed the day
² of his birth. This is what he said:

3 May the day perish when I was born,
   and the night that told of a boy conceived.

---

2 a. The three towns are in Idumaean and Arab territory. Edom and "the East" were proverbailly
the homeland of the sages.

4 May that day be darkness,
    may God on high have no thought for it,
    may no light shine on it.
5 May murk and deep shadow claim it for their own,
    clouds hang over it,
    eclipse swoop down on it.
6 Yes, let the dark lay hold of it,
    to the days of the year let it not be joined,
    into the reckoning of months not find its way.
7 May that night be dismal,
    no shout of joy come near it.
8 Let them curse it who curse the day,
    who are prepared to rouse Leviathan.[a]
9 Dark be the stars of its morning,
    let it wait in vain for light
    and never see the opening eyes of dawn.
10 Since it would not shut the doors of the womb on me
    to hide sorrow from my eyes.
11 Why did I not die newborn,
    not perish as I left the womb?
12 Why were there two knees to receive me,
    two breasts for me to suck?
13 Had there not been, I should now be lying in peace,
    wrapped in a restful slumber,
14 with the kings and high viziers of earth
    who build themselves vast vaults,
15 or with princes who have gold and to spare
    and houses crammed with silver.
16 Or put away like a stillborn child that never came to be,
    like unborn babes that never see the light.
17 Down there,[b] bad men bustle no more,
    there the weary rest.

3 a. The dragon of primeval chaos; he might be roused by a curse against the present order. b. In Sheol, the underworld.

18   Prisoners, all left in peace,
        hear no more the shouts of the jailer.
19   Down there, high and low are all one,
        and the slave is free of his master.
20   Why give light to a man of grief?
        Why give life to those bitter of heart,
21   who long for a death that never comes,
        and hunt for it more than for a buried treasure?
22   They would be glad to see the grave mound
        and shout with joy if they reached the tomb.
23   Why make this gift of light to a man that does not see his way,
        whom God balks on every side?
24   My only food is sighs,
        and my groans pour out like water.
25   Whatever I fear comes true,
        whatever I dread befalls me.
26   For me, there is no calm, no peace;
        my torments banish rest.

Confidence in God

14 Eliphaz of Teman spoke next. He said:

2   If one should address a word to you, will you endure it?
        Yet who can keep silent?
3   Many another, once, you schooled,
        giving strength to feeble hands;
4   your words set right whoever wavered,
        and strengthened every failing knee.
5   And now your turn has come, and you lose patience too;
        now it touches you, and you are overwhelmed.
6   Does not your piety give you confidence,
        your blameless life not give you hope?
7   Can you recall a guiltless man that perished,
        or have you ever seen good men brought to nothing?
8   I speak of what I know: those who plow iniquity
        and sow the seeds of grief reap a harvest of the same kind.

9   A breath from God will bring them to destruction,
    a blast of his anger will wipe them out.

10   The lion's roar, his savage growls,
    like the fangs of lion cubs are broken off.

11   For lack of prey the lion dies at last,
    and the whelps of his lioness are scattered.

12   Now, I have had a secret revelation,
    a whisper has come to my ears.

13   At the hour when dreams master the mind,
    and slumber lies heavy on man,

14   a shiver of horror ran through me,
    and my bones quaked with fear.

15   A breath slid over my face,
    the hairs of my body bristled.

16   Someone stood there—I could not see his face,
    but the form remained before me.
    Silence—and then I heard a Voice,

17   "Was ever any man found blameless in the presence of God,
    or faultless in the presence of his Maker?

18   In his own servants, God puts no trust,
    and even with his angels he has fault to find.

19   What then of those who live in houses of clay,
    who are founded on dust?

20   They are crushed as easily as a moth,
    one day is enough to grind them to powder.
    They vanish for ever, and no one remembers them.

21   Their tent peg is snatched from them,
    and they die for lack of wisdom."

5   Make your appeal then. Will you find an answer?
    To which of the Holy Ones will you turn?

2   Resentment kills the senseless,
    and anger brings death to the fool.

3   I myself have seen how such a one took root,
    until a swift curse fell on his House.

4   His sons at a single blow lose their prop and stay,
      ruined at the gate[a] with no one to defend them;
5   their harvest goes to feed the hungry,
      God snatches it from their mouths,
      and thirsty men hanker after their goods.
6   Grief does not grow out of the earth,
      nor sorrow spring from the ground.
7   It is man who breeds trouble for himself
      as surely as eagles fly to the height.
8   If I were as you are, I should appeal to God,
      and lay my case before him.
9   His works are great, past all reckoning,
      marvels, beyond all counting.
10   He sends down rain to the earth,
      pours down water on the fields.
11   If his will is to rescue the downcast,
      or raise the afflicted to the heights of joy,
12   he wrecks the plans of the artful,
      and brings to naught their intrigues.
13   He traps the crafty in the snare of their own shrewdness,
      turns subtle counselors to idiots.
14   In daylight they come against darkness,
      and grope their way as if noon were night.
15   He rescues the bankrupt from their jaws,
      and the poor man from the hands of the violent.
16   Thus the wretched can hope again
      and wickedness must shut its mouth.
17   Happy indeed the man whom God corrects!
      Then do not refuse this lesson from Shaddai.[b]
18   For he who wounds is he who soothes the sore,
      and the hand that hurts is the hand that heals.
19   Six times he will deliver you from sorrow,
      and the seventh, evil shall not touch you.

5 a. The town gate, at which justice was dispensed. b. Name for God in patriarchal period, here a deliberate archaism.

20 In time of famine, he will save you from death,
and in wartime from the stroke of the sword.
21 You shall be safe from the lash of the tongue,
and see the approach of the brigand without fear.
22 You shall laugh at drought and frost,
and have no fear of the beasts of the earth.
23 You shall have a pact with the stones of the field,
and live in amity with wild beasts.
24 You shall find your tent secure,
and your sheepfold untouched when you come.
25 You shall see your descendants multiply,
your offspring grow like the grass in the fields.
26 In ripe age you shall go to the grave,
like a wheat sheaf stacked in due season.
27 All this, we have observed: it is true.
Heed it, and do so to your profit.

Only the sufferer knows his own grief

¹6 Job spoke next. He said:

2 If only my misery could be weighed,
and all my ills put on the scales!
3 But they outweigh the sands of the seas:
what wonder then if my words are wild?
4 The arrows of Shaddai stick fast in me,
my spirit absorbs their poison,
God's terrors stand against me in array.
5 Does a wild donkey bray when it finds soft grass,
or an ox ever low when its fodder is in reach?
6 Can tasteless food be taken without salt,
or is there flavor in the white of an egg?
7 The very dishes which I cannot stomach,
these are my diet in my sickness.
8 Oh may my prayer find fulfillment,
may God grant me my hope!

9   May it please God to crush me,
      to give his hand free play and do away with me!
10 This thought, at least, would give me comfort
      (a thrill of joy in unrelenting pain),
      that I had not denied the Holy One's decrees.
11 But have I the strength to go on waiting?
      What use is life to me, when doomed to certain death?
12 Is mine the strength of stone,
      or is my flesh bronze?
13 Can any power be found within myself,
      has not all help deserted me?
14 Grudge pity to a neighbor,
      and you forsake the fear of Shaddai.
15 My brothers have been fickle as a torrent,
      as the course of a seasonal stream.
16 Ice is the food of their dark waters,
      they swell with the thawing of the snow;
17 but in the hot season they dry up,
      with summer's heat they vanish.
18 Caravans leave the trail to find them,
      go deep into desert, and are lost.
19 The caravans of Tema look to them,
      and on them Sheba's convoys build their hopes.
20 Their trust proves vain,
      they reach them only to be thwarted.
21 So, at this time, do you behave to me:
      one sight of me, and then you flee in fright.
22 Have I said to you, "Give me this or that,
      bribe someone for me at your own cost,
23 snatch me from the clutches of an enemy,
      or ransom me from a tyrant's hand?"
24 Put me right, and I will say no more;
      show me where I have been at fault.
25 Fair comment can be borne without resentment,
      but what is the basis for your strictures?

26 Do you think mere words deserve censure,
  desperate speech that the wind blows away?
27 Soon you will be casting lots for an orphan,
  and selling your friend at bargain prices!
28 Come, I beg you, look at me:
  as man to man, I will not lie.
29 Relent, and grant me justice;
  relent, my case is not yet tried.
30 Is falsehood to be found on my lips?
  Cannot my palate tell the taste of misfortune?

¹7 Is not man's life on earth nothing more than pressed service,
  his time no better than hired drudgery?
2 Like the slave, sighing for the shade,
  or the workman with no thought but his wages,
3 months of delusion I have assigned to me,
  nothing for my own but nights of grief.
4 Lying in bed I wonder, "When will it be day?"
  Risen I think, "How slowly evening comes!"
  Restlessly I fret till twilight falls.
5 Vermin cover my flesh, and loathsome scabs;
  my skin is cracked and oozes pus.
6 Swifter than a weaver's shuttle my days have passed,
  and vanished, leaving no hope behind.
7 Remember that my life is but a breath,
  and that my eyes will never again see joy.
8 The eye that once saw me will look on me no more,
  your eyes will turn my way, and I shall not be there.
9 As a cloud dissolves and is gone,
  so he who goes down to Sheol never ascends again.
10 He never comes home again,
  and his house knows him no more.
11 No wonder then if I cannot keep silence;
  in the anguish of my spirit I must speak,
  lament in the bitterness of my soul.

12 Am I the Sea, or the Wild Sea Beast,[a]
    that you should keep me under watch and guard?
13 If I say, "My bed will comfort me,
    my couch will soothe my pain,"
14 you frighten me with dreams
    and terrify me with visions.
15 Strangling I would welcome rather,
    and death itself, than these my sufferings.
16 I waste away, my life is not unending;
    leave me then, for my days are but a breath.
17 What is man that you should make so much of him,
    subjecting him to your scrutiny,
18 that morning after morning you should examine him
    and at every instant test him?
19 Will you never take your eyes off me
    long enough for me to swallow my spittle?
20 Suppose I have sinned, what have I done to you,
    you tireless watcher of mankind?
    Why do you choose me as your target?
    Why should I be a burden to you?
21 Can you not tolerate my sin,
    nor overlook my fault?
    It will not be long before I lie in earth;
    then you will look for me, but I shall be no more.

The unswerving course of God's justice

¹8 Bildad of Shuah spoke next. He said:

2   Is there no end to these words of yours,
    to your long-winded blustering?
3   Can God deflect the course of right
    or Shaddai falsify justice?

7 a. In the Babylonian cosmogonies, the Sea (personified as Tiamat) was conquered and controlled by one of the gods. In popular imagery influenced by this story, Yahweh became the conqueror who held the sea under his control.

⁴ If your sons sinned against him,
   they have paid for their sins;
⁶ᵃ so you too, if so pure and honest,
⁵   must now seek God, plead with Shaddai.
⁶ᵇ Without delay he will restore his favor to you,
   will see that the good man's house is rebuilt.
⁷ Your former state will seem to you as nothing
   beside your new prosperity.
⁸ Question the generation that has passed,
   meditate on the experience of its fathers.
⁹ We sons of yesterday know nothing;
   our life on earth passes like a shadow.
¹⁰ But they will teach you, they will tell you,
   and these are the words they will speak from the heart,
¹¹ "Does papyrus flourish, except in marshes?
   Without water, can the rushes grow?
¹² Pluck them even at their freshest:
   fastest of all plants they wither.
¹³ Such is the fate of all who forget God;
   so perishes the hope of the godless man.
¹⁴ His trust is only a thread,
   his assurance a spider's web.
¹⁵ Let him lean on his house; it will not stand firm;
   cling to it, it will not hold.
¹⁶ Like some lush plant in the sunlight,
   he sprouted his early shoots over the garden;
¹⁷ but his roots were twined in a heap of stones,
   he drew his life among the rocks.
¹⁸ Snatch him from his bed,
   and it denies it ever saw him.
¹⁹ Now he rots on the roadside,
   and from that soil spring others.
²⁰ Believe me, God neither spurns a stainless man,
   nor lends his aid to the evil.
²¹ Once again your cheeks will fill with laughter,
   from your lips will break a cry of joy.

²²   Your enemies shall be covered with shame,
       and the tent of the wicked folk shall vanish."

God's justice is above all law

¹9 Job spoke next. He said:

²   Indeed, I know it is as you say:
       how can man be in the right against God?
³   If any were so rash as to challenge him for reasons,
       one in a thousand would be more than they could answer.
⁴   His heart is wise, and his strength is great:
       who then can successfully defy him?
⁵   He moves the mountains, though they do not know it;
       he throws them down when he is angry.
⁶   He shakes the earth, and moves it from its place,
       making all its pillars tremble.
⁷   The sun, at his command, forbears to rise,
       and on the stars he sets a seal.
⁸   He and no other stretched out the skies,
       and trampled the Sea's tall waves.
⁹   The Bear, Orion too, are of his making,
       the Pleiades and the Mansions of the South.
¹⁰   His works are great, beyond all reckoning,
       his marvels, past all counting.
¹¹   Were he to pass me, I should not see him,
       nor detect his stealthy movement.
¹²   Were he to snatch a prize, who could prevent him,
       or dare to say, "What are you doing?"
¹³   God never goes back on his anger,
       Rahab's minions still lie at his feet.[a]
¹⁴   How dare I plead my cause, then,
       or choose arguments against him?
¹⁵   Suppose I am in the right, what use is my defense?
       For he whom I must sue is judge as well.

9 a. Rahab stands for Chaos, the first enemy conquered by God.

16 If he deigned to answer my citation,
could I be sure that he would listen to my voice?

17 He who for one hair crushes me,
who, for no reason, wounds and wounds again,

18 leaving me not a moment to draw breath,
with so much bitterness he fills me.

19 Shall I try force? Look how strong he is!
Or go to court? But who will summon him?

20 Though I think myself right, his mouth may condemn me;
though I count myself innocent, it may declare me a
hypocrite.

21 But am I innocent after all? Not even I know that,
and, as for my life, I find it hateful.

22 It is all one, and this I dare to say:
innocent and guilty, he destroys all alike.

23 When a sudden deadly scourge descends,
he laughs at the plight of the innocent.

24 When a country falls into a tyrant's hand,
it is he who blindfolds the judges.
Or if not he, who else?

25 My days run hurrying by,
seeing no happiness in their flight,

26 skimming along like a reed canoe,
or the flight of an eagle after its prey.

27 If I resolve to stifle my moans,
change countenance, and wear a smiling face,

28 fear comes over me, at the thought of all I suffer,
for such, I know, is not your treatment of the innocent.

29 And if I am guilty,
why should I put myself to useless trouble?

30 No use to wash myself with snow,
or bleach my hands pure white;

31 for you will plunge me in dung
until my very clothes recoil from me.

32 Yes, I am man, and he is not; and so no argument,
     no suit between the two of us is possible.
33 There is no arbiter between us,
     to lay his hand on both,
34 to stay his rod from me,
     or keep away his daunting terrors.
35 Nonetheless, I shall speak, not fearing him:
     I do not see myself like that at all.

¹10 Since I have lost all taste for life,
     I will give free reign to my complaints;
     I shall let my embittered soul speak out.
2   I shall say to God, "Do not condemn me,
     but tell me the reason for your assault.
3   Is it right for you to injure me,
     cheapening the work of your own hands
     and abetting the schemes of the wicked?
4   Have you got human eyes,
     do you see as mankind sees?
5   Is your life mortal like man's,
     do your years pass as men's days pass?
6   You, who inquire into my faults
     and investigate my sins,
7   you know very well that I am innocent,
     and that no one can rescue me from your hand.
8   Your own hands shaped me, modeled me;
     and would you now have second thoughts, and destroy me?
9   You modeled me, remember, as clay is modeled,
     and would you reduce me now to dust?
10 Did you not pour me out like milk,
     and curdle me then like cheeseª;
11 clothe me with skin and flesh,
     and weave me of bone and sinew?

10 a. The contemporary belief was that an embryo was formed by the congealing of the mother's blood.

12   And then you endowed me with life,
         watched each breath of mine with tender care.
13   Yet, after all, you were dissembling;
         biding your time, I know,
14   to mark if I should sin
         and to let no fault of mine go uncensored.
15   Woe to me, if I am guilty;
         if I am innocent, I dare not lift my head,
         so wholly abject, so drunk with pain am I.
16   And if I make a stand, like a lion you hunt me down,
         adding to the tale of your triumphs.
17   You attack, and attack me again,
         with stroke on stroke of your fury,
         relentlessly your fresh troops assail me.
18   "Why did you bring me out of the womb?
         I should have perished then, unseen by any eye,
19   a being that had never been,
         to be carried from womb to grave.
20   The days of my life are few enough:
         turn your eyes away, leave me a little joy,
21   before I go to the place of no return,
         the land of murk and deep shadow,
22   where dimness and disorder hold sway,
         and light itself is like dead of night."

Job must acknowledge God's wisdom

¹11 Zophar of Naamath spoke next. He said:

2   Is babbling to go without an answer?
         Is wordiness in man a proof of right?
3   Do you think your talking strikes men dumb,
         will you jeer with no one to refute you?
4   These were your words, "My way of life is faultless,
         and in your eyes I am free from blame."

5 But if God had a mind to speak,
     to open his lips and give you answer,
6 were he to show you the secrets of wisdom
     which put all cleverness to shame—
     you would know it is for sin he calls you to account.
7 Can you claim to grasp the mystery of God,
     to understand the perfection of Shaddai?
8 It is higher than the heavens: what can you do?
     It is deeper than Sheol: what can you know?
9 Its length is longer than the earth,
     its breadth is broader than the sea.
10 If he passes, who can stop him,
     or make him yield once he has seized?
11 For he detects the worthlessness in man,
     he sees iniquity and marks it well.
12 And so the idiot grows wise,
     thus a young wild donkey grows tame.
13 Come, you must set your heart right,
     stretch out your hands to him.
14 Renounce the iniquity that stains your hands,
     let no injustice live within your tents.
15 Then you may face the world in innocence,
     unwavering and free from fear.
16 You will forget your sufferings,
     remember them as waters that have passed away.
17 Your life, more radiant than the noonday,
     will make a dawn of darkness.
18 Full of hope, you will live secure,
     dwelling well and safely guarded.
19 No one will dare disturb you,
     and many a man will seek your favor.
20 But the wicked will look around with weary eyes,
     and finding no escape,
     the only hope they have is life's last breath.

God's wisdom is best seen in the dreadful works of his omnipotence

^{1}12 Job spoke next. He said:

2   Doubtless, you are the voice of the people,
        and when you die, wisdom will die with you!
3   I can reflect as deeply as ever you can,
        I am no way inferior to you.
        And who, for that matter, has not observed as much?
4   A man becomes a laughingstock to his friends
        if he cries to God and expects an answer.
        The blameless innocent incurs only mockery.
5   "Add insult to injury," think the prosperous,
        "strike the man now that he is staggering!"
6   And yet, the tents of brigands are left in peace,
        and those who challenge God live in safety,
        and make a god of their two fists!
7   If you would learn more, ask the cattle,
        seek information from the birds of the air.
8   The creeping things of earth will give you lessons,
        and the fishes of the sea will tell you all.
9   There is not one such creature but will know
        this state of things is all of God's own making.
10   He holds in his power the soul of every living thing,
        and the breath of each man's body.
11   The ear is a judge of speeches, is it not,
        just as the palate can tell one food from another?
12   Wisdom is found in the old,
        and discretion comes with great age.
13   But in him there is wisdom, and power, too,
        and decision no less than discretion.
14   What he destroys, none can rebuild;
        whom he imprisons, none can release.
15   Is there a drought? He has checked the waters.
        Do these play havoc with the earth? He has let them loose.

16 In him is strength, in him resourcefulness,
   beguiler and beguiled are both alike his slave.
17 He robs the country's counselors of their wits,
   turns judges into fools.
18 His hands untie the belt of kings,
   and bind a rope about their loins.
19 He makes priests walk barefoot,
   and overthrows the powers that are established.
20 He strikes the cleverest speakers dumb,
   and robs old men of their discretion.
21 He pours contempt on the nobly born,
   and unties the girdle of the strong.
22 He robs the depths of their darkness,
   brings deep shadow to the light.
23 He builds a nation up, then strikes it down,
   or makes a people grow, and then destroys it.
24 He strips a country's leaders of their judgement,
   and leaves them to wander in a trackless waste,
25 to grope about in unlit darkness,
   and totter like a man in liquor.

¹13 I have seen all this with my own eyes,
   heard with my own ears, and understood.
2 Whatever you know, I know too;
   I am no way inferior to your.
3 But my words are intended for Shaddai;
   I mean to remonstrate with God.
4 As for you, you are only charlatans,
   physicians in your own estimation.
5 I wish someone would teach you to be quiet
   —the only wisdom that becomes you!
6 Kindly listen to my accusation,
   pay attention to the pleading of my lips.
7 Will you plead God's defense with prevarication,
   his case in terms that ring false?

8   Will you be partial in his favor,
      and act as his advocates?

9   For you to meet his scrutiny, would this be well?
      Can he be duped as men are duped?

10   Harsh rebuke you would receive from him
      for your covert partiality.

11   Does his majesty not affright you,
      dread of him not fall on you?

12   Your old maxims are proverbs of ash,
      your retorts, retorts of clay.

13   Silence! Now I will do the talking,
      whatever may befall me.

14   I put my flesh between my teeth,
      I take my life in my hands.

15   Let him kill me if he will; I have no other hope
      than to justify my conduct in his eyes.

16   This very boldness gives promise of my release,
      since no godless man would dare appear before him.

17   Listen carefully to my words,
      and lend your ears to what I have to say.

18   You shall see, I will proceed by due form of law,
      persuaded, as I am, that I am guiltless.

19   Who comes against me with an accusation?
      Let him come! I am ready to be silenced and to die.

20   But grant me these two favors:
      if not, I shall not dare to confront you.

21   Take your hand away, that lies so heavy on me,
      no longer make me cower from your terror.

22   Then arraign me, and I will reply;
      or rather, I will speak and you shall answer me.

23   How many faults and crimes have I committed?
      What law have I transgressed, or in what have I offended?

24   Why do you hide your face
      and look on me as your enemy?

25   Will you intimidate a wind-blown leaf,
      will you chase the dried-up chaff;

26 you list bitter accusations against me,
      taxing me with the faults of my youth,
27 after putting my feet in the stocks,
      watching my every step,
      and measuring my footprints;
28 while my life is crumbling like rotten wood,
      or a moth-eaten garment.

¹14 Man, born of woman
      has a short life yet has his fill of sorrow.
2   He blossoms, and he withers, like a flower;
      fleeting as a shadow, transient.
3   And is this what you deign to turn your gaze on,
      him that you would bring before you to be judged?
4   Who can bring the clean out of the unclean?
      No man alive!
5   Since man's days are measured out,
      since his tale of months depends on you,
      since you assign him bounds he cannot pass,
6   turn your eyes from him, leave him alone,
      like a hired drudge, to finish his day.
7   There is always hope for a tree:
      when felled, it can start its life again;
      it shoots continue to sprout.
8   Its roots may be decayed in the earth,
      its stump withering in the soil,
9   but let it scent the water, and it buds,
      and puts out branches like a plant new set.
10   But man? He dies, and lifeless he remains;
      man breathes his last, and then where is he?
11   The waters of the seas may disappear,
      all the rivers may run dry or drain away;
12   but man, once in his resting place, will never rise again.
      The heavens will wear away before he wakes,
      before he rises from his sleep.

13 If only you would hide me in Sheol,
    and shelter me there until your anger is past,
14 fixing a certain day for calling me to mind—
    for once a man is dead can he come back to life?—
    day after day of my service I would wait
    for my relief to come.
15 Then you would call, and I should answer,
    you would want to see the work of your hands once more.
16 Now you count every step I take,
    but then you would cease to spy on my sins;
17 you would seal up my crime in a bag,
    and whiten my fault over.
18 But no! Soon or late the mountain falls,
    the rock moves from its place,
19 water wears away the stones,
    the cloudburst erodes the soil;
    just so do you destroy man's hope.
20 You crush him once for all, and he is gone;
    you mar him, and then you bid him go.
21 Let his sons achieve honor, he does not know of it,
    humiliation, he gives it not a thought.
22 He feels no pain for anything but his own body,
    makes no lament, save for his own life.

B. SECOND SERIES OF SPEECHES

Job's own words condemn him

¹15 Eliphaz of Teman spoke next. He said:

2   Does a wise man answer with airy reasonings,
    or feed himself on an east wind?
3   Does he defend himself with empty talk
    and ineffectual wordiness?
4   You do worse: You flout piety,
    you repudiate mediation in God's presence.

5   A guilty conscience prompts your words,
     you adopt the language of the cunning.

6   Your own mouth condemns you, and not I;
     your own lips bear witness against you.

7   Are you the first-born of the human race,
     brought into the world before the hills?

8   Have you been a listener at God's council,
     or established a monopoly of wisdom?

9   What knowledge have you that we have not,
     what understanding that is not ours too?

10   A gray-haired man, and an ancient, are of our number;
     these have seen more summers than your father.

11   Do you scorn the comfort that God gives,
     and the moderation we have used in speaking?

12   See how passion carries you away!
     How evil you look,

13   when you thus loose your anger on God
     and utter speeches such as these!

14   How can any man be clean?
     Born of woman, can he ever be good?

15   In his own Holy Ones God puts no trust,
     and the heavens themselves are not, in his eyes, clean.

16   Then how much less this hateful, corrupt thing,
     mankind, that drinks iniquity like water!

17   Listen to me, I have a lesson for you:
     I will tell you of my own experience,

18   and of the teaching of the sages,
     those faithful guardians of the tradition of their fathers,

19   to whom alone the land was given,
     with never a foreigner to mix with them.

20   The life of the wicked is unceasing torment,
     the years allotted to the tyrant are numbered.

21   The danger signal ever echoes in his ear,
     in the midst of peace the marauder swoops on him.

22   He has no hope of fleeing from the darkness,
     but knows that he is destined for the sword,

23   marked down as meat for the vulture.
      He knows that his ruin is at hand.
24   The hour of darkness makes him terrified;
      distress and anguish close in on him,
      as though some king were mounting an attack.
25   He raised his hand against God,
      he ventured to defy Shaddai.
26   Blindly he bore down on him
      from behind his massive shield.
27   His face had grown full and fat,
      and his thighs too heavy with flesh.
28   He had taken possession of ruined towns
      and made his dwelling in deserted houses.
29   But all his careful building will go once more to ruin;
      not for him increase of wealth, his riches will not last,
      no longer will he cast his shadow over the land.
30   A flame will wither up his tender buds;
      the wind will carry of his blossom.
31   But he should not trust in his great stature,
      if he would not trust in vain.
32   His boughs will wither before their time,
      and his branches never again be green.
33   Like a vine he will let his unripe clusters fall,
      like an olive shed his blossom.
34   Ah yes, the sinner's brood is barren,
      and fire consumes the tents of the venal.
35   Conceive mischief, and you breed disaster,
      and carry in yourself deceitfulness.

The injustice of man and the justice of God

¹16 Job spoke next. He said:

2   How often have I heard all this before!
      What sorry comforters you are!
3   Is there never to be an end of airy words?
      What a plague your need to have the last word is!

4 I too could talk like you,
   were your soul in the plight of mine.

5 I too could overwhelm you with sermons,
   I could shake my head over you,

6 and speak words of encouragement,
   until my lips grew tired.

7 But, while I am speaking, my suffering remains;
   and when I am not, do I suffer any the less?

8 And now ill will drives me to distraction,
   and a whole host molests me,
rising, like some witness for the prosecution,
   to utter slander to my very face.

9 In tearing fury it pursues me,
   with gnashing teeth.

10 My enemies whet their eyes on me,
   and open gaping jaws.
Their insults strike like slaps in the face,
   and all set on me together.

11 Yes, God has handed me over to the godless,
   and cast me into the hands of the wicked.

12 I lived at peace, until he shattered me,
   taking me by the neck to dash me to pieces.

13 He has made me a target for his archery,
   shooting his arrows at me from every side.
Pitiless, through the loins he pierces me,
   and scatters my gall on the ground.

14 Breach after breach he drives through me,
   bearing down on me like a warrior.

15 I have sewn sackcloth over my skin
   and rubbed my brow in the dust.

16 My face is red with tears,
   and a veil of shadow hangs on my eyelids.

17 This notwithstanding, my hands are free of violence,
   and my prayer is undefiled.

18 Cover not my blood, O earth,[a]
   afford my cry no place to rest.

16 a. Blood, if not covered with earth, cries to heaven for vengence.

¹⁹ Henceforth I have a witness in heaven,
   my defender is there in the height.
²⁰ My own lament is my advocate with God,
   while my tears flow before him.
²¹ Let this plead for me as I stand before God,
   as a man will plead for his fellows.
²² For the years of my life are numbered,
   and I shall soon take the road of no return.

¹17 My breath grows weak
   and the gravediggers are gathering for me,
² I am the butt of mockers,
   and all my waking hours I brood on their spitefulness.
³ You yourself must take my own guarantee,
   since no one cares to clap his hand on mine.^a
⁴ For you have shut their hearts to reason,
   and not a hand is lifted.
⁵ Like a man who invites his friends to share his property
   while the eyes of his own sons languish,
⁶ I have become a byword among the people,
   and a creature on whose face to spit.
⁷ My eyes grow dim with grief,
   and my limbs wear away like a shadow.
⁸ At this, honest men are shocked,^b
   and the guiltless man rails against the godless;
⁹ just men grow more settled in their ways,
   those whose hands are clean add strength to strength.
¹⁰ Come, then, all of you: set on me once more!
   I shall not find a single sage among you.
¹¹ My days have passed, far otherwise than I had planned,
   and every fiber of my heart is broken.
¹² Night, they say, makes room for day,
   and light is near at hand to chase the darkness.

17 a. I.e., to go surety for me. b. Assuming that such suffering is a punishment for guilt.

13 All I look forward to is dwelling in Sheol,
      and making my bed in the dark.
14 I tell the tomb, "You are my father,"
      and call the worm my mother and my sister.
15 Where then is my hope?
      Who can see any happiness for me?
16 Will these come down with me to Sheol,
      or sink with me into the dust?

Anger is powerless against the course of justice.

¹18 Bildad of Shuah spoke next. He said:

2   Will you never learn to check such words?
      Do you think we shall be slow to speak?
3   Why do you regard us as beasts,
      look on us as dumb animals?
4   Tear yourself to pieces if you will
      but the world, for all your rage, will not turn to desert,
      the rocks will not shift from their places.
5   The wicked man's light must certainly be put out,
      his brilliant flame cease to shine.
6   In his tent the light is dimmed,
      the lamp that shone on him is snuffed.
7   His vigorous stride grows cramped,
      his own cunning brings him down.
8   For into the net his own feet carry him,
      he walks among the snares.
9   A spring grips him by the heel,
      a trap snaps shut, and he is caught.
10 Hidden in the earth is a noose to snare him,
      pitfalls lie across his path.
11 Terrors attack him on every side,
      and follow behind him step for step.
12 Hunger becomes his companion,
      by his side Disaster stands.

13 Disease devours his flesh,
    Death's First-Born[a] gnaws his limbs.
14 He is torn from the shelter of his tent,
    and dragged before the King of Terrors.
15 The Lilith[b] makes her home under his roof,
    while people scatter brimstone on his holding.
16 His roots grow withered below,
    and his branches are blasted above.
17 His memory fades from the land,
    his name is forgotten in his homeland.
18 Driven from light into darkness,
    he is an exile from the earth,
19 without issue or posterity among his own people,
    none to live on where he has lived.
20 His tragic end appalls the West,
    and fills the East with terror.
21 A fate like his awaits every sinful house,
    the home of every man who knows not God.

Faith at its height in desertion by God and man

19 Job spoke next. He said:

2 Will you never stop tormenting me,
    and shattering me with speeches?
3 Ten times, no less, have you insulted me,
    ill-treating me without a trace of shame.
4 Suppose that I have gone astray,
    suppose I am even yet in error:
5 it is still true, though you think you have the upper hand of me
    and feel that you have proved my guilt,
6 that God, you must know, is my oppressor,
    and his is the net that closes around me.
7 If I protest against such violence, there is no reply;
    if I appeal against it, judgment is never given.

18 a. The principal disease, probably plague. b. A female demon of popular legend.

8   He has built a wall across my path which I cannot pass,
    and covered my way with darkness.
9   He has stolen my honor away,
    and taken the crown from my head.
10 On every side he breaks through my defenses, and I succumb.
    As a man a shrub, so he uproots my hope.
11 His anger flares against me,
    and he counts me as his enemy.
12 His troops have come in force,
    they have mounted their attack against me,
    laid siege to my tent.
13 My brothers stand aloof from me,
    and my relations takes care to avoid me.
14 My kindred and my friends have all gone away,
    and the guests in my house have forgotten me.
15 The serving maids look on me as a foreigner,
    a stranger, never seen before.
16 My servant does not answer when I call him,
    I am reduced to entreating him.
17 To my wife my breath is unbearable,
    for my own brothers I am a thing corrupt.
18 Even the children look down on me,
    ever ready with a jibe when I appear.
19 All my dearest friends recoil from me in horror:
    those I loved best have turned against me.
20 Beneath my skin, my flesh begins to rot,
    and my bones stick out like teeth.
21 Pity me, pity me, you, my friends,
    for the hand of God has struck me.
22 Why do you hound me down like God,
    will you never have enough of my flesh?
23 Ah, would that these words of mine were written down,
    inscribed on some monument
24 with iron chisel and engraving tool,
    cut into the rock for ever.

25   This I know: that my Avenger[a] lives,
     and he, the Last, will take his stand on earth.
26   After my awaking, he will set me close to him,
     and from my flesh I shall look on God.
27   He whom I shall see will take my part:
     these eyes will gaze on him and find him not aloof.
     My heart within me sinks. . .
28   You, then, that mutter, "How shall we track him down,
     what pretext shall we find against him?"
29   may well fear the sword on your own account.
     There is an anger stirred to flame by evil deeds;
     you will learn that there is indeed a judgment.

The course of justice admits of no exception

[1]20 Zophar of Naamath spoke next. He said,

2   To this my thoughts are eager to reply:
     no wonder if I am possessed by impatience,
3   I found these admonitions little to my taste,
     but my spirit whispers to me how to answer them.
4   Do you not know, that since time began
     and man was set on the earth,
5   the triumph of the wicked has always been brief,
     and the sinner's gladness has never lasted long?
6   Towering to the sky he may have been,
     with head touching the clouds;
7   but he vanishes, like a phantom, once for all,
     while those who saw him now ask, "Where is he?"
8   Like a dream that leaves no trace he takes his flight,
     like a vision in the night he flies away.
9   The eye that looked on him will never see him more,
     his house nevermore sets eyes on him.
10   His sons must recoup his victims,
     and his children pay back his riches.

19 a. "Avenger" and "take his stand" are technical legal terms.

11 With the vigor of youth his bones were filled,
      now it lies in the dust with him.
12 Evil was sweet to his mouth,
      he hid it beneath his tongue;
13 unwilling to let it go,
      he let it linger on his palate.
14 Such food goes bad in his belly,
      working inside him like the poison of a viper.
15 Now he must bring up all the wealth that he has swallowed,
      God makes him disgorge it.
16 He sucked "poison of vipers";
      and the tongue of the adder kills him.
17 He will know no more of streams that run with oil,
      or the torrents of honey and cream.
18 Gone that glad face at the sight of his gains,
      those comfortable looks when business was thriving.
19 Since he once destroyed the huts of poor men,
      and stole other's houses when he should have built his own,
20 since his avarice could never be satisfied,
      now his hoarding will not save him;
21 since there was nothing ever escaped his greed,
      now his prosperity will not last.
22 His abundance at its full, want seizes him,
      misery descends on him in all its force.
23 On him God looses all his burning wrath,
      hurling against his flesh a hail of arrows.
24 No use to run away from the iron armory,
      for the bow of bronze will shoot him through.
25 Out through his back an arrow sticks,
      from his gall a shining point.
26 An arsenal of terrors falls on him,
      and all that is dark lies in ambush for him.
    A fire unlit by man devours him,
      and consumes what is left in his tent.
27 The heavens lay bare his iniquity,
      the earth takes its stand against him.

28   A flood sweeps his house away,
       and carries it off in the Day of Wrath.
29   Such is the fate God allots to the wicked,
       such his inheritance assigned by God.

Facts give the lie

¹21 Job spoke next. He said:

2   Listen, only listen to my words;
       this is the consolation you can offer me.
3   Let me have my say;
       you may jeer when I have spoken.
4   Do you think I bear a grudge against man?
       Have I no reason to be out of patience?
5   Hear what I have to say, and you will be dumbfounded,
       will place your hands over your mouths.
6   I myself am appalled at the very thought,
       and my flesh begins to shudder.
7   Why do the wicked still live on,
       their power increasing with their age?
8   They see their posterity insured,
       and their offspring grow before their eyes.
9   The peace of their houses has nothing to fear,
       the rod that God wields is not for them.
10   No mishap with their bulls at breeding time,
       nor miscarriage with their cows at calving.
11   They let their infants frisk like lambs,
       their children dance like deer.
12   They sing to the tambourine and the lyre,
       and rejoice to the sound of the flute.
13   They end their lives in happiness
       and go down in peace to Sheol.
14   Yet these were the ones who said to God, "Go away!
       We do not choose to learn your ways.
15   What is the point of our serving Shaddai?
       What profit should we get from praying to him?"

16   Is it not true, they held their fortune in their own two hands,
      and in their counsels, left no room for God?

17   Do we often see a wicked man's light put out,
      or disaster overtaking him,
      or all his goods destroyed by the wrath of God?

18   How often do we see him harassed like a straw before the wind,
      or swept off like chaff before a gale?

19   God, you say, reserves the man's punishment for his children.
      No! Let him bear the penalty himself, and suffer under it!

20   Let him see his ruin with his own eyes,
      and himself drink the anger of Shaddai.

21   When he has gone, how can the fortunes of his House affect
      him,
      when the number of his months is cut off?

22   But who can give lessons in wisdom to God,
      to him who is judge of those on high?

23   And again: One man dies in the fullness of his strength,
      in all possible happiness and ease,

24   with his thighs all heavy with fat,
      and the marrow of his bones undried.

25   Another dies with bitterness in his heart,
      never having tasted happiness.

26   Together now they lie in the dust
      with worms for covering.

27   I know well what is in your mind,
      the spiteful thoughts you entertain about me.

28   "What has become of the great lord's house," you say,
      "where is the tent where the wicked live?"

29   Have you never asked those that have traveled,
      or have you misunderstood the tale they told,

30   "The wicked man is spared for the day of disaster,
      and carried off in the day of wrath?"

31   But who is there then to accuse him to his face for his deeds,
      and pay him back for what he has done,

32   when he is on his way to his burial,
      when men are watching at his grave.

33   The clods of the valley are laid gently on him,
       and a whole procession walks behind him.
34   So what sense is there in your empty consolation?
       What nonsense are your answers!

God punishes only to vindicate justice

¹22 Eliphaz of Teman spoke next. He said:

2   Can a man be of any use to God,
       when even the wise man's wisdom is of use only to himself?
3   Does Shaddai derive any benefit from your integrity,
       or profit from your blameless conduct?
4   Would he punish you for your piety,
       and hale you off to judgement?
5   No, rather for your manifold wickednesses,
       for you unbending iniquities!
6   You have exacted needless pledges from your brothers,
       and men go naked now through your despoiling;
7   you have grudged water to the thirsty man,
       and refused bread to the hungry;
8   you have narrowed the lands of the poor man down to nothing
       to set your crony in his place,
9   sent widows away empty-handed
       and crushed the arms of orphans.
10   No wonder, then, if snares are all around you,
       or sudden terrors make you afraid.
11   Light has turned to darkness and it blinds you,
       and a flood of water overwhelms you.
12   Does not God live at the height of heaven,
       and see the zenith of the stars?
13   Because he is far above, you said, "What does God know?
       Can he peer through the shadowed darkness?"
14   The clouds, to him, are in impenetrable veil,
       and he prowls on the rim of the heavens.
15   And will you still follow the ancient trail
       trodden by the wicked?

16   Those men who were borne off before their time,
     with rivers swamping their foundations,
17   because they said to God, "Go away!
     What can Shaddai do to us?"
18   Yet he himself had filled their houses with good things,
     while these wicked men shut him out of their counsels.
19   At the sight of their ruin, good men rejoice,
     and the innocent deride them:
20   "See how their greatness is brought to nothing!
     See how their wealth has perished in the flames!"
21   Well then! Make peace with him, be reconciled,
     and all your happiness will be restored to you.
22   Welcome the teaching from his lips,
     and keep his words close to your heart.
23   If you return, humbled, to Shaddai
     and drive all injustice from your tents,
24   if you reckon gold as dust
     and Ophir as the pebbles of the torrent,
25   then you will find Shaddai worth bars of gold
     or silver piled in heaps.
26   Then Shaddai will be all your delight,
     and you will lift your face to God.
27   You will pray, and he will hear;
     you will have good reason to fulfill your vows.
28   Whatever you undertake will go well,
     and light will shine on your path;
29   for he that casts down the boasting of the braggart
     is he that saves the man of downcast eyes.
30   If a man is innocent, he will bring him freedom,
     and freedom for you if your hands are kept unstained.

God is far off, and evil is victorious

¹23 Job spoke next. He said:

² My lament is still rebellious,
  that heavy hand of his drags groans from me.
³ If only I knew how to reach him,
  or how to travel to his dwelling!
⁴ I should set out my case to him,
  my mouth would not want for arguments.
⁵ Then I could learn his defense, every word of it,
  taking note of everything he said to me.
⁶ Would he use all his strength in this debate with me?
  No, he would have to give me a hearing.
⁷ He would see he was contending with an honest man,
  and I should surely win my case.
⁸ If I go eastward, he is not there;
  or westward—still I cannot see him.
⁹ If I seek him in the north, he is not to be found,
  invisible still when I turn to the south.
¹⁰ And yet he knows of every step I take!
  Let him test me in the crucible: I shall come out pure gold.
¹¹ My footsteps have followed close in his,
  I have walked in his way without swerving;
¹² I have kept every commandment of his lips,
  cherishing the words from his mouth in my breast.
¹³ But once he has decided, who can change his mind?
  Whatever he plans, he carries out.
¹⁴ No doubt, then, but he will carry out my sentence,
  like so many other decrees that he has made.
¹⁵ That is why I am full of fear before him,
  and the more I think, the greater grows my dread of him.
¹⁶ God has made my heart sink,
  Shaddai has filled me with fear.
¹⁷ For darkness hides me from him,
  and the gloom veils his presence from me.

24 Why has not Shaddai his own store of times,
    and why do his faithful never see his Days?[a]
2   The wicked move boundary marks away,
    they carry off flock and shepherd.
3   Some drive away the orphan's donkey,
    and take the widow's ox for a security.
4   Beggars, now, avoid the roads,
    and all the poor of the land must go into hiding.
5   Like wild donkeys in the desert, they go out,
    driven by the hunger of their children,
    to seek, food on the barren steppes.
6   They must do the harvesting in the scoundrel's field,
    they must do the picking in the vineyards of the wicked.
10 They go about naked, lacking clothes,
    and starving while they carry the sheaves.
11 They have no stones for pressing oil,
    they tread the winepresses, yet they are parched with thirst.
7   They spend the night naked, lacking clothes,
    with no covering against the cold.
8   Mountain rainstorms cut them through,
    shelterless, they hug the rocks.
9   Fatherless children are robbed of their lands,
    and poor men have their cloaks seized as security.
12 From the towns come the groans of the dying
    and the gasp of wounded men crying for help.
    Yet God remains deaf to their appeal!
13 Others of them hate the light,
    know nothing of its ways,
    avoid its paths.
14 When all is dark the murderer leaves his bed
    to kill the poor and needy.
16a All night long prowls the thief,
    breaking into houses while the darkness lasts.

24 a. A "store of times" could be used to lengthen a man's life and provide the opportunity to complete his punishment; "his Days" would be like "the Day of Yahweh," a time when he would assert his sovereignty in universal retribution.

15 The eye of the adulterer watches for twilight,
    "No one will see me," he mutters
    as he masks his face.
16b In the daytime they go into hiding,
    these folks who have no love for the light.
17 For all of them, morning is their darkest hour,
    because they know its terrors.
25 Is this not so? Who can prove me a liar
    or show that my words have no substance?

A hymn to God's omnipotence

¹25 Bildad of Shuah spoke next. He said:

2   What sovereignty, what awe, is his
    who keeps the peace in his heights!
3   Can anyone number his armies,
    or boast of having escaped his ambushes?
4   Could any man ever think himself innocent, when confronted
    by God?
    Born of woman, how could he ever be clean?
5   The very moon lacks brightness,
    and the stars are unclean as he sees them.
6   What, then, of man, maggot that he is,
    the son of man, a worm?

⁵26 The Shades tremble beneath the earth;
    the waters and their denizens are afraid.
6   Before his eyes, Sheol is bare,
    Perdition[a] itself is uncovered.
7   He it was who spread the North[b] above the void,
    and poised the earth on nothingness.
8   He fastens up the waters in his clouds—
    the mists do not tear apart under their weight.

26 a. In Hebrew "Abaddon," perhaps originally a deity, here a synonym for Sheol, the under-world. b. The "fixed quarter" of the vault of the sky, on which the heavens were believed to revolve.

9   He covers the face of the moon at the full,
      his mist he spreads over it.

10   He has traced a ring on the surface of the waters,
      at the boundary between light and dark.

11   The pillars of the heavens tremble,
      they are struck with wonder when he threatens them.

12   With his power he calmed the Sea,
      with his wisdom struck Rahab down.

13   His breath made the heavens luminous,
      his hand transfixed the Fleeing Serpent.

14   All this but skirts the ways he treads,
      a whispered echo is all that we hear of him.
      But who could comprehend the thunder of his power?

Bildad's words are empty

1 Job spoke next. He said:

2   To one so weak, what a help you are,
      for the arm that is powerless, what a rescuer!

3   What excellent advice you give the unlearned,
      never at a loss for a helpful suggestion!

4   But who are they aimed at, these speeches of yours,
      and what spirit is this that comes out of you?

Job reaffirms his innocence while acknowledging God's power

27 And Job continued his solemn discourse. He said:

2   I swear by the living God who denies me justice,
      by Shaddai who has turned my life sour,

3   that as long as a shred of life is left in me,
      and the breath of God breathes in my nostrils,

4   my lips shall never speak untruth,
      nor any lie be found on my tongue.

5   Far from ever admitting you to be in the right:
      I will maintain my innocence to my dying day.

6   I take my stand on my integrity, I will not stir:
    my conscience gives me no cause to blush for my life.
7   May my enemy meet a criminal's end,
    and my opponent suffer with the guilty.
8   For what hope, after all, has the godless when he prays,
    and raises his soul to God?
9   Is God likely to hear his cries
    when disaster descends on him?
10 Did he make Shaddai all his delight,
    calling on him at every turn?
11 No: I am showing you how God's power works,
    making no secret of Shaddai's designs.
12 And if you all had understood them for yourselves,
    you would not have wasted your breath in empty words.

The speech of Zophar: the accursed

13 Here is the fate that God has in store for the wicked,
    and the inheritance with which Shaddai endows the man of
    violence.
14 A sword awaits his sons, however many they may be,
    and their children after them will go unfed.
15 Plague will bury those he leaves behind him,
    and their widows will have no chance to mourn them.
16 He may collect silver like dust,
    and gather fine clothes like clay.
17 Let him gather! Some good man will wear them,
    while his silver is shared among the innocent.
18 He has built himself a spider's web,
    made himself a watchman's shack.
19 He goes to bed a rich man, but never again:
    he wakes to find not a penny left.
20 Terrors attack him in broad daylight,
    and at night a whirlwind sweeps him off.
21 An east wind picks him up and drags him away,
    snatching him up from his homestead.

22 Pitilessly he is turned into a target,
  and forced to flee from the hands that menace him.
23 His downfall is greeted with applause,
  and hissing meets him on every side.
24.18acb Headlong he flees from daylight,
  he shrinks from the road which runs on the heights.
19 The lands of his home are under a curse,
  for heat and drought dry up the waters
  and scorch what is left of his corn.
20 The womb that shaped him forgets him
  and his name is recalled no longer.
  Thus wickedness is blasted as a tree is struck.
21 He used to be harsh to the barren, childless woman,
  and show no kindness to the widow.
22 But he who lays mighty hold on tyrants
  rises up to take away that life which seemed secure.
23 He let him build his hopes on false security,
  but kept his eyes on every step he took.
24 The man had his time of glory, now he vanishes,
  drooping like a mallow plucked from its bed,
  and withering like an ear of corn.

D. A HYMN IN PRAISE OF WISDOM

Wisdom is beyond man's reach

28 Silver has its mines,
  and gold a place for refining.
2 Iron is extracted from the earth,
  the smelted rocks yield copper.
3 Man makes an end of darkness
  when he pierces to the uttermost depths
  the black and lightless rock.

⁴ Mines the lamp folk dig
  in places where there is no foothold,
  and hang suspended far from mankind.
⁵ That earth from which bread comes
  is ravaged underground by fire.
⁶ Down there, the rocks are set with sapphires
  full of spangles of gold.
⁷ Down there is a path unknown to birds of prey,
  unseen by the eye of any vulture;
⁸ a path not trodden by the lordly beasts,
  where no lion ever walked.
⁹ Man attacks its flinty sides,
  upturning mountains by their roots,
¹⁰ driving tunnels through the rocks,
  on the watch for anything precious.
¹¹ He explores the sources of rivers,ᵃ
  and brings to daylight secrets that were hidden.
¹² But tell me, where does wisdom come from?
  Where is understanding to be found?
¹³ The road to it is still unknown to man,
  not to be found in the land of the living.
¹⁴ "It is not in me," says the Abyss;
  "Nor here" replies the Sea.
¹⁵ It cannot be bought with solid gold,
  not paid for with any weight of silver,
¹⁶ nor be priced by the standard of the gold of Ophir,
  or of precious onyx or sapphire.
¹⁷ No gold, no glass can match it in value,
  nor for a fine gold vase can it be bartered.
¹⁸ Nor is there need to mention coral, nor crystal;
  beside wisdom, pearls are not worth the fishing.
¹⁹ Topaz from Cush is worthless in comparison,
  and gold, even refined, is valueless.

28 a. In "the waters under the earth," cf. 26:5.

20 But tell me, where does wisdom come from?
Where is understanding to be found?
21 It is outside the knowledge of every living thing,
hidden from the birds in the sky.
22 Perdition and Death can only say,
"We have heard reports of it."
23 God alone has traced its path
and found out where it lives.
24 (For he sees to the ends of the earth,
and observes all that lies under heaven.)
25 When he willed to give weight to the wind
and measured out the waters with a gauge,
26 when he made the laws and rules for the rain
and mapped a route for thunderclaps to follow,
27 then he had it in sight, and cast its worth,
assessed it, fathomed it.
28 And he said to man,
"Wisdom? It is fear of the Lord.
Understanding?—avoidance of evil."

E. CONCLUSION OF THE DIALOGUE

Job's lament and final defense
a. His former happiness

¹29 And Job continued his solemn discourse. He said:

2 Who will bring back to me the months that have gone,
and the days when God was my guardian,
3 when his lamp shone over my head,
and his light was my guide in the darkness?
4 Shall I ever see my autumn days again
when God hedged around my tent;
5 when Shaddai dwelt with me,
and my children were around me;
6 when my feet were plunged in cream,
and streams of oil poured from the rocks?

7 When I went out to the gate of the city,
  when I took my seat in the square,
8 as soon as I appeared, the young men stepped aside,
  while the older men rose to their feet.
9 Men of note interrupted their speeches,
  and put their fingers on their lips;
10 the voices of rulers were silenced,
  and their tongues stayed still in their mouths.

21 They waited anxiously to hear me.
  and listened in silence to what I had to say.
22 When I paused, there was no rejoinder,
  any my words dropped on them, one by one.
23 They waited for me, as men wait for rain,
  openmouthed, as if to catch the year's last showers.
24 If I smiled at them, it was too good to be true,
  they watched my face for the least sign of favor.
25 In a lordly style, I told them which course to take,
  and like a king amid his armies,
  I led them where I chose.

11 My praises echoed in every ear,
  and never an eye but smiled on me;
12 because I freed the poor man when he called,
  and the orphan who had no one to help him.
13 When men were dying, I it was who had their blessing;
  if widows' hearts rejoiced, that was my doing.
14 I had dressed myself in righteousness like a garment;
  justice, for me, was cloak and turban.
15 I was eyes for the blind,
  and feet for the lame.
16 Who but I was father of the poor?
  The stranger's case had a hearing from me.
17 I used to break the fangs of wicked men,
  and snatch their prey from between their jaws.

18 So I thought to myself, "I shall die in honor,
    my days like a palm tree's for number.
19 My roots thrust out to the water,
    my leaves freshened by the falling dew at night.
20 My reputation will never fade,
    and the bow in my hands will gain new strength."

b. His present misery

¹30 And now I am the laughingstock
    of my juniors, the young people,
    whose fathers I did not consider fit
    to put with the dogs that looked after my flock.
2   The strength of their hands would have been useless to me,
    enfeebled as they were,
    worn out by want and hunger.
3   They used to gnaw the roots of desert plants,
    and brambles from abandoned ruins;
4   and plucked mallow, and brushwood leaves,
    making their meals off roots of broom.
5   Outlawed from the society of men,
    who, as against thieves, raised hue and cry against them,
6   they made their dwellings on ravines' steep sides,
    in caves or clefts in the rock.
7   You could hear them wailing from the bushes,
    as they huddled together in the thistles.
8   Their children are as worthless a brood as they were,
    nameless people, outcasts of society.
9   And these are the ones that now sing ballads about me,
    and make me the talk of the town!
10 To them I am loathsome, they stand aloof from me,
    do not scruple to spit in my face.
11 Because he has unbent my bow and chastened me
    they cast the bridle from their mouth.

12 That brood of theirs rises to right of me,
stones are their weapons,
and they take threatening strides toward me.
13 They have cut me off from all escape,
there is no one to check their attack.
14 They move in, as though through a wide breach,
and I am crushed beneath the rubble.
15 Terrors turn to meet me,
my confidence is blown away as if by the wind;
my hope of safety passes like a cloud.
16 And now the life in me trickles away,
days of grief have gripped me.
17 At nighttime, sickness saps my bones,
I am gnawed by wounds that never sleep.
18 With immense power it has caught me by the clothes,
clutching at the collar of my coat.
19 It has thrown me into the mud
where I am no better than dust and ashes.
20 I cry to you, and you give me no answer;
I stand before you, but you take no notice.
21 You have grown cruel in your dealings with me,
your hand lies on me, heavy and hostile.
22 You carry me up to ride the wind,
tossing me about in a tempest.
23 I know it is to death that you are taking me,
the common meeting place of all that lives.
24 Yet have I ever laid a hand on the poor
when they cried out for justice in calamity?
25 Have I not wept for all whose life is hard,
felt pity for the penniless?
26 I hope for happiness, but sorrow came;
I looked for light, but there was darkness.
27 My stomach seethes, is never still,
for every day brings further suffering.
28 Somber I go, yet no one comforts me,
and if I rise in the council, I rise to weep.

29 I have become the jackal's brother
    and the ostrich's companion.
30 My skin has turned black on me,
    my bones are burned with fever.
31 My harp is tuned to funeral wails,
    my flute to the voice of mourners.

Job's apologia[a]

¹31 I made a pact with my eyes,
    not to linger on any virgin.
2   Now, what shares does God deal out on high,
    what lots does Shaddai assign from heaven,
3   if not disaster for the wicked,
    and calamities for the iniquitous?
4   But surely he sees how I behave,
    does he not count all my steps?
5   Have I been a fellow traveler with falsehood,
    or hastened my steps toward deceit?
6   If he weighs me on honest scales,
    being God, he cannot fail to see my innocence.
7   If my feet have wandered from the rightful path,
    or if my eyes have led my heart astray,
    or if my hands are smirched with any stain,
8   let another eat what I have sown,
    and let my young shoots all be rooted out.
9   If I ever lost my heart to any woman,
    or lurked at my neighbor's door,
10 let my wife grind corn that is not mine,
    let her sleep between others' sheets.
11 For I should have committed a sin of lust,
    a crime punishable by the law,
12 and should have lit a fire burning till Perdition,
    which would have devoured all my harvesting.

31 a. The form of this declaration, "a conditional imprecation," is that required by law from an accused person pleading "not guilty."

13 If ever I have infringed the rights of slave
   or maidservant in legal actions against me—
14 what shall I do, when God stands up?
   What shall I say, when he holds his assize?
15 They, no less than I, were created in the womb
   by the one same God who shaped us all within our mothers.

38 If my land calls down vengeance on my head
   and every furrow runs with tears,
39 if without payment I have eaten fruit grown on it
   or given those who toiled there cause to groan,
40a let branches grow where once was wheat,
   and foul weeds where barley thrived.

16 Have I been insensible to poor man's needs,
   or let a widow's eyes grow dim?
17 Or taken my share of bread alone,
   not giving a share to the orphan?
18 I, whom God has fostered fatherlike, from childhood,
   and guided since I left my mother's womb.
19 Have I ever seen a wretch in need of clothing,
   or a beggar going naked,
20 without his having cause to bless me from his heart,
   as he felt the warmth of the fleece from my lambs?
21 Have I raised my hand against the guiltless,
   presuming on my credit at the gate?
22 If so, then let my shoulder fall from its socket,
   my arm be shattered at the joint.
23 God's terror would indeed descend on me;
   how could I hold my ground before his majesty?
24 Have I put all my trust in gold,
   from finest gold sought my security?
25 Have I ever gloated over my great wealth,
   or the riches that my hands have won?
26 Or has the sight of the sun in its glory,
   or the glow of the moon as it walked the sky,

27 stolen my heart, so that my hand
   blew them a secret kiss?

28 That too would be a criminal offense,
   to have denied the supreme God.

29 Have I taken pleasure in my enemies' misfortunes,
   or made merry when disaster overtook them,

30 I who allowed my tongue to do no wrong,
   by cursing them or vowing them to death?

31 The people of my tent, did they not say,
   "Is there a man he has not filled with meat?"

32 No stranger ever had to sleep outside,
   my door was always open to the traveler.

33 Have I ever hidden my sins from men,
   keeping my iniquity secret in my breast?

34 Have I ever stood so in fear of common gossip,
   or so dreaded any family's contempt,
   that I have been reduced to silence, not venturing out of
   doors?

35 Who can get me a hearing from God?
   I have had my say, from A to Z; now let Shaddai answer me.
   When my adversary has drafted hit writ against me

36 I shall wear it on my shoulder,
   and bind it around my head like a royal turban.

37 I will give him an account of every step of my life,
   and go as boldly as a prince to meet him.

40b End of the words of Job.

III. THE SPEECHES OF ELIHU

Elihu joins the discussion

¹32 These three men said no more to Job, because he was convinced
2 of his innocence. But another man was infuriated—Elihu son of
3 Barachel the Buzite, of the clan of Ram. He fumed with rage
against Job for thinking that he was right and God was wrong;
and he was equally angry with the three friends for giving up the

4 argument and thus admitting that God could be unjust. While
5 they were speaking, Elihu had held himself back, because they
   were older than he was; but when he saw that the three men had
   not another word to say in answer, his anger burst out. Thus
6 Elihu son of Barachel the Buzite spoke next. He said:

Prologue

> I am still young,
>   and you are old,
> so I was shy, afraid,
>   to tell you what I know.

7 I told myself, "Old age should speak,
       advancing years will utter wisdom."
8 But now I know that it is a breath in man,
       the inspiration of Shaddai, that gives discernment.
9 Great age does not give wisdom,
       nor longevity sound judgment.
10 And so I ask you for a hearing;
       now it is my turn to tell what I know.
11 There was a time when I hoped for much from your speeches:
       I gave your reasonings a ready hearing,
       and watched you choose your words.
12 I gave you all my attention,
       and I can say that no one gave Job the lie,
       not one of you disproved his statements.
13 So do not dare to say that you have found wisdom,
       or that your teaching is from God not man.
14 I am not going to follow the same line of argument;
       my reply to Job will be couched in different terms.
15 They have been nonplused, baffled for an answer,
       words have failed them.
16 I have been waiting. Since they are silent,
       and have abandoned all efforts to reply,
17 now I will have my say,
       my turn has come to say what I know.

18 For I am filled with words,
　　choked by the rush of them within me.
19 I have a feeling in my heart like new wine seeking a vent,
　　and bursting a brand-new wineskin.
20 Nothing will bring relief but speech,
　　I will open my mouth and give my answer.
21 I shall not show any partiality toward anyone,
　　nor heap on any fulsome flatteries.
22 I have no skill in flattery,
　　my creator would soon silence me otherwise.

Job's presumption

¹33 Now, Job, be kind enough to listen to my words,
　　and attend to all I have to say.
2 Now as I open my mouth,
　　and my tongue shapes words against my palate,
3 my heart shall utter sayings full of wisdom,
　　and my lips speak the honest truth.
4 Refute me, if you can.
　　Prepare your ground to oppose me.
5 See, I am your fellow man, not a god;
　　like you, I was fashioned out of clay.
6 God's breath it was that made me,
　　the breathing of Shaddai that gave me life.
7 Thus, no fear of me need disturb you,
　　my hand will not lie heavy over you.
8 How could you say in my hearing—
　　for the sound of your words did not escape me—
9 "I am clean, and sinless,
　　I am pure, free of all fault.
10 Yet he is inventing grievances against me,
　　and imagining me his enemy.
11 He puts me in the stocks,
　　he watches my every step?"

¹² In saying so, I tell you, you are wrong:
God does not fit man's measure.

¹³ Why do you rail at him
for not replying to you, word for word?

¹⁴ God speaks first in one way,
and then in another, but not one notices.

¹⁵ He speaks by dreams, and visions that come in the night,
when slumber comes on mankind
and men are all asleep in bed.

¹⁶ Then it is he who whispers in the ear of man,
or may frighten him with fearful sights,

¹⁷ to turn him away from evil-doing,
and make an end of his pride;

¹⁸ to save his soul from the pit
and his life from the pathway to Sheol.

¹⁹ With suffering, too, he corrects man on his sickbed,
when his bones keep trembling with palsy;

²⁰ when his whole self is revolted by food,
and his appetite spurns dainties;

²¹ when his flesh rots as you watch it,
and his bare bones begin to show;

²² when his soul is drawing near to the pit,
and his life to the dwelling of the dead.

²³ Then there is an Angel by his side,
a Mediator, chosen out of thousands,
to remind a man where his duty lies,
to take pity on him and to say,

²⁴ "Release him from descent into the pit,
for I have found a ransom for his life";

²⁵ his flesh recovers the bloom of its youth,
he lives again as he did when he was young.

²⁶ He prays to God who has restored him to favor,
and comes, in happiness, to see his face.
He publishes far and wide the news of his vindication,
singing before his fellow men this hymn of praise,

27 "I sinned and left the path of right,
       but God has not punished me as my sin deserved.
28 He has spared my soul from going down into the pit,
       and is allowing my life to continue in the light."
29 All this God does
       again and yet again for man,
30 rescuing his soul from the pit,
       and letting the light of life shine bright on him.
31 Job, give me your attention, listen well;
       keep silence: I have more to say.
32 If you have anything to say, refute me,
       speak out, for I would gladly recognize your innocence.
33 If you have not, then listen:
       keep silence, while I teach you wisdom.

The three Sages have failed to justify God

¹34 Elihu continues his speech. He said:

2   You men of wisdom, listen to my words:
       lend me your ears, you learned men.
3   The ear is a judge of speeches,
       just as the palate can tell one food from another.
4   Let us discover together where justice lies,
       and settle among us what is best.
5   Now Job has said, "I am in the right,
       and God refuses to grant me justice.
6   The judge who judges me is ill-disposed,
       and though I have not sinned, my wounds are past all cure."
7   Are there many men like Job,
       who drink scurrility like water,
8   who keep company with evildoers,
       and march in step with the wicked?
9   Did he not say it was useless
       for man to try to please God?

10 Listen then to me, like intelligent men.
    So far is God removed from wickedness,
        and Shaddai from injustice,
11 that he requites a man for what he does,
        treating each one as his way of life deserves.
12 God never does wrong, do not doubt that!
        Shaddai does not deflect the course of right.
13 It is not as if someone else had given him the earth in trust,
        or confided the whole universe to his care.
14 Were he to recall his breath,
        to draw his breathing back into himself,
15 things of flesh would perish all together,
        and man would return to dust.
16 If you have any intelligence, listen to this,
        and lend your ear to what I have to say.
17 Could an enemy of justice ever govern?
        Would you dare condemn the Just One, the Almighty,
18 who can tell kings that they are good for nothing,
        and treat noblemen like criminals,
19 who shows no partiality to princes
        and makes no distinction between the rich and the poor,
    all alike being made by his own hands?
20 They die, they are gone in an instant,
        great though they are, they perish in the dead of night:
        it costs him no effort to remove a tyrant.
21 His eyes, you see, keep watch on all men's ways,
        and he observes their every step.
22 Not darkness, nor the deepest shadow,
        can hide the wrongdoer.
23 He serves no writ on men
        summoning them to appear before God's court:
24 he smashes great men's power without inquiry
        and sets up others in their places.
25 He knows well enough what they are about,
        and one fine night he throws them down for men to trample
    on.

26 He strikes them down for their wickedness,
      and makes them prisoners for all to see.

27 You may say, "They have so turned from him,
      and so ignored his ways,

28 that the poor have cried out to him against them
      and the wailing of the humble has assailed his ears,

29 yet he is unmoved, and nothing can touch him;
      he hides his face and nobody can see him."

30 But nonetheless he does take pity on nations and on men,
      freeing the godless man from the meshes of distress.

31 If such a man says to God,
      "I was led astray, I will sin no more.

32 If I did wrong, tell me about it,
      if I have been unjust, I will be so no more"—

33 in such a case, do you thing he ought to punish him,
      you who reject his decisions?
      Since it is you who make this choice, not I,
      let us all share your knowledge!

34 But this is what all sensible folk will say,
      and any wise man among my hearers,

35 "There is no wisdom in Job's speech,
      his words lack sense.

36 Put him unsparingly to the proof
      since his retorts are the same as those that the wicked make.

37 For to sin he adds rebellion,
      calling justice into question in our midst
      and heaping abuse on God."

God is not indifferent to what happens on earth

¹35 Elihu continued his speech. He said:

2   Do you presume to maintain that you are in the right,
      to insist on your innocence before God,

3   even to ask him, "How does it affect you,
      what harm has it done you if I have sinned?"

⁴   Well then, this is how I will answer you,
       and your friends as well.

⁵   Look up at the skies, look at them well,
       and see how high the clouds are above you.

⁶   If you sin, what do you achieve against him?
       If you heap up crimes, what is the injury you do him?

⁷   If you are just, what do you give him,
       what benefit does he receive at your hands?

⁸   Your fellow men are the ones to suffer from your crimes,
       humanity is the gainer if you are good.

⁹   When people groan under the weight of oppression,
       or cry out under the tyranny of the mighty,

¹⁰   no one thinks to ask, "Where is God, my maker,
       who makes glad songs ring out at dead of night,

¹¹   who makes us cleverer than the earth's wild beasts,
       wiser than the birds in the sky?"

¹²   Then they cry aloud, but he does not answer
       because of man's base pride.

¹³   How idle to maintain that God is deaf,
       that Shaddai notices nothing!

¹⁴   You even claim, "He does not see me:
       my cause is exposed before him, and yet I wait and wait."

¹⁵   Or even, "His anger never punishes,
       he does not seem to know of men's rebellion."

¹⁶   Hence when Job opens his mouth, it is for idle talk:
       his spate of words comes out of ignorance.

The real meaning of Job's sufferings

¹36 Elihu went on speaking. He said:

²   Be patient with me a little longer while I explain,
       for I have more to say on God's behalf.

³   I will range far afield for my arguments
       to prove my Maker just.

⁴   What I say contains no fallacies, I assure you,
       you see before you an enlightened man.

5   God does not spurn the blameless man
       or let the sinner live on in all his power.
6   He accords justice to the poor,
       and upholds the good man's rights.
7   When he raises kings to thrones,
       if they grow proud of their unending sway,
8   then he fetters them with chains,
       binding them in the bondage of distress.
9   He shows them all that they have done,
       and all the sins of pride they have committed.
10 He whispers a message in their ears,
       urging them to amend themselves.
11 If they listen and do as he says,
       their days end in happiness,
       and their closing years are full of ease.
12 If not, then a thunderbolt destroys them,
       and death comes on them unawares.
13 Yes the stubborn who cherish anger,
       and when he shackles them, do not ask for help:
14 they die in their youth,
       or lead a life despised by all.
15 The wretched, however, he saves by their very wretchedness,
       and uses distress to open their eyes.
16 For you, no less, he plans relief from sorrow.
       Once you lived in luxury unbounded,
       with rich food piled high on your table.
17 But you did not execute justice on the wicked,
       you cheated orphaned children of their rights.
18 In future beware of being led astray by riches,
       or corrupted by fat bribes.
19 Prosecute the rich, not merely the penniless;
       strong-armed men as well as those who are powerless.
20 Do not trample on those you do not know
       to install your relations in their place.
21 Avoid any tendency to wrong-doing,
       for such has been the true cause of your trials.

A hymn to God's wisdom and omnipotence

22 Look, by reason of his power God is supreme,
   what teacher can be compared with him?
23 Who has ever told him which course to take,
   or dared to say to him, "You have done wrong?"
24 Turn your mind rather to praising his works,
   a theme that many men have sung;
25 a sight that everyone can see,
   that man may gaze on from afar.
26 Yes, the greatness of God exceeds our knowledge,
   the number of his years is past computing.
27 He it is who keeps the raindrops back,
   dissolving the showers into mist,
28 which otherwise the clouds would spill
   in floods over all mankind.
31 Thanks to them he nourishes the nations
   with generous gifts of food.
29 And who can fathom how he spreads the clouds,
   or why such crashes thunder from his tent?
30 He spreads out the mist, wrapping it about him,
   and covers the tops of the mountains.
32 He gathers up the lightning in his hands,
   choosing the mark it is to reach;
33 his thunder gives warning of its coming:
   wrath overtakes iniquity.

37 At this my own heart quakes,
   and leaps from its place.
2 Listen, oh listen, to the blast of his voice
   and the sound that blares from his mouth.
3 He hurls his lightning below the span of heaven,
   it strikes to the very ends of the earth.
4 After it comes the roar of his voice,
   the peal of God's majestic thunder.

He does not check his thunderbolts
  until his voice resounds no more.
5 No doubt of it, but God reveals wonders,
  and does great deeds that we cannot understand.
6 When he says to the snow, "Fall on the earth,"
  or tells the rain to pour down in torrents,
7 he brings all men's strivings to a standstill
  so that each must acknowledge his hand at work.
8 All the beasts go back to their dens,
  taking shelter in their lairs.
9 The storm wind comes from the Mansion of the South,
  and the north winds usher in the cold.
10 God breathes, and the ice is there,
  the surface of the waters freezes over.
11 He weighs the clouds down with moisture,
  and the storm clouds radiate his lightning.
12 He himself guides their wheeling motion,
  directing all their seasonal changes:
they carry out his orders to the letter
  all over his inhabited world.
13 Whether for punishing earth's peoples
  or for a work of mercy, he dispatches them.
14 Listen to all this Job: no backsliding now!
  Meditate on God's wonders.
15 Can you tell how God controls them
  or how his clouds make the lightning flash?
16 Can you tell how he holds the clouds in balance:
  a miracle of consummate skill?
17 When your clothes are hot to your body
  and the earth lies still under the south wind,
18 can you help him to spread the vault of heaven,
  Or temper that mirror of cast metal?
19 Tell me what to say to him:
  . . . .
20 Can my words carry weight with him?
  Do man's commands reach his ears?

21 There are times when the light vanishes
    behind darkening clouds;
then comes the wind, sweeping them away,
    and brightness spreads from the north.
22 God is clothed in fearful splendor:
    he, Shaddai, is far beyond our reach.
23 Supreme in power, in equity,
    excelling in justice, yet no oppressor—
24 no wonder that men fear him,
    and thoughtful men hold him in awe.

IV. THE SPEECHES OF YAHWEH

FIRST SPEECH

Job must bow to the creator's wisdom

¹38 Then from the heart of the tempest Yahweh gave Job his answer.
He said:

2 Who is this obscuring my designs
    with his empty-headed words?
3 Brace yourself like a fighter;
    now it is my turn to ask questions and yours to inform me.
4 Where were you when I laid the earth's foundations?
    Tell me, since you are so well informed!
5 Who decided the dimensions of it, do you know?
    Or who stretched the measuring line across it?
6 What supports its pillars at their bases?
    Who laid its cornerstone
7 when all the stars of the morning were singing with joy,
    and the Sons of God in chorus were chanting praise?
8 Who pent up the sea behind closed doors
    when it leaped tumultuous out of the womb,
9 when I wrapped it in a robe of mist
    and made black clouds its swaddling bands;
10 when I marked the bounds it was not to cross
    and made it fast with a bolted gate?

11 Come thus far, I said, and no farther:
here your proud waves shall break.

12 Have you ever in your life given orders to the morning
or sent the dawn to its post,

13 telling it to grasp the earth by its edges
and shake the wicked out of it,

14 when it changes the earth[a] to sealing clay
and dyes it as a man dyes clothes;

15 stealing the light from the wicked men[b]
and breaking the arm raised to strike?

16 Have you journeyed all the way to the sources of the sea,
or walked where the Abyss is deepest?

17 Have you been shown the gates of Death
or met the janitors of Shadowland?

18 Have you an inkling of the extend of the earth?
Tell me about it if you have!

19 Which is the way to the home of the light,
and where does darkness live?

20 You could then show them the way to their proper places,
or put them on the path to where they live!

21 If you know all this, you must have been born with them,
you must be very old by now!

22 Have you ever visited the place where the snow is kept,
or seen where the hail is stored up,

23 which I keep for times of stress,
for days of battle and war?

24 From which direction does the lightning fork
when it scatters sparks over the earth?

25 Who carves a channel for the downpour,
and hacks a way for the rolling thunder,

26 so that rain may fall on lands where no one lives,
and the deserts void of human dwelling,

38 a. The "clay" is red in color. b. The light, or natural element, of the wicked, is the darkness of night.

27 giving drink to the lonely wastes
   and making grass spring where everything was dry?
28 Has the rain a father?
   Who begets the dewdrops?
29 What womb brings forth the ice,
   and gives birth to the frost of heaven,
30 when the waters grow hard as stone
   and the surface of the deep congeals?
31 Can you fasten the harness of the Pleiades
   or untie Orion's bands?
32 Can you guide the morning star season by season
   and show the Bear and its cubs which way to go?
33 Have you grasped the celestial laws?
   Could you make their writ run on the earth?
34 Can your voice carry as far as the clouds
   and make the pent-up waters do your bidding?
35 Will lightning flashes come at your command
   and answer, "Here we are?"
36 Who gave the ibis wisdom
   and endowed the cock with foreknowledge?[c]
37 Whose skill details every cloud
   and tilts the flasks of heaven
38 until the soil cakes into a solid mass
   and clods of earth cohere together?
39 Do you find a prey for the lioness
   and satisfy the hunger of her whelps
40 when they crouch in their dens
   and lurk in their lairs?
41 Who makes provisions for the raven
   when his squabs cry out to God
   and crane their necks in hunger?

¹39 Do you know how mountain goats give birth
   or have you ever watched the hinds in labor?

---

38 c. Both birds credited with foresight; the ibis heralds the flooding of the Nile, the cock announces the dawn.

2   How many months do they carry their young?
      At what time do they give birth?

3   They crouch to drop their young,
      and let their burdens fall in the open desert;

4   and when the calves have grown and gathered strength
      they leave them, never to return.

5   Who gave the wild donkey his freedom,
      and untied the rope from his proud neck?

6   I have given him the desert as a home,
      the salt plains as his own habitat.

7   He scorns the turmoil of the town:
      there are no shouts from a driver for him to listen for.

8   The mountains are the pastures that he ranges
      in quest of any type of green blade or leaf.

9   Is the wild ox willing to serve you
      or spend a night beside your manger?

10   If you tie a rope around his neck
      will he harrow the furrows for you?

11   Can you rely on his massive strength
      and leave him to do your heavy work?

12   Can you depend on him to come home
      carrying your grain to your threshing floor?

13   Can the wing of the ostrich be compared
      with the plumage of the stork or falcon?

14   She leaves her eggs on the ground
      with only earth to warm them;

15   forgetting that a foot may tread on them
      or a wild beast may crush them.

16   Cruel to her chicks as if they were not hers,
      little she cares if her labor goes for nothing.

17   God, you see, has made her unwise,
      and given her no share of common sense.

18   Yet, if she bestirs herself to use her height,
      she can make fools of horse and rider too.

19 Are you the one who makes the horse so brave
   and covers his neck with flowing hair?
20 Do you make him leap like a grasshopper?
   His proud neighing spreads terror far and wide.
21 Exultantly he paws the soil of the valley,
   and prances eagerly to meet the clash of arms.
22 He laughs at fear; he is afraid of nothing,
   he recoils before no sword.
23 On his back the quiver rattles,
   the flashing spear and javelin.
24 Quivering with impatience, he eats up the miles;
   when the trumpet sounds, there is no holding him.
25 At each trumpet blast he shouts "Hurrah!"
   He scents the battle from afar
   hearing the thundering of chiefs, the shouting.
26 Does the hawk take flight on your advice
   when he spreads his wings to travel south?
27 Does the eagle soar at your command
   to make her eyrie in the heights?
28 She spends her night among the crags
   with an unclimbed peak as her redoubt
29 from which she watches for prey,
   fixing it with her far-ranging eye.
30 She feeds her young on blood:
   wherever men fall dying, there she is.

1,3140 Then Yahweh turned to Job, and he said:

2,32 Is Shaddai's opponent willing to give in?
   Has God's critic thought up an answer?
3,33 Job replied to Yahweh:
4,34   My words have been frivolous: what can I reply?
   I had better lay my finger on my lips.
5,35 I have spoken once. . .I will not speak again;
   more than once. . .I will add nothing.

SECOND SPEECH

God is master of the forces of evil

^{6,1} Yahweh gave Job his answer from the heart of the tempest. He said:

^{7,2} Brace yourself like a fighter,
   now it is my turn to ask questions and yours to inform me.

^{8,3} Do you really want to reverse my judgment,
   and put me in the wrong to put yourself in the right?

^{9,4} Has your arm the strength of God's
   can your voice thunder as loud?

^{10,5} If so, assume your dignity, your state,
   robe yourself in majesty and splendor.

^{11,6} Let the spate of your anger flow free;
   humiliate the haughty at a glance!

^{12,7} Cast one look at the proud and bring them low,
   strike down the wicked where they stand.

^{13,8} Bury the lot of them in the ground,
   shut them, silent-faced, in the dungeon.

^{14,9} I myself will be the first to acknowledge
   that your own right hand can assure your triumph.

Behemoth

^{15,10} Now think of Behemoth;
   he eats greenstuff like the ox.

^{16,11} But what strength he has in his loins,
   what power in his stomach muscles!

^{17,12} His tail is as stiff as a cedar,
   the sinews of his thighs are tightly knit.

^{18,13} His vertebrae are bronze tubing,
   his bones as hard as hammered iron.

^{19,14} He is the masterpiece of all God's work,
   but his maker threatened him with the sword,

^{20,15} forbidding him the mountain regions
   where all the wild beasts have their playground.

21,16 So he lies beneath the lotus,
    and hides among the reeds in the swamps.
22,17 The leaves of the Lotus give him shade,
    the willows by the stream shelter him.
23,18 Should the river overflow on him, why should he worry?
    A Jordan could pour down his throat without his caring.
24,19 So who is going to catch him by the eyes
    or drive a peg through his nostrils?

Leviathan

25,20 Leviathan, too! Can you catch him with a fishhook
    or run a line around his tongue?
26,21 Can you put a ring through his nose
    or pierce his jaw with a hook?
27,22 Will he plead and plead with you,
    will he coax you with smooth words?
28,23 Will he strike a bargain with you
    to become your slave for life?
29,24 Will you make a pet of him, like a bird,
    keep him on a lead to amuse your maids?
30,25 Is he to be sold by the fishing guild
    and then retailed by merchants?
31,26 Riddle his hide with darts?
    Prod his head with a harpoon?.
32,27 You have only to lay a finger on him
    never to forget the struggle or risk it again!

1,2841Any hopes you might have would prove vain,
    for the mere sight of him would stagger you.
2,1 When roused, he grows ferocious,
    no one can face him in a fight.
3,2 Who can attack him with impunity?
    No one beneath all heaven.
4,3 Next I will talk of his limbs
    and describe his matchless strength.

5,4 Who can unloose the front of his coat
  or pierce the double armor of his breastplate?
6,5 Who dare open the gates of his mouth?
  Terror dwells in those rows of teeth!
7,6 His back is like rows of shields,
  sealed with a seal of stone,
8,7 touching each other so close
  that not a breath could pass between;
9,8 sticking to one another
  to make an indivisible whole.
10,9 When he sneezes, light leaps forth,
  his eyes are like the eyelids of the dawn.
11,10 From his mouth come fiery torches,
  sparks of fire fly out of it.
12,11 His nostrils belch smoke
  like a caldron boiling on the fire.
13,12 His breath could kindle coals,
  so hot a flame issues from his mouth.
14,13 Strength has made a home in his neck,
  fear leaps before him as he goes.
15,14 The folds of his flesh stick together,
  firmly set in it, immovable.
16,15 His heart is as hard as rock,
  unyielding as a millstone.
17,16 When he stands up, the waves themselves take fright,
  the billows of the sea retreat.
18,17 Sword may strike him, but cannot pierce him;
  no more can spear, javelin or lance.
19,18 Iron means no more to him than straw,
  nor bronze than rotten wood.
20,19 The arrow does not make him run,
  sling stones he treats as wisps of hay.
21,20 A club strikes him like a reed,
  he laughs at the whirring javelin.
22,21 He has sharp potsherd underneath,
  and moves across the slime like a harrow.

23,22 He churns the depths into a seething caldron,
      he makes the sea fume like a scent burner.
24,23 Behind him he leaves a glittering wake—
      a white fleece seems to float on the deeps.
25,24 He has no equal on earth,
      being created without fear.
26,25 He looks the haughtiest in the eye;
      of all the sons of pride he is the king.

Job's final answer

¹42 This was the answer Job gave to Yahweh:

2   I know that you are all-powerful:
      what you conceive, you can perform.
3   I am the man who obscured your designs
      with my empty-headed words.
     I have been holding forth on matters I cannot understand,
      on marvels beyond me and my knowledge.
4   (Listen, I have more to say,
      now it is my turn to ask questions and yours to inform me.)
5   I knew you then only by hearsay;
      but now, having seen you with my own eyes,
6   I retract all I have said,
      and in dust and ashes I repent.

V. EPILOGUE

Yahweh rebukes the three Sages

7   When Yahweh had said all this to Job, he turned to Eliphaz of Teman. "I burn with anger against you and your two friends,"
8 he said, "for not speaking truthfully about me as my servant Job has done. So now find seven bullocks and seven rams, and take them back with you to my servant Job and offer a holocaust for yourselves, while Job, my servant, offers prayers for you. I will listen to him with favor and excuse your folly in not speaking of
9 me properly as my servant Job has done." Eliphaz of Teman, Bildad of Shuah and Zophar of Naamath went away to do as Yahweh had ordered, and Yahweh listened to Job with favor.

Yahweh restores Job's fortunes

10
11   Yahweh restored Job's fortune, because he had prayed for his friends. More than that, Yahweh gave him double what he had before. And all his brothers and all his sisters and all his friends of former times came to see him and sat down at table with him. They showed him every sympathy, and comforted him for all the evils Yahweh had inflicted on him. Each of them gave him a silver

12   coin, and each a gold ring. Yahweh blessed Job's new fortune even more than his first one. He came to own fourteen thousand sheep, six thousand camels, a thousand yoke of oxen and a thou-

13,14 sand she-donkeys. He had seven sons and three daughters; his

15   first daughter he called "Turtledove," the second "Cassia" and the third "Mascara." Throughout the land there were no women as beautiful as the daughters of Job. And their father gave them inheritance rights like their brothers.

16   After his trials, Job lived on until he was a hundred and forty

17   years old, and saw his children and his children's children up to the fourth generation. Then Job died, an old man and full of days.

NOTES

¹ Dr. William Brugh Joy is a physician and healer who conducts residential workshops aimed at expanding conscious awareness and stimulating the healing journey. See his *Joy's Way* (Los Angeles: J.P. Tarcher, 1979), and *Avalanche* (New York: Ballantine, 1990). Dr. Harold Stone is a psychologist and healer who conducts workshops worldwide to raise consciousness about the living process. See his *Embracing Heaven and Earth* (Marina del Rey: De Vorss, 1985), and *Embracing Ourselves* (San Rafael: New World Library, 1989).

² From *The Jerusalem Bible, Reader's Edition*. A Jones, Ed. (New York: Doubleday, 1968). All other citations from the text, unless otherwise noted, are from *The Book Of Job* in this edition.

³ *Hashem* is the Hebrew name for God.

⁴ See Marie-Louise Von Franz, *Puer Aeternus* (Sigo Press, 1981), p.3.

⁵ See Gerard Manley Hopkins' "Felix Randal, "*Norton Anthology of English Literature, Vol. 2*, M. H. Abrams, Ed. (New York: W.W. Norton, 1974).

⁶ I have used "Elihu/Hashem" to suggest that Higher Wisdom is speaking through Elihu.

⁷ See C.G. Jung, *Collected Works, Vol. 9* (Princeton: Princeton University Press, 1969, pp. 70-71.

⁸ Elihu serves here as a psychic function that allows for the discordant worlds of ordinary man and the transordinary deity to interrelate. This "angel" is neither one's ordinary conscious self nor the raw, untamed, unconscious ocean within. Rather, it is a psychological function aware of polar opposites but not identified with either, a part that supports the diversity of life and serves as a buffer between people and their Creator.

⁹ See William James, *The Varieties of Religious Experience* (New York: Longman's 1902), p. 36.

¹⁰ This does not mean that I dogmatically exclude the possibility that outside our psychic lives there are superior forces coordinating and supervising the whole universe. Such an idea, however, is unnecessary for understanding what occurs to us psychospiritually and, hence, for explanation of our experience of the world.

[11] Elihu/Hashem refers to the Ten Commandments that are a blue-print for our inner lives. When we follow them, he says, our days end in happiness and ease, but if we don't, then we can expect an early death or a life despised, in the psychological sense of guilt, shame, fear, or remorse (36:10-14).

[12] See Marie-Louise Von Franz, *Alchemy* (Toronto: Inner City Books, 1980). p. 158.

[13] *Shaddai* is a Hebrew acronym for the expression "And He said to His world: enough!"

[14] In my estimation, the first sequence of human development unfolds during the first 24 months of life. The second occurs between the ages of 2 and 9, the third between 10 and 18, the fourth from 19-36, the fifth between 37 and 54, the sixth between 55 and 72, and the last, usually, after we reach 72. It is precisely during the final sequence, elderhood, that we attain the freedom of being that allows us to enjoy and participate in life with a minimum of concern or worry. This is a time when we do not need to perform or prove anything to anyone, or to compete with others for power or supremacy. It is a time of great joy and appreciation—one in which we can genuinely smell the roses and in which no dark clouds lurk over our horizon. When we reach this state of being, we are like an open book for all to read. Nothing is concealed or defended. Fear is a foreigner in our tent, and all there is, is suchness of living and harmony.

ACKNOWLEDGEMENT

To my wife and children who had to endure the many contortions of my healing journey and the great uncertainty that surrounded my being.

ABOUT THE AUTHOR

Jacob Zighelboim, M.D. is a physician/scientist. He is the author of some eighty peer-reviewed scientific research papers and co-author of ten books, most of them having to do with the immunology of cancer and the application of immunological principles to the treatment of human cancer. Formerly professor at the medical school, UCLA, his discovery of his own cancer led to a philosophical, spiritual and professional search for knowledge and understanding and a renewal of his own ideas about health, illness, and the healing process.

For the last ten years he has been practicing Integrative Oncology, a type of medicine whose objectives are to help people with cancer reach the highest potential for recovery and well-being available to them. He has recently opened a fully integrated medical oncology clinic in Beverly Hills—The Anchor Clinic—where his work continues to evolve and expand.